Planning and the Economy

Since World War II, the way economic policy has been formed both in Canada and abroad has changed radically. In this book, political scientist Hugh Thorburn shows that the different courses that have been taken in Canada and most other industrial nations have much to do with the crsis in the Canadian economy.

In various ways, the economies of the U.S., the European Economic Community and Japan have become more organized: some have a high degree of cooperation between government and industry, and even labour; others have powerful central planning agencies; and some are home to powerful global corporations. All of them have unimpeded access to large home markets like the EEC, and vigorously promote their own industries in an increasingly competitive global marketplace.

In this same period Canada has headed in the opposite direction. It has a small home market, and is left outside the major trading blocs. The division of power between the federal and provincial levels has had a number of consequences that have prevented the development of an effective Canadian economic presence: "province-building" has lead to provinces competing with one another; the federal government has attempted to placate regional grievances by propping up or creating inefficient industries in disadvantaged parts of the country; and the lack of a central vision has meant that various federal agencies have pursued sometimes contradictory objectives, while coordination of policy with the provinces is stymied by an atmosphere of acrimony and competition.

Thorburn examines the response of other Western nations to the changing economic order of the postwar world, and then turns to an analysis of Canadian economic policy-making at the federal level and in all ten provinces. Separate chapters are devoted to the federal-provincial economic relations and Ottawa's brief experiment in building a consensus with business and labour on the economy. Considering possible scenarios for the future, Thorburn points to the need for a central planning agency to correct the drift in Canada's economic policy.

Hugh Thorburn teaches politics at Queen's University, and is the author or editor of several books, including *Party Politics in Canada*.

Planning and the Economy

The Canadian Institute for Economic Policy has been established to engage in public discussion of fiscal, industrial and other related public policies designed to strengthen Canada in a rapidly changing international environment.

The Institute fulfills this mandate by sponsoring and undertaking studies pertaining to the economy of Canada and disseminating such studies. Its intention is to contribute in an innovative way to the development of public policy in Canada.

Canadian Institute for Economic Policy
Suite 409, 350 Sparks St., Ottawa K1R 7S8

Planning and the Economy

Building Federal-Provincial Consensus

H.G. Thorburn

James Lorimer & Company, Publishers
in association with the
Canadian Institute for Economic Policy
Toronto 1984

The opinions expressed in this study are those of the author alone and are not intended to represent those of any organization with which he may be associated.

ISBN 0-88862-695-9 paper
ISBN 0-88862-696-7 cloth

6 5 4 3 2 1   84 85 86 87 88 89

Canadian Cataloguing in Publication Data
Thorburn, Hugh G., 1924–
    Planning and the economy

1. Canada - Economic policy -1945–1971.*   2. Canada - Economic policy - 1971–   *I. Canadian Institute for Economic Policy.   II. Title.

HC115.T56 1984   338.971   C84-098177-5

Additional copies of this book
may be purchased from:
James Lorimer & Company, Publishers
Egerton Ryerson Memorial Building
35 Britain Street
Toronto, Ontario M5A 1R7
Printed and bound in Canada

Contents

Figures

Foreword

The formulation of a national economic policy is not easy in Canada. Each province has its own economic comparative advantage. The interests of the industrial heartland are not easily reconciled with those of the resource-rich provinces.

In this study, Hugh Thorburn focuses on the dilemma of economic policy-making in our federated state and proposes the establishment of a federal-provincial cooperative institution that would elaborate a truly national economic policy.

The institute is publishing this study to encourage discussion of Professor Thorburn's proposal. However, like all our studies, the views expressed here are those of the author and do not necessarily reflect those of the institute.

Roger Voyer
Executive Director
Canadian Institute for Economic Policy

Preface

I undertook to examine the question of the drift in Canada's economic policy by first piecing together from available literature and from interviews with senior public servants in Ottawa and the provincial capitals, the story of how we organize and practise our economic development policy. I agreed not to quote these people directly, but to put together from what they told me an account of the decision-making structures and the policy outputs of all the provincial governments and of the federal government. Obviously I owe a great debt of gratitude to those I interviewed. They will find in the pages that follow the pictures they drew for me, duly interpreted by me with, I hope, a minimum of distortion.

One person who helped me greatly need not remain anonymous. Guy Heywood acted as my research assistant during the summer of 1980. The work he did in interviewing in western Canada and reviewing literature was of great value to me. Also I wish to thank Leisa McDonald, who typed the manuscript through three versions.

The policy suggestions and the structural changes in governmental machinery that I propose are my own responsibility. They may appear to some as radical, unrealistic, utopian, and to others as conservative. While I consider substantial changes to be necessary, I am also convinced that we must start from the conditions of here and now. Thus I begin with our pluralist, federal system, and suggest the grafting of new institutions to it, along with more-cooperative attitudes. I think I have avoided visionary utopianism on the one hand, and conventional incrementalism on the other. But the reader will have to decide that for himself. I can only say with Luther, *Hier steh' ich, ich kann nicht anders* ("Here I stand, I can do no other").

H. G. Thorburn

Introduction

This study is inspired by a mounting concern regarding Canada's failure to organize itself effectively to meet the much stronger economic competition in the world market that has accompanied the recovery of the powers defeated in the Second World War and the arrival of new competition from the newly industrializing countries. In the immediate postwar period, Canada was riding the wave of worldwide demand for both staple products and processed goods following the wartime shortages. We perceived the issue as one of production first, with concerns for cost second. This attitude was appropriate to the immediate postwar period, when Canada and the U.S. were almost the only countries whose productive capacities were not only intact, but were actually improved compared to the prewar period.

However, European and Japanese recovery drastically changed the world economic environment. With new plants and equipment, and with newly created organizations for production, these prewar industrial states were formidable competitors. They had built up mechanisms to create a national consensus for production. The French pioneered indicative planning; the Germans, worker-management co-determination and industrial coordination through the banking system; the Japanese, their remarkable concertation of government, business and labour. Successful states developed intensive research and development programs, and integrated these with production. Also, since they were rebuilding "from scratch," they were spared the networks of vested interests defending their positions of acquired advantage that hobbled the countries whose social and economic structures had survived the war. As it turned out, the defeated nations had certain advantages following their humiliation in war.

Moreover, the structure of the international market changed. Large trading blocs formed or consolidated to challenge the U.S. — the European Economic Community (EEC), Japan and Comecon; other regional groupings formed in Latin America, South East Asia and so on. Canada was left out of these, and saw the Commonwealth trading system collapse and its own special relationship with the U.S. attenuate. The world, for Canadian business and industry, became a much harsher place.

At the same time as these external changes were occurring, Canada proceeded to weaken its competitiveness by its own actions. Quebec nationalism and a growing awareness of regional economic inequalities led Canadian governments to perceive Canada's primary problem as one of internal dissent, which had to be appeased by programs of equalization of services between regions and by the institution of costly programs of bilingualism and equality of opportunity for minorities.

Moral and laudable as such programs were, and in many cases necessary to preserve the nation, they had the effect of diminishing the competitiveness of the Canadian economy. Many nonviable enterprises in disadvantaged regions were begun or were shored up at the taxpayers' expense. Generous social security programs were put in place that encouraged people to remain in uneconomic jobs and in disadvantaged parts of the country. The Canadian economy became an increasingly high-cost one compared to the international competition.

In the postwar years Canadian industry became more and more dominated by foreign capital, much of which entered from the United States for the annexation of the Canadian market through the setting up of branch plants to sell U.S.-type products. Some of these undertakings operated as part of great multinational empires, and were difficult to enlist in initiatives of primarily Canadian concern. Some were natural resource recovery operations, supplying raw materials for processing in the U.S. and overseas. All of these activities tended to encourage the balkanization of the Canadian economy, since each industry developed in relation to its foreign head office. The old east-west axis of the National Policy was undermined.

Federal-provincial relations after 1945 reflected these changes. Regional tensions grew, and provincial premiers, often goaded on by substantial investor interests within their provinces, adopted uncompromising and demanding stances. Federal-provincial relations were played as a zero-sum game, where one's loss was the other's gain, and the country moved away from an integrated common market towards a competitive market of communities "province-building" themselves into separate economic units. The communities increased their demands on the federal government, which found itself bypassed by the provinces as a spender of tax dollars at the same time as it was driven deeper into deficit. Its capacity to exert leadership declined in phase with this change.

Now it is occurring to many Canadians that our concern with equalization, plus our zero-sum approach to national economic questions, is leading us to disaster. Therefore we must make some basic changes.

It is the concern of this study to argue for a process of institutional innovation in which a federal-provincial economic development commission would be created. It would be answerable to both the federal and provincial governments; staffed by recognized economic specialists, with a board of directors named equally by both levels of government, it would be charged with the task of elaborating policies and plans for economic development. It would rely on the expert knowledge of its staff, and its primary commitment would be to the development of acceptable policy. We would thus escape from the trap of the federal-provincial conference in which all participants are responsible to the provincial or federal side — so the meeting is confrontational rather than consensus-building. Of course, there would be many tradeoffs and tense negotiations; but at least the environment would be favourable, and there would be adequate time for discussion and compromise. With such an arrangement Canada would be able to compete more effectively with its trading partners, who have adopted more centrally directed and aggressive economic systems than ever before.

Part 1

The Canadian Setting

The Problem   1

Canada is facing an economic crisis. The problem lies in the increasing estrangement between the federal government and the provinces on the one hand, and among the different regions of Canada on the other, this latter manifesting itself in a failure on the part of the provincial premiers to agree on much beyond a common determination to resist the federal government. This smouldering dispute came to a head in the standoff over constitutional amendment before the repatriation of the Constitution in 1982 — a standoff with all the attributes of conflict: deadlock, unilateral action, reference to the courts, and a war of advertising campaigns.

The estrangement between the central and provincial governments can be viewed as a sign of maturity. No longer is the federal government alone equipped with skilled policy staffs to develop subtle and complex proposals for economic development or taxation structures to influence investment, buttressed by sophisticated and reasonably complete statistical data. Now the provinces (in some cases as a result of federal transfer payments) have developed their own specialist agencies, with experts in economic analysis, industrial policy and, ultimately, skilled advocacy, and legal and economic argumentation. Each participant in the federal-provincial system is equally or similarly equipped and ready to do battle to protect its turf and seize all advantages on behalf of its jurisdiction.

However, this is a shallow approach to the Canadian reality. Why should the members of a federation be concerned about besting one another in the process of negotiation, rather than seeking to improve the lot of all by cooperative action? Here the reasons are complex, and can best be seen in terms of the role the participants see themselves playing in this particular game and in terms of the real options that appear to be available to the participants.

The Development of Federal-Provincial Relations

At the time of Confederation the federal and provincial governments were considerably removed from each other, not only in terms of the inadequate communications of the day, but also because both levels of government functioned so minimally that there were few problems raised by overlapping jurisdictions. The Fathers of Confederation structured the institutions to reflect their expectation that the federal government would dominate, especially in the areas of economic activity, such as communications and transportation. At the beginning, the federal government was assertive in using its powers to disallow provincial legislation and to enact laws, indicating its aggressive position in the economic development of the country. The National Policy was clearly a policy of federal domination, aimed at building a strong country united by a costly and ambitious transportation network. The major instrument for economic development in the early years was the tariff, which encouraged the development of the manufacturing industry located mainly in central Canada.

The Confederation settlement provided for the dominance of the federal government in the field of public finance: the provinces were to rely upon subsidies paid out of the federal treasury (the eighty cents per capita grant, plus the debt allowance and exceptional grants for short-term periods). In addition, the provinces could impose direct taxes, fees and levies on their public lands. These modest sources did not prove sufficient when the provinces developed to the point where they required better roads and urban services. With the development of a modern urbanized economy, the provinces were led into social security programs, enlarged education commitments, and so on. Also, provincial expenditures mounted when federal subsidies were made available to encourage industry. By 1913 the provinces were spending more than half as much as the federal government, reflecting a considerable enlargement of the role they then played. This in turn forced them to rely upon direct taxation, which, of course, showed up the provinces' different capacities to pay and produced a great variation from province to province in the standard of services offered.

After the First World War prosperity tempted the provinces to expand their debt and spend on public works and services. This was the era of the introduction of the motor car and the development of hydroelectric power. Therefore, the provinces had to provide roads and power distribution systems. The development of industry meant a growth in the need for public welfare during economic downturns;

4

consequently, the provinces became increasingly dependent upon the federal government to assist them in rendering this newly expanded level of services. The result was a great gap between conditions in one province and those in another. The Prairie provinces were heavily dependent on a single staple crop — wheat; its varied yields and prices introduced instability into the public finances of those provinces. The Maritimes in turn suffered a chronic depression after the First World War, which forced them to offer a level of services well below those available in central Canada. Generally speaking, the federal government was unwilling to do much to help the provinces except in cases of real privation. On the other hand, the provinces were not able to live adequately off the subsidies and tax base that they possessed. Regional feelings of discontent began to develop as the inequality between the provinces was manifested in the different levels of service.

However, it was during the Depression that these problems became serious. Those provinces depending upon exports were the hardest hit, although problems of mass unemployment imposed on all provinces a burden of poor relief beyond their capacity. The federal government had to step in with grants-in-aid to the provinces, paying 40 per cent of the costs of relief between 1930 and 1937. In addition, the federal government extended over $100 million in loans to the provinces during that period.

To meet the crisis, the federal government, not surprisingly, set up a royal commission to investigate "dominion-provincial relations." In its studies the commission pointed to the uneven development of Canada. Large corporations were doing business from coast to coast but were located mainly in central Canada, where their profits were made and taxed, although their earnings were secured from transcontinental trade. Pools of economic surplus developed that could only be tapped by the federal government and the provincial governments of Ontario and Quebec. The argument was advanced that the federal government should tax these pools of wealth and pass a portion of the yield to the outlying provinces. The same argument was made with respect to private wealth, much of which was concentrated in the large central Canadian cities. The commission suggested a general overhaul of federal-provincial public finance, with the federal government taking responsibility for unemployed employables, and undertaking a general responsibility for integrating the Canadian tax structure across the country in order to stimulate the national income, simplify the taxation schedules and balance the provincial budgets. It was hoped

5

that the taxation, borrowing and spending policies of the two levels of government could be coordinated with the monetary, exchange, tariff and trade policies.

However, war broke out before the final report of the commission was tabled, and the federal government was led to implement many of the recommendations of the commission as emergency wartime measures. The provinces had to "rent" much of their taxing power in the field of income and corporation taxes to the federal government in exchange for subsidies for the duration of the war. This practice led to the tax rental agreements and the subsequent tax-sharing arrangements that have been in effect since the Second World War in varying forms. Thus, with greater provincial financial capacity, there came to be a complex interpenetration of federal and provincial activities, with the inevitable possibilities for friction and dispute.

The war changed the attitudes of many Canadians towards the responsibilities of government. There was a growing awareness of the need for comprehensive social security arrangements. Attitudes towards employment changed: if a government could spend enormously for war, surely it could spend for peace and prosperity. The government responded with plans for full employment and social security. The White Paper on Employment and Income published by the federal government in 1945 summarized this new philosophy. There were four major groups of proposals in this document:

- The federal government should take steps to expand world trade by lowering trade barriers and stabilizing exchange rates, thereby furthering international economic stability and encouraging the development of foreign markets for Canadian staple products.
- The government should undertake to stimulate private business through taxation and monetary policies that encourage low interest rates. It should also intervene in the market to encourage the sale of Canadian products, and it should conduct research for improving production and distribution.
- There should be a program of planned public investment along Keynesian lines to maintain full employment and to prevent deflation of the currency.
- The government should stabilize, and if necessary subsidize, consumption expenditures through transfer payments, such as family allowances, old age pensions and unemployment assistance.

These proposals were in contrast to prewar arrangements and caught the provinces somewhat off guard. At a federal-provincial conference in 1945 the provinces were ill-equipped to deal with these complex issues; so leadership fell to the federal government. While the provinces did not want to give up their constitutional powers, they were prevailed upon to continue to rent their basic taxes to the federal government in exchange for subsidies so that the federal government could undertake a coherent policy of national development.

The provinces found themselves at a serious disadvantage at the 1945 conference because during the war the federal government had developed a highly sophisticated senior bureaucracy with high-level skills in economics. It prepared the complex and sophisticated schemes for financial management and tax revenue sharing that the relatively traditional provincial bureaucracies were not able to discuss competently. In the conferences in 1945 and 1946 provincial representatives were compelled either to accept the federal proposals holus-bolus or simply to say no. Naturally the provincial political leaders determined to rectify the situation so that they could deal more effectively with the federal government in future.

Since provincial revenues did in fact increase with the prosperity of the times, and the new services and facilities demanded by the expanding and modernizing economy fell under provincial jurisdiction, there was a substantial increase in the provincial governments' revenues and commitments. It was not long, therefore, before the provinces were able to match the federal government in sophisticated discussion of these complex financial matters, and each side developed what in effect was a kind of team for federal-provincial negotiation of financial questions.

As so often happens in such circumstances, this did not only represent a new capacity on the part of the provinces but also a commitment to a vigorous defence of their own turf. Teams of people in such adversary situations are inexorably drawn into defending the interests of their side as if they were playing a zero-sum game. Each was determined to defend its jurisdiction and enhance its available revenues.

In the early postwar years, apart from some friction caused by flamboyant provincial leaders (for example, premiers Duplessis and Drew of Quebec and Ontario respectively), federal/provincial relationships were fairly harmonious, partly because the federal government still possessed considerable advantage in terms of the competence of its negotiators and advisers. Also, the fact that the federal government was the supplier of the funds being transferred to the provinces tended to permit it to initiate policy. However, as time went on and any initial feelings of gratitude had had time to dissipate, the provinces came to consider the federal transfers part of their rightful domain and they became increasingly disposed to take issue with the federal government.

In the immediate postwar period economic expansion occurred most strongly in the central Canadian industrial area of southern Ontario and southwestern Quebec. Since this was the area that produced industrial goods for the whole Canadian market, there was little voter resistance in the region to transferring some of the surplus to the outlying provinces, which, as customers, were contributing to the economic development of central Canada. The federal government simply followed a strategy in the 1950s of concocting options for tax rental, among which the provinces could choose. These were successful in attracting all the provinces but Quebec by the 1952–57 period. Quebec remained outside despite considerable loss to its own treasury because of the concern of the Quebec government to defend its role as protector of French Canada.

While the other provinces were accepting federal leadership in the sharing of tax revenues, the example of Quebec was having an important impact on the consciousness of other provincial leaders.

When Quebec refused what were quite generous terms in 1952, the federal government instructed its experts to devise a scheme whereby Quebec would be able to retain the beneficial features of the old tax rental agreements signed by the other provinces without it actually having to sign an agreement. Thus Quebec's participation in a passive sense was obtained and the gross financial injustice to the taxpayers of the province was ended. However, the province was still clearly going its own way, while the federal government was maintaining its financial leadership and was introducing equalization grants in order to bring the per capita yield of the three major taxes (personal income tax, corporate income tax and succession duties) up to the average yields of the two provinces with the highest per capita yield (Ontario and British Columbia).

In this way the arrangements between the federal and provincial governments left the initiative with the federal government and introduced an element of equalization and stabilization into provincial government revenues so that the provinces could plan their own programs with the confidence that the monies would be there when needed. The arrangements also, of course, introduced an element of rigidity into the federal government's budget, limiting its ability to take initiatives to deal with shifts in unemployment, inflation and the rate of exchange of the Canadian dollar.

An ongoing relationship between the federal government and the provinces developed in which the federal government dominated the public finances of the country and became the arbiter between the competing provincial claims. The poor provinces kept advancing their argument for increased revenues on the basis of their fiscal need, whereas the more prosperous provinces countered by an argument based on their tax potential — that is to say, provinces with a growing economy should not be hobbled by taxes that interfere with their ability to be even more productive in the future, and therefore able to provide jobs and pay taxes. By the early 1960s there was general resignation to equalization schemes as the only means of preventing the citizens of the poorer provinces from becoming second class in terms of the services available to them. Quebec was the only province not to fall in line, still attaching greater importance to its role as the guardian of French Canadian society and culture. The English-speaking provinces sided with the federal government, since the equalization grants guaranteed all a reasonable level of revenue. The change from the 1950s was that the provinces were now bargaining on the basis of equality with the federal government and had developed a competence to do this through the upgrading of their public services.

As provincial assertiveness grew, it was necessary to devise a formula that would not entail the provinces' formally giving up their taxing powers. Therefore, in 1957 the tax-sharing arrangement was introduced. Under it, the provinces could choose between the tax rental arrangement and another scheme in which they would levy their own taxes and their taxpayers would profit by an abatement of the federal tax to make room for the new provincially levied taxes, therefore paying the same total taxation as under the tax rental arrangement. Of course, the equalization and stabilization arrangements were continued and amplified. In 1962 the arrangement was further modified under the Federal-Provincial Fiscal Arrangements Act. Under this, the provinces levied their own personal and corporate income taxes, although they could still have the federal government act as tax collector, provided they used the same base as the federal government. The federal government was to partially withdraw from the personal income tax field progressively. This arrangement also included a broader basis for equalization by basing it on the national average yield of the three standard taxes plus 50 per cent of the average provincial revenue from natural resources. This was in recognition of the growing revenues being received by some provinces from natural resource royalties.

The leadership role of the federal government has continued in that it has initiated various shared-cost programs, especially in relation to health and welfare and postsecondary education. These programs have become extremely expensive, and the federal government has gradually been taking steps to limit its financial commitments and, if possible, to withdraw to some degree. This, of course, has led the provinces to be critical of the federal government for leading them into these commitments and then abandoning them, or at least reducing its support. This perception is particularly acute in the poorer provinces where the locally raised revenues are not sufficient to support an increasing burden. This tendency for the costs of shared-cost programs to grow, has caused the federal government to move away from them in favour of block funding to the provinces, thus freeing it from specific commitments and yet enabling it to continue its overall support of provincial activity. Block funding also appeals to the provinces, since it leaves them free to assign their own priorities to public expenditure, rather than being committed to federally initiated ones.

While in a certain sense these cooperative fiscal arrangements can be considered to be satisfactory, they did produce growing resentment on the part of the poorer provinces, which had to levy higher taxes in order to raise the revenues necessary to permit them to participate in shared-cost programs. Furthermore, the wealthier, resource-rich provinces resented the level of federal interference involved. In addition, over the years with the development of the sophisticated bureaucratic arrangements at the provincial and federal level, there came to be a kind of ongoing game in which each party attempted to maximize the return to its own level of jurisdiction. This encouraged a spirit of rivalry with deep-seated resentments and emotional commitments.

While Quebec was at first the sole objector to federal initiatives in the fiscal field, it tended to lead other provinces to follow its example. Its policies appeared to be paying off, since the federal government paid the province greater attention and was more generous to it in order to win it over to agreement. While Quebec, with its obligation to look after the interests of French Canada, could be expected to make particular demands, its economy is nevertheless more integrated into the Canadian economy than any other province except Ontario. Moreover, while there is considerable dispute in the matter, it is probably correct to say that Quebec is a net financial beneficiary of federal policy — and of Canadian federalism generally. In short, it is

10

not likely that Quebec would be better off going its own way from an economic point of view, at least in the short term.

The same cannot be said for the western resource-rich provinces. They are essentially primary producers exporting to a world market (or to a Canadian market at artificially low prices in the case of hydrocarbons). Therefore, it is not in their interests to protect the Canadian common market, and they deeply resent the trade and tariff policies of the federal government. The complaint is often heard that they pay high protected prices for Canadian manufactured goods, while they must sell their primary products in international competitive markets. Moreover, it is easy to perceive the natural resources beneath the topsoil of an area as belonging to the people who live there; so there is a tendency to resent federal taxation to recover a share of the rents from these resources. One cannot be sure that these attitudes in the West would not have developed anyway, with the confirming of these enormous resources and the beginning of a substantial cash flow into the public treasury of the provinces. However, the example of Quebec has been readily followed, and the country now faces very serious problems of regional resentment on the fiscal front.

The growing assertiveness of the provinces as their economies have matured has led them to be tempted into protectionist policies in order to develop certain of their industries. While the Constitution is clear in prohibiting interprovincial tariffs, this has not prevented the kind of protectionism utilizing nontariff barriers.

When one considers that Canada is virtually the only modern industrial state that does not have direct access to a market of a hundred million or more, the detrimental consequences of these restrictive practices become particularly serious in that they greatly reduce the ability of Canada to compete in international markets. These restrictions interfere with the mobility of goods, capital and labour between the regions of Canada; as the economy becomes increasingly mature, governments are called upon by interest groups to come to their defence by protecting them from outside competition.

There is pressure on provincial governments to protect the provincial market. Moreover, since these governments are now such important purchasers of goods and services, they can play a crucial role by adopting policies that discriminate in favour of goods produced in their own territory. The result appears to be a growing tendency of provincial governments to protect their own markets by imposing regulations that would prevent competition from other provinces. Recent examples are the prohibition by the Newfoundland government against employing out-of-province personnel on the offshore oil rigs and Quebec's refusal to allow Ontario workers to secure jobs in the construction industry in the province. The cumulative effect of such measures is to reduce the economic efficiency of the overall Canadian productive community and to increase costs.

Economic Divergence

There have long been substantial differences in per capita income among the provinces and regions of Canada. Such differences were easier to bear before the consumer society and modern communications centred people's attention on the availability of consumer goods and made per capita income statistics generally known. With the development of a wage- and salary-earning economy and the relative decline in importance of self-employed activities, such as farming, fishing, trapping and wood cutting, the regional incidence of unemployment has become a serious problem. Ever since the First World War, the Atlantic provinces have usually had a considerably higher percentage of their labour force unemployed than the rest of Canada. Unemployment, added to low per capita incomes for those employed, has created a feeling of deprivation, further discouraging investment. The result is chronic economic stagnation.

The situation in Quebec, while generally better than in the Maritimes, remains behind Ontario and western Canada in terms of per capita income and unemployment. Quebec and Ontario have the lion's share of secondary manufacturing, which for a long time gave them great advantages over the outlying regions because this provided generally steady work at relatively high wages. The economic problems of the early Eighties have revealed soft spots in this economy and the West has appeared as the more prosperous part of the country.

The resource boom in the West has created much higher levels of prosperity there than in the rest of the country. There is a general perception of economic strength in the West in contrast to a relative levelling off or even decline in the East. This creates disquieting conditions in the country because the old power base in central Canada appears threatened and the new West appears to be aggressively on the rise. This, of course, exacerbates conflicts over resource rents.

The vulnerable and declining eastern industrial complex seems threatened by the West, which is seeking to industrialize on the basis of its own natural resources. To protect itself, the East claims the right to lower than the world prices for these resources. This is resented in the

West, an area which has been nursing its own grievances against what it perceives to be eastern exploitation of the protected western market for manufactured goods.

Reconciliation or Conflict

These differing regional perceptions of the economic realities of present-day Canada are protected and articulated by the provincial governments. Ontario has become the major defender of the Canadian secondary manufacturing industries and is supported in its efforts by Quebec and the Atlantic provinces, all of which are concerned about the supply and price of hydrocarbons. This is now conditioned by a changing attitude in Newfoundland, which sees itself as an emerging oil producer with greater common interests with Alberta than with Ontario. While the federal government is caught in the middle of this conflict of interests between the regions, it is probably nudged to favour eastern Canadian manufacturing industry because of the fact that since the majority of the population of the country is concentrated there, the political voting strength of that region (given its tendency to favour the federal Liberals) is greater than that of the West. In addition, the established economic interest groups that have longstanding relationships with the federal government are mainly those located in central Canada. Moreover, the deficit area east of the Ottawa River has long relied upon the federal government to carry out the equalization policies to support their provincial revenues up to the level of the richer provinces. This in turn sets the federal government on a collision course with the resource-rich provinces.

Three possible outcomes of this situation are:

- a return to federal domination as it existed before the First World War;
- growing provincial autonomy in economic affairs, with the provinces undertaking to protect their own interests; or
- federal-provincial collaboration to work out arrangements.

While it is likely that whatever happens is not going to be any single one of the three courses but rather some complex combination, it is important to consider the implications of each of these eventualities.

The federal government may succeed in asserting itself in some areas where it has clear constitutional authority, especially where it enjoys the support of a substantial majority of the Canadian people. Federal domination is likely to continue if the area concerned is one in which it has an established legitimacy already. Interprovincial

13

transportation and communication probably fall in this category. However, it is probably true to say that the legitimacy of the federal government today has declined considerably from what it was during the Second World War, and therefore it is unlikely that it will be able to reassert its domination in areas that are not clearly under its control at present.

On the other hand, a recourse to increasing provincial autonomy in economic affairs is likely to produce a series of begger-my-neighbour policies that could only add to the general impoverishment of all, with increasing bitterness between the populations of the different regions. However tempting it may be for currently prosperous areas of the country to follow this course, it is shortsighted in the extreme.

As a general course, it is clearly advisable for all concerned to seek some sort of collaboration. The difficulty here is that the recent practices and attitudes are not conducive to this. The general perception of intergovernmental relations as a zero-sum game, with each government defending its own interests against the others, creates a situation where the political process itself appears to be biased in favour of friction and deadlock. The problem, then, is how to elaborate institutions and practices that will move in the opposite direction. How can we induce Canadians generally, and governmental officials and politicians in particular, to favour the greater good of the country over the particular advantage of their own area of jurisdiction and interest? Present institutions and practices are not accomplishing this, and therefore we must turn our attention to an elaboration of new institutions of a collaborative, cooperative kind.

Part 2

The International Setting

The Changing Environment   **2**

Canada in the World Trading System

The world trading system as it appeared in the seventeenth and eighteenth centuries saw the rival British, French, Spanish and Dutch colonial empires competing along mercantilist lines to amass bullion — the sinews of war. The protectionist British trading empire model, based on the Navigation Acts, gave way in the nineteenth century to a system of free trade under British supremacy through Britain's sea power and superiority in commerce and manufacturing and guided by the philosophy of liberalism. An international division of labour ensued based on comparative advantage. The system was policed by the Royal Navy and facilitated by the London money market and the willingness of British investors to export capital. Free trade encouraged wide participation in the world trading system — a kind of pluralism of economic participation under British guidance.

This system was challenged by the rise of economic nationalism, especially in the newly created German Empire, which responded to British supremacy with a policy of protectionism and naval construction. Friedrich List replaced Adam Smith as the guiding economic philosopher on the Continent, and tariffs (under the iron and rye deal) replaced free trade.

In the nineteenth century Canada traded as part of the British Empire trading system, although even before Confederation the colonies that were to become Canada had begun to erect tariff barriers against imports. When Britain repealed the Navigation Acts in the 1840s, it ended the protectionist old colonial system and adopted free trade. This ended Canada's privileged position in the British market; so it had to cast about for alternative arrangements. From 1854 to 1866 there was reciprocity with the United States, but with its abrogation British North America was thrust upon its own resources.

This was a major factor leading to Confederation in 1867, which was followed twelve years later by the introduction of the National Policy. This was a plan for national development based on tariff protection. Nation-building required the creation of an east-west economy based on the transcontinental railway. The settlement of the West and the growing of wheat for export would create a market for eastern manufactured goods on the Prairies and stimulate further settlement there. A protective tariff would encourage the building up of a manufacturing complex in central Canada, and revenue from customs duties would provide a surplus to the government for investment in further national development projects, such as railway extensions.

While the depression that ran from 1873 to 1896 prevented the Conservatives, who introduced the policy, from seeing it succeed, the subsequent boom up to the First World War brought success.

> [It was] a national programme expressed in terms of staples and transportation, tariffs and railways, land and immigration policies, and the buttressing of enterprise by government ownership and support. It was unfortunate that efforts to fit Canada more effectively into a pattern of world trade increased the vulnerability of the economy to external changes beyond her control and to unpredictable shifts in commercial policy on the part of those with whom she traded.[1]

This development strategy for Canada based on east-west trade and integration with Britain and Europe as a major market for staple products was challenged after the First World War. New technologies and the discovery of new resources created a new economic era for Canada. The development of the pulp and paper industry, which exploited the forests of the Precambrian Shield, the Maritime provinces and British Columbia, plus the development of the metal mining industry in the hinterland, gave rise to a new trading relationship with the United States, which supplied most of the capital for these developments.

The growth of secondary manufacturing that had been stimulated by the needs of the First World War continued with the development of the steel industry. The establishment of large manufacturing empires in the United States led to their expansion into Canada to profit from the nearby Canadian market, where tastes were similar to those in the U.S. because of the spillover of advertising and sales activities. The beginning of this development of the miniature replica economy in Canada occurred between the two world wars and was completed soon after the end of the Second World War. For consumer durables, therefore, Canada was effectively annexed to the U.S. market and production system.

This was our new industrialism. By the 1920s Canada was no longer dependent entirely upon coal and iron and steam power, but turned rapidly to hydroelectric power, and the internal combustion engine.

Growing instability following the First World War meant the breakdown of the nineteenth-century world trading system, which assumed a high level of security, thereby permitting countries to become heavily reliant upon distant foreign sources of cheap food and raw materials. The need for security compelled countries to seek assured sources of raw materials in readily accessible regions. This led to substantial American investment in Canadian raw material development at a time when, because of Britain's economic weakness, British investment was withdrawing. Canadian industrialization has taken place within these new technologies and these new conditions of security.

The result has been a reorientation of the Canadian economy from a predominantly east-west one, serving European markets, to a north-south one, where the various regions of Canada are each developing trading relationships with nearby states of the American union. The new industrialism has meant a rapid urbanization of the society and the appearance of manufacturing as a major source of employment for Canadians. By 1950 manufacturing accounted for over 50 per cent of the total value of production in the nine major sectors of the Canadian economy.[2]

With the decline of British power, upon which the somewhat artificial east-west economic axis was based, geography began to assert itself. Canada's long frontier with the United States meant its proximity to the most dynamic industrial economy in the world, and was bound to have its effect. While the country had a protective tariff and effective east-west communications, these turned out to be of little consequence in resisting the inroads of American capital into Canada. Indeed the tariff served as a magnet drawing American manufacturing industry into Canada in order to profit by the protected market and gain access to other parts of the British Empire trading system. Once Canada's trade shifted to a predominant reliance upon American markets and sources of supply, Canada became extremely vulnerable to the impact of American monetary and fiscal policies.

The Postwar World

The world has been passing through periods of security followed by periods of instability. The former have encouraged countries to seek their economic advantage by specializing in the goods and services they do best. During the period of the Pax Britannica in the nineteenth century up to the First World War, Britain, secure behind the shield of the Royal Navy, converted itself into a commercial, industrial and banking country that imported the bulk of its food and raw materials from overseas and paid for them with manufactured products, banking, insurance and transportation services. This pattern was emulated to some extent by other industrializing countries on the Continent so that there was a large international trade on a worldwide basis. Canada played its part by exporting wheat and timber to the British and European markets in exchange for finished goods and services. Britain was clearly the hegemonic power guaranteeing and profiting from this system of worldwide seaborne trade.

However, the period from 1914 until 1945 was one of insecurity and war. Countries could no longer afford the vulnerability of relying heavily on distant supplies of essential products. Protectionist measures in some countries provoked retaliation in others, and the pattern of international trade was drastically changed as some countries retired into autarky and developed mobilization economies, typified by Nazi Germany and the Soviet Union. The reaction in North America was for the United States to seek increased security by developing sources of raw materials nearby, which, as we have seen, meant in Canada and other areas in the Americas.

This period of about thirty years of war and depression and general economic dislocation ended with a world economically dominated by the United States but politically divided between that country and its allies, and the Communist bloc. With the development of nuclear weapons on both sides, a new military situation presented itself: a balance of terror in which each side possessed the power to obliterate the defences and productive facilities of the other. So complete was this relationship that it became clear that all-out nuclear war would be madness, and therefore the nuclear stalemate served as a kind of umbrella conveying a tense security upon the world in that it seemed to guarantee that there would be no all-out war between the superpowers. This situation in turn produced a new international competition on the basis of economic power. If the rest of the world was to escape from American domination on the economic level, it would have to build up

20

its strength. In Western Europe this took the form of the development of the European Economic Community, which has a larger population than the United States itself. This has been such a success that it has attracted the application of countries that originally had refused to join, such as the United Kingdom, which had been relying on the European Free Trade Association with other peripheral countries in order to retain its preference for the international and Commonwealth commitments that it had maintained before the Second World War. Once Britain had joined the EEC, it was clear that it would constitute a powerful rival on the international economic front to the United States; and so it has developed. At the same time Japan, resurrected from the devastation of war, has rebuilt its productive capacity and become the second largest national economy in the world. For practical purposes the Communist countries have withdrawn into their own Comecon economic association. Following these examples of regional integration, there have been other groupings of countries coming together for mutual protection in the economic struggles of the world.

Canada has a higher proportion of foreign ownership and control in its industry than any other country in the world.[3] Indeed, in Canada's nonrenewable-resource sector, foreign ownership is overwhelming: eight of the ten largest resource firms in Canada are more than 50 per cent foreign owned.[4] This situation has meant that the dynamic sectors of the Canadian economy have come to be dominated by large firms controlled mainly in the United States. Given the pluralist nature of Canadian political democracy, a very substantial influence over Canadian governments has been exercised by these powerful economic interests. Therefore, it has become difficult for Canada to take an independent and self-interested position in policy-making. The brokerage political party system operating in Canada has favoured a process of elite accommodation, which gives these large foreign-controlled interests substantial leverage over Canadian governments.

The polarized international situation between the United States and the Soviet Union that emerged after the Second World War intensified Canadian integration with the U.S. Military integration through the North American Air Defence (NORAD) and the North Atlantic Treaty Organization (NATO), with the defence-sharing agreements for pooling military procurement, meant close collaboration between the armed services of the two countries. The development of Canada as a major source of raw materials for American industry led to an effective diminution of Canadian autonomy, while at the same time contributing to Canadian prosperity. Canadian industry developed in relation to the U.S. to the point that about 70 per cent of its imports and 75 per cent of its exports were with that single country.

Canadian attitudes towards this overwhelming commitment were somewhat mixed. Generally speaking, the business community favoured the association because it was good for business. However, in the community at large there were serious misgivings, which manifested themselves in the development of a kind of defensive nationalism demonstrated by the Committee for an Independent Canada and the Waffle movement within the New Democratic Party (NDP). Both of these appeared in about 1970, when the United States was perceived as a fairly aggressive country on the world stage. After the U.S. withdrawal from Vietnam and the decline of its military preponderance over the Soviet Union Canadians began to show less nationalistic concerns. The Waffle was expelled from the NDP and disappeared from the political scene, and the Committee for an Independent Canada was dissolved in 1981.

The attention of Canadians has been drawn to their own internal problems: Quebec nationalism led to the election of the Parti Québécois (PQ) in 1976. Canadian governments were preoccupied with the relationship between Quebec and the rest of the country, and attempts were made to reconcile differences.

After the failure of the PQ referendum option in 1980, attention shifted to the growing regional discontent within the country, culminating in the confrontation between the federal government and the government of Alberta over the National Energy Program in 1980. These factors, combined with the economic difficulties of increasing unemployment, persistent inflation and the decline in the value of the Canadian dollar, led to less emphasis on nationalistic considerations and a greater concern about restoring the country to prosperity.

As noted, an increasing reliance upon the American market has increased the susceptibility of the country to influence from the United States. In addition, economic integration through the Canada-U.S. Auto Pact, the defence-sharing arrangements and the growing domination of important sectors of the Canadian economy by American corporations have likewise increased the vulnerability of Canada. On the other hand, the country has not accepted the arguments that have been made in favour of free trade with the U.S. As a result, Canada is in a somewhat contradictory position, trying to retain its political independence, while at the same time appearing to be losing its capacity to defend itself against the increasingly chill economic winds blowing across the border.[5]

In this latter part of the twentieth century the international economic environment is one of powerful trading blocs. If we contemplate the industrialized world, we find that all these countries each have access to a market of about a hundred million people, either within their own borders or within the common market of which they form a part. Canada, almost alone, is in the more traditional position of attempting to trade with the whole world from the vantage point of a small nation-state. Canada has been reluctant to allow itself to be drawn into free trade arrangements with the United States because of its fear of political absorption and its apprehension that its own protected industries would be destroyed when forced to compete with American producers. Indeed, the fact that much of Canadian industry has been controlled by American firms has tended to support this status quo situation, because such firms have often found it possible to collect and pocket the rents available to them from Canadian tariff protection, which allowed higher prices and, as a consequence in some cases, higher profits for Canadian operations, or profits to be made on intrafirm transfers despite a generally low level of productivity in Canada. In fairness it must be admitted that this situation is passing with the decline of tariffs and the obsolescence of the branch plant. This, of course, presents Canada with other problems.

When Canada found itself caught in this situation, it sought to escape by developing a "third option," that is, a "contractual link" with the EEC, which would permit Canada to develop trading relationships large enough to offset its heavy commitment to the United States. This arrangement, negotiated with considerable diplomatic difficulty by the Trudeau government, has in fact turned out to be largely a diplomatic gesture with very little economic content.

Canada in the mid-1980s finds itself largely alone in a competitive world of giant trading blocs. It lacks the advantages of both the large domestic market and access to other markets on a preferred basis. Moreover, it suffers from the failure to organize its own economic affairs on a coherent basis to confront vigorous competition from abroad. The federal system has developed in such a way that the provinces have become centres of economic initiative themselves and compete with one another, and an effective Canadian concerted economic presence has so far failed to develop.

In the international trading world, events have been developing rapidly. Not only are there large and powerful trading blocs following aggressive self-interested trading policies, but large multinational corporations are operating in their own interests on a transnational basis. The resource-rich but balkanized Canadian presence is a somewhat lumbering and uncoordinated beast in the highly competitive world of modern international trade. Neither is it the headquarters of multinational corporations, which operate very often in the interests of their country of national origin, nor is it a powerful economic player in the world market as a producer of competitive finished goods. At the level of international trade, Canada is largely a supplier of unfinished or semi-processed raw materials and plays the role of a price taker for these products rather than a price setter. Much of this trade is handled by large trading organizations controlled outside the country.

The economic crisis following the oil shocks of the 1970s has seen competition in international trade increase, and countries and corporations are seeking to gird themselves with effective organizations to meet these challenges. The economic consequences for the losers in the trade battles of the present era are extremely serious. Grave economic dislocations are already being suffered by those countries that have not succeeded in developing competitive economies. The problems of the U.K. are well known, and the serious difficulties of the American automobile and other industries are illustrating the advantages that go to countries and corporations that plan their affairs carefully and maximize the potentiality for increased productivity and competitiveness. This is a condition which is new for Canada, and one with which the country is relatively poorly equipped to cope. Not only is its economy largely controlled outside its own borders, at least in the most dynamic areas of the private sector, but its own decision-making units are politically balkanized and in competition with each other.

The Response of Other States   **3**

A third of a century has passed since the Second World War. This period has witnessed a profound transformation in the international trading system. One can now with justification speak of a world economy. Of course, there are some holdouts, notably the Communist countries, but even they are being drawn into the new economic system, albeit on a rather restrictive and centrally controlled basis. For the rest, there has evolved an international system of markets and production in which the large players have been the multinational corporations and the governments of nation-states. This has meant a high degree of integration of production and distribution around the world, with the decline of tariff restrictions, the growth of nontariff barriers, and the concentration of market power in the hands of the largest players. The prizes for the winners have been very large, and the adverse consequences visited upon the losers have also been serious. Some corporations, notably those dominating the market for key commodities such as petroleum, food stuffs, chemicals and high-technology products, have become great concentrations of economic power to rival the governments of even middle-sized countries.

This development has constituted a challenge to the power and authority of governments, which have generally reacted with much more assertive or interventionist policies than those before the Second World War. The result is a rivalry between highly integrated systems of power.

At the end of the Second World War the world economy was in shambles. Destruction had been so widespread and catastrophic that all the major powers in the Eurasian land mass were virtually prostrate, whether victors or vanquished. Only in North America did the economy emerge, not only unscathed, but strengthened as a consequence of the war. American domination of the world was dramatized by U.S. exclusive control of the ultimate thermonuclear weapon, but it was apparent also in the immense U.S. economic strength compared to its crippled neighbours in the rest of the world.

It was obvious, however, that simply to preside over an impoverished world would be not only an immoral but a vain pursuit; so the United States undertook a policy of assistance to the shattered industrial powers in Europe and Asia. Generous credits were extended, making possible the export of substantial quantities of foodstuffs, raw materials and equipment. This was intended to restore the shattered economies, but could only do so if organized along coherent lines to re-equip the productive capacities of the war-ravaged countries. These countries undertook to develop plans for the effective use of the substantial credits made available to them so that they would be able to harness the skilled manpower, organizational capacity and resources in their possession.

Of course, each individual country was responsible for its own development efforts; some were much more successful than others. Germany relied upon a currency reform followed by a free market economy, whereas France developed a system of indicative planning of the national economy. Britain, one of the victor powers that had escaped occupation by the German army, appeared to be in a stronger position than the continental European countries at first, and therefore it did not feel the necessity to undertake such drastic measures. In any event, the British tradition from the nineteenth century of economic hegemony was to rely upon a liberal, free market approach. This conformed to the American preference, leading the British to see themselves as enjoying a special relationship with the United States.

The Americans were convinced that the reasons for the international hostilities that led to the Second World War were to be found in restrictive trading arrangements; they thought that by being the champions of a liberal international economy they would open the door to a new prosperity. They advocated free trade and free investment. Since the United States was much the most powerful country, this would mean it would have the whole world for its markets, and at the same time it would be a champion of equal treatment for all. Thus the importance of political boundaries would be diminished and a new era of economic interdependence would be introduced. To shore up this arrangement the Americans fostered a series of international institutions, collectively known as the Bretton Woods System, which established the framework for multilateralism. These included the International Monetary Fund (IMF), the General Agreement on Tariffs and Trade (GATT), the International Bank for Reconstruction and Development (the World Bank), the International Trade Organization (ITO) and a survival from the prewar period, the Bank for International Settlements. In addition, there were key rules of the game involving fixed exchange rates and the convertibility of currency.

With decreases in transportation costs, improved communications and lower trade barriers, countries were much more sensitive to flows of international trade and were rendered insecure because of the vagaries of foreign competition and their vulnerability to external disruptions of economic activity. The result was the very extensive integration of the national economies of the participating countries through the actions of multinational corporations, most of which were American centred. Thus, the trading world became interdependent, not only in regard to finance and money, but in regard to production itself. In reaction to this, many host countries felt their values threatened and resorted to various forms of economic nationalism.

In this new system, governments began to intervene more in markets, and economic relations became increasingly politicized.[1] This liberal, free market, international system was perceived by many of the weaker countries as merely being an excuse for the economic domination of the United States, and therefore, in order to protect themselves and build up their power, they resorted to various devices, such as combining with other states to form economic blocs, to challenge the hegemonic power. They also resorted to various forms of economic nationalism to curtail the extension of the power of the multinational corporations and of the United States within their territories.

The major one of these economic combinations was formed in Europe and was not primarily intended as a means of resisting American hegemony. Indeed, the United States was enlisted in support of the developing community whose priorities were to prevent a return to European international conflict.

The major initiative in this respect came from France, which was particularly susceptible to fears of a renewed German revanchist power threatening it once again. The solution envisaged by such French leaders as Robert Schumann and Jean Monnet was to favour the international economic integration of the major European powers. The first step was the establishment of the European Coal and Steel Community, which combined the coal and steel industries of Germany, France and the Benelux countries, producing an integrated, international industry. It was thought that this would have the additional effect of making it impossible for any one country to engage in a war against its neighbours, since it would not have an autonomous source of coal and steel. This idea of integration was carried further with the suggestion of a European defence force, which would have meant an integration of the military forces of the European powers. This proposal was defeated in the French Parliament. The other integrative suggestion was for an extension of the coal and steel community to a broader range of products and a larger number of countries — a common market that would permit longer production runs, greater specialization and therefore greater economic efficiency. This was consummated in the Treaty of Rome in 1957 creating the European Economic Community, which initially consisted of Germany, France, Italy, the Netherlands, Belgium and Luxembourg.

While initially invited to join, the United Kingdom decided for various reasons to remain outside. It already had its connections with the overseas Commonwealth countries — connections that would be jeopardized by British membership. The U.K. had its special relationship with the United States based on a comradeship in arms in the Second World War, an attitude in favour of liberal, international trading relations, and an apprehension, particularly among some British socialist leaders, lest the Common Market be too conservative, since it was dominated by the Christian Democratic governments of Germany, France and Italy.

Britain therefore turned to other small European countries and formed the European Free Trade Association. This experiment, however, soon turned out to be abortive, and Britain was obliged to seek admission to the Common Market under less favourable circumstances. Initially rebuffed by de Gaulle, Britain succeeded in achieving entry in 1972 along with Denmark and Ireland. In 1981 Greece entered, and it is expected that Spain and Portugal will be admitted soon. Therefore, the bulk of non-Communist Europe now constitutes a large common market, a powerful force in the international trading community. More important, it is able to offer a large and prosperous market to its producers of industrial goods. This in turn favours specialization and low unit costs of production.

The European Economic Community, however, is still very far from being a political unit. The individual states remain, and each carries out its own economic policies within the framework of the larger EEC. This has permitted differing approaches to the problems imposed by prevailing international economic conditions.

The Germans have rebuilt their country following a currency reform on the basis of a free market economy, a high level of social security and high taxes. There is considerable national solidarity in the German economy, with the trade unions preferring to share in management through co-determination over confrontation with their employers. The economy is highly concentrated, with the banks exercising a leading role, as is discussed in chapter 5. The French, on the other hand, consistent with their tradition of centralized *dirigiste* control and with a highly competent and technically sophisticated senior civil service, have developed the system of indicative planning, which is elaborated in chapter 4. British policy has remained more in line with the national tradition of a world trader, with the City of London playing a leading role as international banker (see chapter 4).

The other countries of the Common Market have all followed their own policies with varying degrees of success. It is beyond the scope of this study to do more than simply sample in passing various approaches that have been adopted, and no attempt at comprehensive analysis will be undertaken.[2] One thing does appear to be consistent. Among the economic policies of the developed countries is their interest in promoting economic growth and the efficiency of industry. This is leading them all, one way or another, to greater centralization and in most cases also to industrial concentration. The state is coming to exercise a more important role in directing the orientation of investment either by participating itself, inducing industrial participants to act according to its policies, or by encouraging the private market to accomplish objectives of which it approves. The French make the needed distinction here between *faire* (action), *faire faire* (getting someone to do it) and *laisser faire* (leaving the market free). The first is normally accomplished through nationalized industries, such as our crown corporations in Canada, or through special public-private organizations, which take many forms. The second is often accomplished by the state giving grants and other assistance for various economic activities, or making technical information or expertise available in order to advance specific activities. Other means are special tax credits, tariff protection or the use of government regulations to encourage particular activities. The third option needs no elaboration.

It is now common for the government to participate in economic activities, but there are great differences between the means taken by one country and another. Some large enterprises facing bankruptcy have been taken over by the state in order to preserve employment and avoid economic dislocation. The Italian Institute for Industrial

Reconstruction (IRI) is a good example of this, as is the British Leyland automobile manufacturing enterprise. Other countries have become involved in the support of high technology, such as Britain and France in aerospace industries. The computer industry and naval construction are other examples where government intervention is common. Government aid is often undertaken in order to facilitate regional development or to encourage progress in what are perceived to be the key industries of modern technology. Generally it is the stable traditional industries that tend to be left alone; the technologically sophisticated and those facing bankruptcy are the ones most often supported.

The state is often motivated to bring about industrial concentration in order to produce viable industries to meet foreign competition. Another common reason is the furtherance of strategic considerations, such as support of an armaments industry, a space program or an aerospace industry. Finally, industrial concentration frequently serves to encourage new capital investments or certain types of research that appear to be promising for future economic development. State assistance normally goes to large corporations in order to further economic growth and, therefore, generally tends to favour industrial concentration.

Another approach often followed by governments is to reduce taxes so as to encourage industrial development. This technique has been particularly popular in the U.S., Canada and Germany. It represents a general tendency for governments to shift the burden of taxation from industry to other bases, such as personal income tax and taxes on consumption. Such assistance often takes the form of permitting a rapid write-off of industrial installations and of tax concessions to encourage research and development. These approaches tend to be concentrated in a limited field, such as high technology, energy and communications.

Then there is the traditional technique of tariff protection, which really constitutes a form of subsidy paid by the general consumer through higher prices. In general, the tendency is for tariffs to decline in line with the general adoption of the GATT tariff reductions. This has often opened the door to the erection of new nontariff barriers (NTBs), which frequently constitute more effective barriers to trade than the older tariff mechanism. It is usually the manufacturing industries that are protected by these two devices in order to preserve jobs and build up diversified, advanced economies.

This "liberalization of international trade" has facilitated the expansion of large multinational corporations, thereby bringing about a greater concentration of economic power in their hands at the international level. There are other devices for state intervention in the economy, such as antitrust laws and foreign investment review, which have generally played a relatively minor role in Western economies since the Second World War. Most countries are showing concern about massive investments in their economies from abroad because of the potential external control that this may involve. As a result government intervention tends to increase as foreign investment grows.

In general, there is a tendency for state intervention in the economies to increase, and for it to involve intervention in individual sectors rather than to be confined to macroeconomic methods. In some ways governments' actions appear paradoxical, as when they participate in tariff reduction while simultaneously increasing financial aid to individual sectors. Although they have generally left the free market in operation, they have tended to influence it by increasing interventions, both direct and indirect.

The United States has been particularly active in the movement to reduce tariff barriers, which of course are substantially beneficial to multinational corporations, most of which are centred in that country. The general condemnation, then, of economic nationalism must be seen as a defence of the interests of these corporations. Periods of economic growth generally have been periods of economic liberalization, and therefore the crisis of the late Seventies and early Eighties has seen the return to more protectionist measures, particularly nontariff barriers. All states attempt to improve the export possibilities of their own industries, and this has by and large meant an increase in financial aid in order to make them more competitive. Such aid serves to compensate for the loss of protection due to tariff reductions.

Generally speaking, states have encouraged economic concentration so that their own corporations are made competitive. Mergers have therefore been tolerated without significant question in most advanced industrial countries, and the state has moved in support of large industrial enterprises because these are the most likely to be internationally competitive.

As to declining industries and underdeveloped regions, governments generally have been supportive in order to preserve employment and avoid worsening regional disparities. This has meant greater efforts to protect manufacturing industries with large employment commitments. It can be said that government intervention is a conservative influence slowing down the pace of change. It acts to counteract the market forces favouring certain industries and regions over others. The state therefore is involved in a rather paradoxical pattern of activity in that it is trying to encourage innovation and technological development, while at the same time it is struggling to preserve declining industries lest serious employment problems result. Generally, however, it is inclined to support industries where capital is forthcoming for investment.

A main concern of governments is to improve the balance of payments, which can be achieved either by increasing exports or by substituting domestic products for imports. Since all countries tend to follow the same policy, there is increasing competition in the field of high technology so that substantial deficits in this area can be avoided. There is a tendency to see these industries as progressive and prestigious, and they tend to be readily adaptable to national defence priorities. This is particularly true, of course, of the communications and aerospace industries. In order of priority, then, there is general concern with industrial growth (which means supporting large national industries), with the multinationals located in one's own country, and, finally, with small national companies.

The picture is one of some incoherence, with a basic commitment to economic growth and technological advance. In summary, governments tend to exert a priority for aiding industries with a high level of visibility — usually large corporations or corporations experiencing rapid change (whether this be decline or possible improvement through high technology). Therefore, the smaller and less exciting industries whose performance is more stable are inclined to be neglected. On a regional basis, the state tends to come to the aid of the most retarded regions and to do relatively little for those regions that are neither seriously backward nor very dynamic.

The dramatic rises in rates of unemployment in the early Eighties in both Europe and North America are making governments anxious to protect the jobs of workers in their countries. This is giving a striking stimulus to protectionist policies. Since the cause of the unemployment is partly structural (the substitution of robots for workers or the introduction of highly productive equipment, such as computer-aided design and manufacture, word processors and other computer-based office equipment), governments are trying to develop policies to provide employment for displaced workers. More government intervention is bound to occur, although its nature is not yet clear.

Some countries prior to the recession of the 1980s have shown serious apprehension about the invasion of foreign capital (notably from Japan and France), and since 1974 Canada has erected its foreign investment review arrangements. There is, however, a curious ambivalence here: governments attempt to favour their own national corporations while at the same time giving support to multinationals in order to attract their technology and employment. It is perhaps natural that bureaucratic organizations should try to enlarge their own sphere of activity and their capacity for monitoring activities within their domain. What is clear is a general tendency for governments to adopt interventionist policies in support of their own industrial activity, and to do this with increasingly effective measures emanating from centralized government authority.[3]

Indicative Planning in France and the U.K. 4

We shall now look at the problems of managing the national economy from the internal perspective of the states in question. Western countries have all developed over the years a pattern of institutions and a system of relationships between the state and the other instruments and organizations of society. There is a general acceptance of the pluralist political system, in which a democratically elected government receives political inputs from interest groups that consist of private, voluntary associations. The most important of these, of course, are the business associations and corporations, the trade unions, the professional associations, and then the various voluntary groups organized to defend particular interests or to advocate particular causes. Moreover, each country has its own distinctive pattern of institutions, such as a cabinet, a parliament, a political party system, a bureaucracy and so on. The society develops deeply rooted traditions. We note in the English-speaking countries, for example, a tendency to assign an important role to the free market economy and to restrict the intervention of government to the regulation and support of it. On the other hand, the French tradition, going back to such historic personalities as Colbert and Napoleon, emphasized a more important role for the state as a leader in economic development and an architect not only of economic policy but of the shape of the economy itself. Given these dissimilar traditions, it is not surprising that the responses of countries to the problems of postwar reconstruction and economic crisis would differ.

The Depression of the 1930s resulted in a general disenchantment with the workings of the free market economy, and the Second World War put substantial bureaucratic machinery in place to control economic activity. However, with the return of peace in 1945, countries tended to revert to their traditional patterns. Britain, with a

Labour government in power, might have been expected to adopt a system of socialist planning. However, the power of the City of London, the bureaucracy and the tradition of empire led to a preoccupation with the defence of sterling as a reserve currency and with prestige spending, such as defence installations throughout the world. An impressive diplomatic presence meant substantial commitment to the role of an imperial power despite straitened economic circumstances. After all, Britain was a victor and had to act like one. Moreover, Britain was the partner of the United States in the leadership of the Western world. Given the predominance of American economic and military power, Britain was compelled to adopt American policies to facilitate this relationship. The result, therefore, was to assign a low priority to planning and rely as much as possible on the free market.

In contrast, France, while technically a victor nation, emerged from German occupation with widespread devastation of its productive facilities. It was therefore in much greater need of an ordering of its infrastructure and the rebuilding of facilities. Moreover, France's *dirigiste* traditions and the presence of a competent and authoritative civil service made it easy to rely upon government intervention.

The French Experience

No study of economic development in a democratic context would be complete without some consideration of the path-breaking experience of France since the Second World War. The Allied victory brought about the restoration of the French state and a reconstitution of the essentials of the prewar political system, with all the governmental instability and deep partisan divisions that had existed before the war. After the Communists left the government in 1947, it looked as if the country was to be the victim of a paralyzing internal division that would produce ineffective government, political weakness and general economic stagnation.

This, however, did not develop because of crucial decisions made by French leaders in the immediate aftermath of the war. In 1946 the General Planning Commissariat was created by decree. Jean Monnet, the designer of the new mechanism, believed that the state should not only have an active role rebuilding the economy, but should modernize and direct it in a coherent, orderly way. It was therefore necessary to create planning machinery independent of the vacillating and unstable governmental leadership. Monnet proposed to employ the expert French bureaucracy in the vital role of formulating economic policy. It would have to be involved not only in the daily management of the country, but also in the development of policies for economic growth and prosperity. By elevating economic planning above the realm of party warfare, he was able to gain the acceptance of all political parties for his planning objectives. In effect the politicians agreed that since they couldn't compromise on long-term development policies, they would simply turn the matter over to the planning authorities, who would report to Parliament and the various private decision-makers in the country.

Central to the concept of economic planning in France was the belief that a coherent government-supported program, setting out the possibilities for expansion of each industrial sector, would provide industry with the assurance that would encourage it to divert both business and personal savings from short-term, safe investments to more productive but longer-term, riskier investments. The purpose of economic planning was not just to forecast and describe the spontaneous developments of the French economy, but to guide it towards the attainment of chosen objectives. The plan encompassed not only the nationalized industries. It also sought to draw the private sector into the process of centralized economic decision-making. Economic incentives, such as tax subsidies, exemptions from regulations and lower interest rates on loans, were seen as necessary to secure private industry's cooperation with the plan. The state's most effective stimulant for sectors of the economy earmarked for rapid development was the use of credit through the nationalized banks. Monnet envisaged a permanent exchange of ideas between the planning commission and the nation in a pluralist economy. Modernization Commissions were created to attract input from interests in all sectors of French society. Some of these commissions would deal with particular sectors of the economy, others had broader economic concerns. Their role was advisory, involving forecasting the development of production for their respective industries and providing information on structural changes in the conditions governing investment and finance.

The planning commission was the key organ for coordinating the government's economic policy. It consisted of a small group of young, imaginative, highly trained civil servants, who prepared the basic projections for the Modernization Commissions to consider. Then it would coordinate their activities, producing a draft of a four-year economic plan. Technically the commission had no formal powers of its own; so it was dependent on government laws regarding each plan to give it the legal authority required. However, it controlled the allocation of funds from the Marshall Plan. Since these were independent of the Ministry of Finance, the planning commission had autonomy from both government and Parliament.

The first plan, approved in 1947, chose six priority sectors for development: coal, electricity, steel, transportation, cement and fertilizers, and agricultural machinery. These constituted the infrastructure on which the economy would be rebuilt. The plan was an outstanding success on both economic and psychological fronts.[1]

The second plan faced new problems, such as the need to favour new sectors of the economy, to re-arm and to deal with the balance-of-payments deficit. The plan accordingly was extended to cover all productive activities. The commission developed skills to predict not only sectoral growth, but that of the economy as a whole. It analyzed each sector from an economic, psychological and social standpoint, emphasizing the need for improved quality and efficiency of national production, as well as an increasing growth rate. It sponsored scientific and technical research, and prepared training programs and marketing techniques for manpower development.

The emphasis was on creating a rapidly growing but balanced national economy, drawing input from all the sectors and gaining thereby their support and assistance. After the signing of the Treaty of Rome in 1957, the planners studied the implications of the Common Market arrangements and made plans to cope with the problems involved. The planning techniques were particularly successful in the early years because of the clear and explicit economic development objectives involved. These were generally supported in the community. As time went on, however, the second and third plans lacked this clear sense of strategic choice, and economic priorities became less self-evident. Issues became more complex and more controversial. By the middle of the 1950s, the plan had ceased to be an exercise in social pioneering; it had become transformed into a conservative institution. Under the Gaullist Fifth Republic (beginning in 1958), planning became more subject to the political preferences of the government, tending simply to express its medium-term economic and social policy. Interest group participation became more important in the fourth and later plans because of the greater difficulty in building consensus. The plan continued to be submitted to Parliament in order to have its support, although little detailed debate took place. The government perceived the plan as representing a consistent whole so that amendments would destroy its overall balance. As a result the plan was approved *en bloc*.

Under the Fifth Republic the number of Modernization Commissions has been increased so that all sectors affected by the plan are represented by a commission. These are composed of selected representatives of management, the trade unions, agricultural interests, consumer groups, the financial community, government officials and, of course, the planners and economic experts themselves. There is no fixed proportion of seats allotted to particular groups. In practice the managers of big business, the planners, the higher civil servants and the economic experts constitute the majority on these commissions. Therefore Parliament, the trade unions, small business, consumer groups and agricultural interests have very little influence, but their involvement and assent assists in the production of a national consensus.

The crucial contact is between industry and the state, and these two effectively exclude the unions from serious discussions. The government at times acted decisively to shape certain elements of industrial strategy, notably in the computer industry and in steel production. The state really is in a position to determine which industries will prosper and which will not, by deciding on the level of support to be given to them under the plan. Here control over investment funds is the decisive lever.

During the Giscard presidency (beginning in 1974), weaknesses have appeared in the planning mechanism. There has been more political interference with it, and the economic crisis has led it to be ignored by the political process, especially when the budget was being formulated. The planning mechanism has settled down to a kind of routine; so some of the participation by interest groups has become almost ceremonial. Moreover, the trade unions have become disenchanted with their minimal role in the process and have been withdrawing some of the support previously given. By the time the international economic crisis developed in the mid-Seventies, the plan had become downgraded in importance. The crisis has forced the government to divert its attention from the medium-range projections of the plan to current economic questions. In some instances the plan has conflicted with the budget.

Giscard's finance minister was struggling to contain inflation, and his efforts pitted the government against the growth-oriented policies of the plan. He attempted to harmonize the two by imposing a system of rationalization on the budgetary process and the planning machinery by setting up the Central Planning Council, which shifts responsibility to the presidential level.[2] This involved applying a variant of the

American planning, programming and budgetary systems to produce a program budget, using quantitative and analytical techniques and methods of modern management. The result was a serious attempt to harmonize short-term and medium-term expenditure decisions, and the plan now is less of a strategy for development than it was. On the other hand, it does encourage rational, comprehensive economic management in a time of uncertainty. Consensus-building is being downgraded, and "technocratic planning" (i.e., medium-term budgeting) is growing more important.

The lesson of the French experience surely is to show how serious economic difficulties can be confronted in a democratic context by the application of rational economic analysis combined with consultation, thus accomplishing the building of consensus among the various participants in the national economy. To succeed, the plan requires the support of all concerned. This is a kind of "ardent obligation." However, when the consensus weakens and when the clarity of objectives is obscured, planning seems to be less dramatically successful but still valuable.

The British Experience

Britain offers a striking contrast to France in the area of economic planning. It emerged from the war with immense prestige as one of the three major Allies who shared the victory over the Axis powers. Morale was high, although the economic weakness of the British economy was far greater than was generally realized. The partnership with the United States, which the government wished to maintain, meant accommodation to policy preferences held by the more powerful partner. This, combined with the traditions of empire, world commerce and banking, created a preference for macroeconomic policies and economic liberalism generally. The Labour government was determined to maintain full employment with rising living standards; yet it feared a balance-of-payments deficit. With rising public expectations, the government was led to make frequent changes of policy with serious disruptive effects. These were the so-called "stop-go" policies that have plagued the country ever since. The monopoly power of organized labour increased substantially, and the government came to rely mainly on fiscal policy as its short-term stabilization tool. There were experiments also with incomes policies, and concerted efforts were made to encourage exports and investment in the British economy. The influence of Lord Keynes was great in the postwar years, making substantial public sector deficits respectable. These were financed by monetary expansion, which sowed the seeds of inflation.

From the 1961–73 period it became clear that the country was not investing enough in the economy and was unable effectively to carry the great burden of a world power with substantial overseas defence commitments. In order to build up investment, the government undertook policies of stimulation through tax incentives for corporations. This, of course, meant a greater degree of economic planning and a conscious copying of some of the techniques France used to achieve a rapid rate of economic growth. In 1962 the National Economic Development Council was set up, bringing together government, unions and employers. The policy aim was economic growth, but unfortunately it was not possible to achieve sufficient consensus on specific policies. Spurts of economic growth took place in 1963–64 and 1971–73, only to be followed by periods of crisis and setback.

Because of the overexpansion of the money supply, the government had to resort to tight budgtary policy and was forced to rely on the Phillips curve, that is, allowing unemployment to rise in an attempt to dampen inflationary wage demands. In 1970 and 1972 it undertook to reduce the overall role of government to "set the people free." This meant cutting the burden of taxation and moving away from direct taxes to indirect ones. The government undertook to "make a dash for growth" and seek rapid economic expansion. This, however, created serious wage inflation. After making a decision to allow the pound to float in international markets, the government found itself forced to introduce an incomes policy to regain control over the economy.

By mid-1973 the government had to act. It negotiated arrangements with the unions for the so-called social contract. This was an approach to a corporate state with the government, unions and business agreeing to control wages and prices.

The oil shocks of the early 1970s brought serious inflationary effects. By 1975 inflation hit 25 per cent, and the country faced the worst recession since the war, with shattered business confidence. This meant a return to an incomes policy to control inflation, and the pound fell.

As the oil from the North Sea came on stream, there was a boost in the balance of payments, resulting in the pound being maintained at unrealistically high rates vis-à-vis other currencies. This occurred despite substantial domestic inflation, which in turn made British exports expensive and threatened jobs in Britain. The result was high unemployment, low productivity and a relative failure to adapt to rapidly changing conditions. The British industrial structure has revealed a state of senescence, and exports have been declining.

It appears that the benefit of the North Sea oil is being lost. World demand for British products is low because of the international crisis, and the attack by the government on inflation through a monetarist policy has increased the rate of business failures and heightened the unemployment problem. The result is that the country must pay more and more attention to microeconomic matters and try to improve economic and industrial efficiency. The search is on for an industrial strategy.

The contrast with France is very striking. Instead of a relatively consistent long-term plan for economic development, Britain has gone through three and a half decades of stop-go economic policies, in which no real success has been attained in long-term investment in the economy to modernize and make it more productive. Burdened by external obligations and by its own traditional preferences for liberal economic policies, the government's priority has been the maintenance of the value of sterling rather than industrial investment. Experiments with economic planning have been too short-lived to bring success.

Immediate government priorities always took precedence over longer-term economic plans. After elections governments always tried to carry out their commitments to the electorate. This was usually followed by a period of economic difficulty because the state was doing more than it could afford and it therefore had to borrow abroad. Trade unions' demands have become increasingly assertive, and this has pushed the government into increasing wages beyond what the economy could support. The Keynesian influence tended to lead people to see public expenditure as, on the whole, a good thing. However, recent experience with inflation has converted people in high places to the ideas of Milton Friedman, who emphasizes the need to control the money supply. The result has been tight money and increasing unemployment. Inflation, however, is well down from its 25-per-cent-a-year height in the late Seventies.[3]

To sum up, British experience since the war has involved considerable vacillation in policy; commitment to planning has been short term and relatively ineffectual. British economic policies have been dominated by its foreign policy goals, and this has led to policy choices that were beyond the means of the British economy. Policies have been inadequate in dealing with some of the structural problems, such as the country's inefficiently organized industries and its dated capital structures. Both its trade union and management practices have inhibited industrial modernization, and, consequently, it has had to contend with a vulnerable international financial position and recurring balance-of-payments crises. In this sense, Britain's problems have been more political than economic, profound rather than superficial.

Samuel Beer has advanced an interesting hypothesis on British economic difficulties: "pluralistic stagnation."[4] He sees "a new group politics" in which powerful interests such as trade unions and industrial associations have become extremely powerful as counterbalances to the growing and increasingly centralized nature of the government. The result is a kind of *immobilisme* preventing the government from taking the necessary rational measures to remedy the country's economic difficulties. This situation has left the initiatives in economic policy-making to corporatist veto groups. Thus, the government has been restricted to manipulating the levers of fiscal and monetary policy and has not had the freedom to undertake overall structural economic planning. Commitment to imperial defence and diplomatic obligations have continued, whereas the trading system of the empire has crumbled rapidly. The position of Britain as a world banker has been jealously guarded, which has meant a high priority for protecting the international position of the pound. This has meant a neglect of the domestic economy, producing crises that have led to serious confrontations with labour.

Indicative Planning in a Democratic Setting: The Issues

The above sketchy outline of the experience of Britain and France with planning for economic development brings out certain contrasts. By the 1960s it had become clear in both countries, and indeed in most others, that capitalism can be humane, can produce a rising standard of living and a high rate of economic output. Planning seemed to be the obvious way of controlling the boom-and-bust cycle so as to assure an orderly pattern of investment, as well as reasonable levels of consumption. While this sort of planning need not necessarily be done by the state, the government alone has the democratic legitimacy to speak for the whole community. Large business organizations have long been planning their own operations over the long run. Only in the Sixties did it become clear that the democratic state too should assume a planning role, either directly, as in the case of France and for a short time Britain, or indirectly, through public industrial and financial institutions or through the banking system, as tends to occur in

Germany. On the whole the English-speaking countries (Britain, the United States, as well as Canada) have involved themselves very little in economic planning, whereas the counties of continental Europe have been much more active.

The central issue here is the reconciliation of material progress with the sustaining of democratic institutions. This can be attained through the development of institutions of popular control over the planning process. Only with such institutions can we be assured of achieving both planning objectives: the social democratic one of maintaining a reasonable level of equality of consumption, and the liberal-conservative one of maintaining a satisfactory level of production. Planning enterprises are undertaken as a response to the general pressure to modernize industry. As seen in chapter 3, this usually means fostering industrial concentration and emphasizing high technology. The government becomes involved in providing technical and financial assistance, and may also establish public enterprises modelled on the private capitalist corporation. Industrial concentration brings industry and government closer together and encourages planning for managerial problem-solving.

Planning requires the development of policies that are consistent with each other and coherently implemented. Therefore, emphasis must be placed upon the coordination of both governmental and private activity, with the close collusion of private and public managers in elaborating and carrying out the plan. This activity requires highly qualified professionals, who must make their objectives and strategies known to political leaders and who can count on the politicians' general support. However, political intervention can be disruptive; it can produce short-term *ad hoc* pressures that interrupt the long-term application of the planning arrangements. Clearly this is a difficult matter, since the policy process must be sustained in an evenhanded and continuing way. Therefore government must work closely with the planning authority. In France the planning commission is attached to the prime minister's office and thus has the clout necessary to command respect; its people work closely with the decision-making bodies.

It takes time and patience to develop general support for planning arrangements; the general socialization necessary to support the planning process has to be developed before success can be achieved. The planners therefore have to be more than just neutral, rational agents. They have to make allies among the leaders of government and business. This usually involves sectoral planning, which brings planners and business leaders together to elaborate detailed arrangements for investment and production. Beyond this, the process of consensus-building is difficult, involving not only the planners and the business leaders, but also government employees, trade union representatives and sometimes representatives of local governments, consumers and so on.

Sometimes it is extremely difficult to enlist the support of trade union leaders, especially in societies where they are accustomed to a confrontational posture. This is particularly true when the level of distrust between industrial managers and trade union leaders is great. The thrust of planning activity has tended to emphasize close collaboration between the planning authorities and business leaders. In other words, the prevailing authority structure of the society is accepted as given. The cooperation of the trade union leaders is sought to obtain the legitimation of the process and lessen the possibilities of disruption. This, however, can only be attained if these leaders can be convinced that the interests of their members will be better served by their supporting the planning operation than by their opposing it.

Essentially then, planning is a professional activity involving highly qualified people who are widely trusted. It is a device for excluding demagogy and irrational demands, and it has the inevitable consequence of strengthening the professional managerial elite in the society. Also, it enhances the role of the concentrated large industrial organizations, private and public, whose leaders are closely involved with the planning authority.

The need for close cooperation between industrial and planning leaders tends to conflict with the need for general public acceptance. Therefore, successful planning demands a high level of trust by the general population and by the bulk of the interest groups in the society for the planning operation, which itself is a highly elitist function.

Achieving this trust is particularly difficult at a time of serious inflation. In economies dominated by large corporations and large unions, inflation is the likely by-product of the exercise of the monopoly power of such large-scale bodies. Wage rises tend to be passed on in price increases. Inflation often serves the interests of large financial groups, who can use their market position to raise prices. It is here, however, that the legitimacy of public authority must be called in to impose policies that are in the general interest, such as incomes or prices policies. Such policies often demand substantial institutional change in order to make possible the effective planning of economic and social development in the context of democratic control.

44

Ultimately, of course, it is the political order that must prevail over the economic one, but if the governments are to intervene they must do so competently; that is, they must use qualified personnel to approach the problems in a long-term fashion, and they must develop a reasonable level of public trust and support in order to make this development possible. The French experience is probably the best known of the successful attempts at doing this, but even it has encountered considerable difficulty in meeting the problems of the economic crisis of the early Eighties, particularly the problems posed by stagflation.

The Free Market Option 5

There are, particularly in North America, very mixed views as to the virtues of indicative planning. The prevailing attitude appears to favour the free market economy in which business will constitute the major engine of economic growth, with the government playing a supportive but subordinate role. This attitude reflects the general North American philosophical bias towards traditional free enterprise or a capitalist economy. The prejudice is common and widespread that governments are generally so incompetent in economic affairs that whatever they can do could be done much better by private business. In support of this view, one often sees reference to the Canadian post office or other notoriously high-cost and inefficient government operations. However, in fairness it must be admitted that there is nothing *inherently* inefficient about government operations, and indeed there are well-run and efficient ones.

Another reason for favouring the free market option is the fact that it is particularly advantageous to those who are powerful in the marketplace. This applies both to countries — for example, the United States in the twentieth century, and Great Britain in the nineteenth — and to corporations. The largest corporations, because of their market power, are particularly advantaged in a free market situation.

The U.S.A.
Socialistic ideas have always been unpopular in the United States, and there many people identify planning with socialism. While the indicative planning practised in France has been anything but socialist, this prejudice in North America persists nonetheless.

Another factor is the power of business vis-à-vis government in the United States. American government has always been relatively weak and fragmented when confronting business. The separation of powers, the division between state and federal authority, the great power of interest groups especially in the legislative branch, the great power remaining in the hands of the judiciary, all tend to fragment governmental power and make it vulnerable to initiatives taken by business. Under these conditions it makes little sense to advocate a system of government-initiated planning because the government simply does not have the concentrated authority and power to make such an enterprise successful in the face of an extremely powerful business community.

However, most important of all is the fact that the United States has been for almost half a century the undisputed, predominant economic power in the Western world. It has greater weight in the international economic system than any other country and therefore has every advantage in favouring the free market option.

At the end of the Second World War American producers were the only ones who could compete vigorously in any market in the world; hence they were disposed to favour the "open door" and the free convertibility of currencies into dollars. It was their objective to force the colonial powers to end their protected, closed trading systems and allow free competition among producers. This would greatly favour the then more efficient American industrial complex. The American rationale for this was the maximization of productivity as a principle in its own right. Americans argued that with free trade and convertibility of currencies people would be able to buy in the most advantageous markets and thus raise their living standards more rapidly than would otherwise be the case. They championed lowering tariff barriers and preached the gospel of comparative advantage. There was much propaganda about "the century of the common man" and the liberalism of abundance. Since there was a kind of superficial plausibility about this argument, it was difficult for other nations to resist. Moreover, they were not in a position to do so because many of them were dependent upon the United States for economic aid through the Marshall Plan and through loans and grants made by the American government.

This free market approach was seen as a means of defeating the appeal of communism by bringing about the general enrichment of the people of the world. It would permit productive abundance without a radical redistribution of economic power and would encourage a partnership between business and government.

A similar argument was made in defence of stable values and convertibility of currencies. The argument was that this would enhance the welfare of all — and of course it would also guarantee the predominance of the United States because the American dollar then was the major reserve currency. Foreign countries held dollars to settle their international accounts and in doing so were giving interest-free loans to the United States.

The dependence of Europe and Japan upon American support assured the enormous influence of the United States. It meant they could not resist the American sponsorship of a capitalist West German federal state, which condemned the left wings of both the Social Democratic and Christian Democratic parties to oblivion. The Americans abandoned their policy of breaking up cartels in both Germany and Japan as the emphasis went to increasing productivity as the first consideration.

During the 1950s and 1960s the American policy seemed to be successful. Capital formation was high, and as a result, class conflict was held in check by rising incomes through economic growth.

In the late 1960s America's relative economic power began to decline as Europe and Japan re-entered the world trading system with renewed strength. The Americans could no longer impose their will on others. Some of these states had the advantage of highly centralized and efficient governmental structures, which contrasted sharply with the decentralized and open American system. American government decision-makers had little power to change the behaviour of private domestic actors and had little command of material resources, such as credit, that could be used as a lever to compel compliance. Their major instrument, therefore, has had to be simple exhortation and a resort to ideology, which has produced a rather overemphasized and simplistic anti-Communist rhetoric.

As the American economy came to be effectively challenged by the revived Japanese and EEC economies, American support for economic liberalism tended to diminish in favour of a new protectionism. There was serious disagreement within the United States about the level of tariffs and nontariff barriers needed to protect American industry. Some large multinational corporations at this time had invested substantially abroad and thus opposed protectionist measures in the United States, lest they expose themselves to retaliation. This was true not only of resource industries and manufacturing, but also of the American banks, which had made extensive commitments to foreign countries.

This new American weakness vis-à-vis the outside world and its internal divisions have been translated into international monetary disorder. The American dollar played a central role as a reserve currency in the 1950s and 1960s. However, as American balance-of-payments deficits grew, the willingness of foreign countries to hold dollars diminished. The U.S. was coming to resort increasingly to protectionist nontariff measures, while at the same time carrying out a liberal policy under the Trade Expansion Act of 1972 involving generous tariff cuts. The protectionist measures were highly selective and at first appeared to be mere exceptions to a generally prevailing liberal attitude. Eventually the American economy proved to be not strong enough to sustain both the Vietnam War and high domestic expenditures. The result was serious balance-of-payments deficits. The crisis came in August 1971 when the Americans devalued their currency and refused to redeem it for gold. There was a state of monetary instability; exchange rates fluctuated and "dirty floats" occurred, as countries attempted to manipulate the value of their currencies in their own interests.

The oil shocks of the early Seventies made the situation increasingly unstable. The flood of petro-dollars onto the world market gave new economic power to hitherto weak states such as Saudi Arabia and the other oil producers of the Third World. These events have served to shake the confident American commitment to the free market system. About 75 per cent of the holdings of U.S. raw materials corporations located in Third World countries have been nationalized, and firms directly controlled by governments are playing a prominent role in the world economy.[1]

In short, the free market option which paid off so handsomely for the United States in the Fifties and Sixties has encountered heavy weather in the Seventies and Eighties, and apparently the system is beginning to flounder. The American governments are now manning the protective devices to look after the strength of the American currency and the American productive economy. The inflationary and employment crisis of the 1980s sees the United States abandoning many of its cherished liberal values in favour of individual acts of protectionism in support of industries in difficulty. The ideological commitment to the free market remains, but it tends to be carried out by the Reagan administration in perverse governmental acts to support business in meeting its problems, sometimes at the cost of the ordinary citizen. The simple pattern of free market policies that was advocated in the Forties and Fifties has been succeeded by a confusing *mélange* of general free market policies that a hegemonic power would find beneficial, combined with individual acts of protectionism.

West Germany: Concertation through the Banks

When West Germany emerged from military occupation in the late Forties, it was especially subject to American influence because it depended upon American aid to assist in rebuilding its economy. The Americans favoured a decentralized federal government with a large number of firms in vigorous competition with each other. However, this conflicted with the German tradition of centralization in industry; so the industrial enterprises began to form cooperative associations. In order to amass sufficient venture capital, industrial concentration moved ahead quickly.

The Federation of German Industry (BDI) was established in 1949, based on thirty-nine national industrial federations. This greatly facilitated the collaboration of corporations in developing their investments and management practices. However, at the same time there was resistance against government-sponsored planning on the French model, partly because of apprehension about the consequences for Germany of too much centralized governmental authority, and also because of the desire of the industrialists to control economic matters themselves.

The leadership role has largely been played by the three major banks: the Deutsche Bank, the Dresdner Bank and the Commerz Bank. Through them the economic decisions were largely centralized. They have been prepared to make long-term loans for industrial development, but when doing so, they also exercise a role of control over the corporations concerned. This is often done through the *Aufsichtsrat,* or the supervisory board of the company, originally intended as a device for giving extra representation to shareholders, but these bodies have come to be dominated by senior bank executives. They have usually become allied to the company management, thereby increasing the concentration of effective economic power. Since the bank officials are the only people, other than brokers, who are allowed to trade on the floor of German stock exchanges, and because it is impossible to solicit investors' funds for a new enterprise unless it has at least a year's trading as a public company behind it, the banks have come to be used as agents for the large corporations. During this probationary period the corporation is entirely dependent on bank finance. Given these powers, the banks act as prefects controlling German industry, using the proxies of the German investing community. The effectiveness of this has been increased by the banks' practice of exchanging proxies so as to give a given bank predominant authority over an industry in which it is particularly interested. Banks normally try to get at least 25 per cent control of the shares of any such company.

This situation has permitted the banks to play the role of grand strategists of the nation's industry. They have acted to develop a consensus of German big business, and are therefore in a position to plan the economy should they choose to do so. Because the banks have assumed such an important role, they have become the trusted allies of the public authority. For example, they have been the agents for distributing government subsidies to industry to develop certain types of activity. Since the government imposes a high level of taxation to pay both for social security schemes and for industrial subsidies, the result is a relatively high level of industrial investment, about a third of which is financed by the government.

Since the Constitution formally charged the government with the duty of balancing its budget *each year*, there has been a tendency to overtax in order to maintain a kind of orderly governmental housekeeping and to avoid budgetary deficits. This practice in turn gave the government considerable influence in determining investment patterns because such a large portion of investment came from public funds. The KW (*Kreditanstalt für Wiederaufbau*), a government financing agency, has played a large role in funnelling public funds into private investment. Often on the basis of low-cost loans, these funds are extended to business via the banks.

The government has been prepared to discriminate among industries, granting favours such as tax concessions to some but not others. For example, the basic industries (steel, coal and iron) were given early concessions in order to facilitate their rebuilding after the war. This sort of policy favoured the large industries that were able to develop close relations with government and banking officials. This policy has meant that the German government has consistently undertaken responsibility for the composition of the national economy. It has been prepared to enter the fray and make crucial choices — something that Canadian governments have been conspicuously unwilling to do — and it has done it with a vengeance, spending about a quarter of all budgetary expenditure on fiscal discrimination.[2] Germany has endowed itself with the powers and equipment necessary for economic planning, although it has avoided the French pattern of elaborating a detailed plan through a governmental institution.

The concern of the German government has consistently been with the maintenance of exports so as to sustain continued economic growth. This in turn has led the government to favour price stability even at the cost of some periods of substantial unemployment. The early success of the "free market economy" under the leadership of Ludwig Erhard legitimized the newly established German capitalism as the creator of the economic miracle. From 1970 to 1973 Germany was the world's second largest trading nation. The high level of economic activity, with virtually full employment engaged in the task of national reconstruction, created a remarkable sense of national dedication. The trade unions played a constructive and cooperative role. Everyone seemed to share the view that success would come through export performance as long as inflation could be avoided. The trauma of the inflation of 1923 was still recalled with horror. The Deutschmark was kept undervalued in order to guarantee that German exports would remain competitive.

The key government agency overseeing the economic developments has been the Ministry of Economics working in close association with the Bundesbank, or central bank. It has favoured a liberal regime of foreign trade, always with the state backing the national champions in the international market. Business interest groups have worked in close collaboration with the governmental bureaucracy to the point that they would be informed of the government's proposed policies before the members of the Parliament themselves.[3] Thus, the bargaining process between the BDI and the government has been extremely important in policy-making. Interest group influence is often institutionalized in the numerous ministerial advisory councils that help formulate policy. The labour unions too have been part of the "grand coalition" that has supported export expansion, but generally they have played a passive and supportive role, with wages increasing at a rate lower than productivity.

There has been a considerable reliance upon monetary policy in the strategy of export expansion. With inflation rates kept low, export surpluses were long maintained, putting Germany at a strong competitive advantage over her trading partners. This has meant considerable power resting in the hands of the Bundesbank, which is, like most central banks, in some measure independent of the government. With floating exchange rates the power of the central bank has increased. Generally the relations between the Bundesbank and the government involve close consultation and cooperation. In the council of the central bank, the presidents of the state or Land banks are more numerous and therefore more important than the directors appointed by the federal government. This dual representation serves economic integration and enlists the support of both state and federal governments for current monetary policy.[4]

The surpluses earned in international trade have facilitated a growth in capital export by German industries. The government favours this over importing labour because the country has already assimilated as large a proportion of foreigners as it thinks it safely can. Much of this investment has been in order to secure supplies of raw materials. However, since about 1970, the industrial sector has shrunk while the service sector has grown, with total employment declining by 1.4 million.[5] This has led to a conservation-oriented structure and a regional policy to keep marginal producers in operation. The government has followed a *Struktur Politik* (sectoral policy) as a strategy of selective competitiveness, with the government favouring those industries which are highly competitive, such as the machine-building, chemical and pharmaceutical industries. It also has favoured high technology, such as the data-processing and electronics industries. This interventionist policy has its emphasis on maintaining a high level of investment and therefore has involved an attempt to control undue increases in the level of wages.

Germany has combined in a particular way central direction, which one associates with French planning, with a competitive liberal economy. This has been done by allowing a considerable free play for industrial concentration, leaving the initiative to the businessmen of the country. The result is a concerted and dynamic economy able to fend effectively for itself in international trade.

Part 3

Canadian Responses

Federal Central Agencies 6

Postwar Social and Economic Changes

Canada is one of the world's most profoundly federal countries. Not only is governmental jurisdiction divided among the federal government in Ottawa and the ten provinces, but the country is composed of regions with their own peculiar cultures, economies and attitudes. Quebec is in many ways the most distinctive province and region, with its French culture and language. The four western provinces are sometimes perceived as a region in themselves and at other times as two regions: British Columbia, with its mountains and coastline, in contrast to the Prairie provinces. They have in common a dynamism that comes from new wealth based on natural resources. In the 1980s it is here that the main challenge to federal authority is to be found, centring on the provincial governments' determination to maximize their share of the return from these resources. This has had the inevitable effect of challenging the federal government, and also of creating a certain estrangement from eastern Canada, which western Canada perceives as seeking more than its share of nature's bounty in the West.

The Atlantic provinces remain in a relatively poor economic situation, although they have been encouraged by the example of Alberta and Saskatchewan as well as by indications of substantial natural resources of their own, particularly in the form of offshore petroleum deposits. Their poverty makes them relatively vulnerable, with a weak bargaining position; but on the other hand, in the case of Nova Scotia and Newfoundland, their hoped-for oil and gas resources encourage them to claim the full benefits of natural resource wealth for the provinces — that is, for themselves.

Ontario finds itself in a changing situation. From Confederation on, it became the most important province economically, and with the development of industry it became the major centre of secondary manufacturing, trade and commerce, as well as being a leader in the field of natural resource development. The result was that the province took on the role, in some respects, of an imperial power in relation to the outlying parts of the country. It became richer and more populous in relation to them, and it was of course resented because of its power and wealth. Its economic preponderance was interpreted by some as exploitive. As the major powerhouse within Confederation and the province where the federal capital is located, there came to be a certain identity between the federal government and the province of Ontario. The pan-Canadian concerns of the federal government were mirrored in the pan-Canadian concerns of the Ontario-centred industrial complex.

More recently, however, the direction of development has changed. Before the 1982 crisis, although Ontario continued to grow in population and investment, its relative rate of growth was well behind that of Alberta, British Columbia and Saskatchewan. Canada has been experiencing the same kind of shift of economic activity from the East to the West as the United States; this could mean a relative decline for Ontario.

Politicians, in dealing with regional economic tension and rivalry, are defending their own jurisdictional turf and attempting to expand it at the expense of the others. This development comes at the same time as individuals and groups in the society are growing more assertive, claiming every advantage for themselves. The wartime commitment to the overall national interest has been attenuated by newer loyalties closer to the individual to maximize his or her own welfare. The power of interest groups has become more manifest in relation to government, and great corporations have increased their hold on power and economic strength, using advertising and taste-moulding influences in their products and public presentations. Corporations and governments have been challenged by the growth of powerful trade unions, which have come to possess and to exercise the right to disrupt substantial economic activities not only in the private sector but also in government. The arrival of the "me generation" among the youth of the Western world corresponds also to the development of these interest groups, some possessing considerable monopoly power to claim ever larger shares of the national income.

All this has been happening in Canada at the same time as international trade rivalries have become more acute, with the development of highly sophisticated processing methods in not only

58

Western Europe but now in Asia. As noted above, the appearance of dynamic and successful concerted economies in France and, in a different way, Germany, and more recently the development of the extremely successful Japanese economy place the relatively divided and disorganized Canadian economic community at a disadvantage in world trade. It is obvious that in a contest between societies organized to maximize their economic effectiveness and those preoccupied with internecine struggles for dominance, the former have the advantage. On the other hand, North America has the benefit of long years of economic development uninterrupted by war, as well as some of the world's most generous endowments of natural resources.

In the years since the Second World War, the Canadian government has been drawn more and more into providing services to strengthen the economic position of Canadian producers. We shall in the following pages sketch the most important of these.

As already noted, the end of the Second World War brought a new approach to the role of government. Fear of a return to the miseries of the Depression, combined with a general leftward policy orientation in the world and the new policy revolution of Keynesian economics, led the government to shoulder a new responsibility for employment, income and economic growth. This involved a considerable enlargement in the scale of government and the elaboration of new mechanisms to deliver services, plan policy and generate information. The objective was to make the government capable of affecting economic activity in the country within the general structure of individual freedom and private ownership of the bulk of the productive assets. The process was essentially pragmatic, but it involved the government in certain important but limited areas of economic activity. The policy goals were full employment, price stability, economic growth, balance-of-payments equilibrium, equitable distribution of income, and the alleviation of regional economic disparities. Some of these inevitably conflicted with others — a problem that has become increasingly acute in recent years — and substantial tradeoffs have had to be made.

The immediate postwar period was prosperous. Satisfactory levels of economic growth bred a certain complacency about the economy, under the general surveillance of the federal government. However, after 1957 a recession occurred and unemployment increased. There grew a need for government spending to relieve distress and create jobs. This ushered in a new era of government programs to deal with the various ills of the society. Pensions and equalization payments to the provinces were increased. Special programs for winter employment and others to facilitate regional development were introduced. The government took the pulse of the country through a series of royal commissions looking at energy, government organization, taxation, health services, banking and finance.

After 1962 there was a substantial increase in social security arrangements, such as the Canada Pension Plan and Medicare. These raised public expenditure and thus conflicted with policies for economic development. In this latter area, the government established the Economic Council of Canada, the Department of Industry, the Department of Forestry and Rural Development, and separated the Treasury Board from the Department of Finance.

Paralleling this federal interventionism were increased activities at the provincial level, particularly in economic areas. The federal government became increasingly sensitive to the differential rates of economic development among the provinces and regions of Canada; new departments were created, notably the departments of Manpower and Immigration, Consumer and Corporate Affairs, Industry, Trade and Commerce, and Regional Economic Expansion. Policy ministries were also created: Science and Technology, and Urban Affairs.

In the Seventies there was greater concentration on problems of the national economy, as high inflation and unemployment both became serious and chronic problems. The country also became concerned with the extremely high level of foreign ownership and control of Canadian industry, although little was done to correct the situation apart from the creation of the Foreign Investment Review Agency (FIRA) to monitor the development.

After the failure of voluntary wage and price guidelines in 1975, the government introduced mandatory controls administered by the Anti-Inflation Board (AIB). This program gave rise to considerable controversy and was dropped after it ran its three-year course, although the problem of inflation proceeded thereafter to become increasingly acute. There is evidence of considerable disagreement within the policy-making circles over the means to deal with inflation. While the prime minister expressed the need for controls because of the power of big business and big labour to pass price increases on to the consumer, others, especially in the Finance Department, showed greater confidence in the forces of the market and favoured controlling the supply of money and cutting down on government expenditures as more appropriate remedies.

It became apparent that the stated goals of the government as articulated in 1945 were leading to contradictory government policies — government proceeded to pursue its various priorities at one and the same time. Add to this the debates about the appropriate economic theories to inform policy and the attempts to reform the political processes through internal governmental machinery, and one has virtually insurmountable problems of government.

The Central Agencies

Before 1968 the prime minister presided over a cabinet made up of relatively independent ministers who developed their own policies. The cabinet itself looked after what coordination there was. C. D. Howe was a kind of super minister over the economy until his defeat in 1957. The subsequent Diefenbaker and Pearson periods were times of loose central coordination in the Department of Finance in the areas of economic policy; yet it was during the Pearson period that the beginnings of a committee system in cabinet were instituted.

However, it was after 1968 with Pierre Trudeau as prime minister that a much more structured and highly integrated decision-making system was built up.[1] The guiding principle was to get power into the hands of the ministers and away from the powerful deputy ministers. The practical application was joint responsibility between ministers.[2] To accomplish this, a system of cabinet committees was put in place. The first five committees attempted to divide the major substantive policy spheres into sectors. The key committee, the Priorities and Planning Committee, was chaired by the prime minister. It set the overall tone and direction of government policy by choosing the priorities, initiating policy reviews, assigning responsibilities to the other committees, and considering the most pressing and politically important issues.[3] The committees were equipped with competent secretariats drawn from the Privy Council Office. After the Federal-Provincial Relations Office was created in 1975, its representatives often attended. They reported back to the full cabinet where the final decisions would be taken. "The Prime Minister, through the Secretary to the Cabinet, is the final arbiter of the content of the Records Decision."[4] Each committee met once a week when carrying a full work load, and each minister was normally a member of two or three committees. While the major coordinating committee was the Priorities and Planning Committee, other major committees were the Legislation and House Planning Committee, which charted the legislative program of the government, the Federal-Provincial Relations Committee and, of course, the Treasury Board, which was

61

responsible for advising the cabinet on the allocation of funds, in addition to its statutory functions. The other committees were sectoral and tended to group the government's concerns such as social development, economic development, foreign and defence policy, and miscellaneous government operations. There were special committees which met when they were needed, such as the committees on labour relations, western affairs (since 1980), the public service, security and intelligence. The overall effect of this system was to have some policy questions bouncing back and forth between committees of ministers without a clear allocation of responsibility. The prime minister, however, was in a powerful position to influence the play, as indeed were his close associates, both staff and ministerial.

Of course, this structure has undergone a change over the years since 1968, and especially during the short-lived Conservative government of Joe Clark in 1979–80. However, the structure has remained fairly constant, even if the nomenclature has changed. Mr. Clark's inner cabinet really fulfilled the same role as Mr. Trudeau's Priorities and Planning Committee except that the latter's decisions required cabinet confirmation. The major recent change (1978), is the introduction of the "envelope system" or PEMS (Policy and Expenditures Management System), which, for purposes of financial control, groups departments together in "envelopes," each of which receives a given overall amount of money to meet its commitments. Transfers can be made between departments in the same envelope but not between envelopes. This has turned out to be an effective means of forcing tradeoffs and therefore of setting priorities. It is superior to the previous Treasury Board system in that both policy and expenditure decisions are taken in one forum, and not bounced back and forth between Treasury Board and policy committees.

For such a system to work, it requires a competent support system. Some support comes from the new ministries of state for social and for economic development, but most is to be found in the expanded central agencies of the Privy Council Office (PCO), the Treasury Board, the Finance Department, plus the Prime Minister's Office (PMO). All of these bodies have been expanded over the past decade or more and have become centres of planning and reflection on government policy in both the short and long term. Their mandates extend over the whole spectrum of government, and therefore they have become checks on the sectoral thrusts of the individual departments. Their rise reflects the importance of the newer style — planning-oriented and often technocratic experts — over the traditional mandarinate in the line

62

departments. They are identified with the newer budgeting techniques and planning arrangements — although each developed its own special approaches and emphasis.

The Prime Minister's Office

The most partisan and *ad hoc* of these bodies is the Prime Minister's Office, whose staff has grown to over a hundred (1983) from about thirty under St. Laurent and Diefenbaker. While the PMO is not technically a central agency, it has a political staff that changes with each prime minister and is thus concerned about the survival of the government. It has not, therefore, been a major source of policy innovations in recent years, although since it has the ear of the prime minister in an intimate sense, it has considerable power of initiative. It is the means by which the prime minister can centralize power in emergencies, to act effectively before opposition crystallizes. By strengthening the PMO and the PCO and by using the cabinet committee system, the prime minister has been able to give himself alternative sources of policy advice, and thus make himself less dependent upon the mandarins — the senior corps of deputy ministers and their assistants.

The Privy Council Office

The Privy Council Office is staffed by career public servants and is a much more nonpartisan and therefore more professional body than the Prime Minister's Office. Its role is to service the cabinet committees, provide secretarial support and coordinate the various aspects of government policy. This gives it power to act as a kind of arbiter between departments and as an assembler of information. It can be thought of as the prime minister's department. The clerk of the privy council is the highest-ranking public servant in the federal government, and is the director of the PCO. He is, of course, also the secretary to the cabinet.

When the Trudeau government came to power in 1968, concerned to avoid control by the deputy ministers and other senior members of the line departments, it decided to build up the PCO as an alternative source of policy advice. Equipped with its expertise, the government would be able to gain a degree of independence from the mandarinate. This meant developing a substantial staff of able, highly trained people for general policy advice. Soon the PCO became the centre of government planning in Ottawa. It had the initial advantage of being closest to the prime minister and his nearest advisors, and was built around the

Committee on Priorities and Planning of the cabinet. It was not committed to any particular intellectual discipline or planning theory. Rather it was "based on an eclectic mixture of corporate planning theory, cybernetics and systems with a smattering of technological forecasting and futurology."[5] Its approach tended to reject the more personalized manner of policy-making from the past. The problem was to find the right structure. Its approach was essentially rational, with a deductive approach to planning, focusing on the future: "What kind of Canada do we want in the year 2000?" Thus it was very general; Michael Pitfield claimed the object of the planning undertaking was "to help ministers to know what they were doing."[6] The PCO had the advantage over the departmental deputy ministers and the other planning agencies (see below). It operated through planning documents whose function was to catalogue, define, schedule, monitor and update various categories of issues facing the government.[7]

In the first Trudeau government (1968–72) the planning team was optimistic and felt that it was breaking new ground. It did much to elaborate the cabinet committee system in close cooperation with the prime minister and the Priorities and Planning Committee. It identified the government priorities, such as the language policy and the problem of removing regional economic disparities, as well as the fight against inflation. These became lists of policy areas ranked in order of priority. However, the first years of optimism were followed by fatigue and prudence, as the government encountered serious opposition in the inevitable difficulties of governing. The setback in the election of 1972, when the Liberals were put into a minority position, shook the confidence of the planners and the PCO. The government felt it could no longer afford the luxury of long-term planning, and shifted its attention to day-to-day survival in the minority government situation. This has meant that the cabinet Committee on Priorities and Planning became the allocator of major policies, as well as a general management committee to keep government forces together.

In the planning process a very select group of people exercised a very important role: the officers of the Priorities and Planning Secretariat of the Plans Division of the Privy Council Office kept in touch with the ministers and discussed their policy ideas, synthesized these and worked out schedules for implementation and packaging of the ideas. The result would be a cabinet memorandum going to the prime minister for his approval. After the cabinet committees and the full cabinet had had their discussions, these people drafted the resulting

Records of Decision, and interpreted them for the departments. In this process, while the group represented itself as simply the instrument of the cabinet, it inevitably developed a kind of agency philosophy. It identified the priority problem which required analysis and perhaps action. "In 1970, the list of priority problems included inflation, pollution, national unity, information, the public service, participatory democracy, education, social justice, urban growth and housing, tax reform and the ownership and control of Canadian resources."[8] Later such matters as regional economic expansion, bilingualism, foreign investment and cartels were added. The effect was to see these problems dealt with either by the setting up of special machinery, such as new departments of government, and/or in the studying of the questions directly so as to deal with them appropriately. Such matters, for example, as participatory democracy and social justice were too amorphous to produce tangible results.

This Cabinet Planning System also produced a departmental policy review to stimulate departments to reflect on their plans and to share these ideas with the cabinet. In the early years such matters as constitutional reform, foreign policy, defence policy and northern development were the focus of the review.[9] This activity reflected the enormous faith in "the power and persuasiveness of rational analysis" that the Cabinet Planning System involved. Also it was an attempt to bring the weight of cabinet behind the designation of particular policies for evaluation.

In 1974–75 the Cabinet Planning System became involved in the "Priorities Exercise" — an attempt to articulate the highest priority tasks to be accomplished by the government of Canada when the Trudeau government returned with a parliamentary majority. This was the most ambitious attempt by this body to elaborate the future tasks of government and play a coordinating function within government. It was an attempt to involve the departments far more thoroughly than in the past in the development of priorities. The idea was that a small policy group in the Prime Minister's Office would interview each minister in the new cabinet to obtain his views as to what the government should do during its mandate. These interviews resulted in a list of objectives. It was hoped that a set of five to ten priorities would emerge from this exercise. However, with the benefit of hindsight, it appears to have been an overly grand plan, as well as being a somewhat naive and simplistic approach to the problem of establishing policy objectives.

In the cabinet meeting to discuss this question in November of 1974, five policy themes were articulated:

- a more just, tolerant Canadian society;
- a greater balance in the distribution of people, and the creation and distribution of wealth between and within regions;
- the more rational use of resources and a sensitivity to the natural and human environment;
- the acceptance of new international responsibilities, particularly with regard to assisting developing countries; and
- an evolving federal stake in national policy, as well as sensitive, responsive and competent government at all levels.

Under these five general points were elaborated sixteen priority policy areas. These were an equally general list of "motherhood" items. This vague, optimistic exercise really was the beginning of the end for the Cabinet Planning System. It failed to define real priorities in any meaningful sense, instead resorting to generalities and platitudes. This is no doubt because of the dynamics of the committee system, in which all participants wished to make their contribution and in which there was no structured sense of procedure that could be clearly agreed upon and articulated. The priorities had a certain naive optimism about them that did not square with the harsh realities of the international economy in the 1970s. Inflation was not mentioned, and no attempt was made to deal with the election promise made by the Liberals in 1974 not to implement wage and price controls. The process of elaboration, general and pedestrian, of these objectives dragged on as departments were consulted and each attempted to make its contribution, without making suggestions that would disturb its own tranquility. The result was a set of defensive and unimaginative responses, which amounted to the aggregate ambitions of the departmental middle managers and the personal policy ideas of the ministers. General objectives were stated, but they were largely devoid of politically tangible initiatives. As a result, the government drifted somewhat listlessly as the country faced accelerating inflation and unprecedented wage settlements. "At the moment which should have been its greatest triumph, the Cabinet's Planning System was at the point of collapse."[10] Within the year the government was to set up a system of wage and price controls; the results of the priorities exercise were simply ignored. The government embarked on its own initiatives, with the economy and "law and order" as its two priorities.

The Cabinet Planning System largely disappeared with the priorities exercise. Since that time, the initiative in planning has passed to other bodies, which we shall discuss below. The Privy Council Office has remained with a somewhat lower profile than in its pre-1975 heroic period. Also the jealousies that inevitably were directed against the dynamic upstart formation have had time to cool, and no attempt to add specialized planning expertise has been attempted since. There was a reluctance to create yet another central agency "monster." The initiative therefore passed to other bodies.

The Treasury Board and the Treasury Board Secretariat

Another child of the early Trudeau government was set up in 1969 in the Planning Branch of the Treasury Board Secretariat. Douglas Hartle, the deputy secretary of the Treasury Board, directed this small but dynamic operation. Here the emphasis was upon rigorous analysis and appraisal of government programs to measure their effectiveness and test their policy thrusts in terms of modern economic analysis. The work of this body fitted in with the general aim of modernizing government management, following in the wake of the Glassco Commission on Government Organization. The watchword here was the Planning, Programming, Budgeting System (PPBS) — management by objectives and the operational performance measurement system. The concern was with efficiency and effectiveness. The techniques were rational, objective measurement.[11] The Treasury Board Planning System was based on the belief that government programs should be tested for efficiency and for their effectiveness in achieving the government's objectives. This would permit the systematic elimination of the wasteful and ineffective programs, which in turn would provide resources for more useful and efficient ones. To test these programs, modern methods of economic analysis, including econometric model building, would be employed. This would force the operating departments to scrutinize their own programs and clarify their objectives. The result would come (through reliance upon quantitative methods) in the form of an objective and precise accounting of the expenditure of public money through programs operated by the departments.

Al Johnson became the secretary to the Treasury Board in 1970. His task was to help achieve a systematic approach to government decision-making. This in turn carried the Treasury Board Secretariat beyond simple scrutiny of efficiency into policy questions. The Planning Branch was led with dynamism and ethusiasm by Hartle and Johnson into an aspect of planning at the same time as the Privy

Council Office and the Department of Finance were launched on their own attempts at economic planning. However, the fact that the wave of planning enthusiasm was being ridden by these three central agencies, plus many planning bodies in most of the line departments, meant that there was inevitable competition among them, and the great expectations developed by each could not possibly be fulfilled.

As Richard French comments, the Treasury Board Planning System "appears as an intellectual *tour de force* without an audience to appreciate it . . . all dressed up with no place to go."[12] Still, of all the planning systems, the Treasury Planning System was the most intellectually sophisticated and determined effort to introduce rational analysis into the traditional incremental process of policy-making in the federal government. However, the new rationalistic tools had turned out to be somewhat disappointing in what they could in fact produce. This disenchantment is not peculiar to Canada, but is a general one that represents the inevitable letdown following over-enthusiastic adoption of the new methods.

The concepts in forming the budgetary restructuring as defined in the Treasury Board manual of 1969 were:

> a) the setting of specific objectives; b) the systematic analysis to clarify objectives and to assess alternative ways of meeting them; c) the framing of budgetary proposals in terms of programs directed toward the achievement of the objectives; d) the projection of the costs of these programs a number of years in the future; e) the formulation of plans of achievement year by year for each program; and f) an information system for each program to supply data for the monitoring of achievement of program goals, and to supply data for the reassessment of program objectives and the appropriateness of the program itself.[13]

The emphasis, in short, was on resource allocation in a departmental context, or between programs and functions of government, instead of the traditional annual increases in expenditure items.

Hartle, in tackling this difficult assignment, was optimistic and aggressive; he thought that if relatively few changes in the system could be made, great returns would follow. Objective measurement and analysis would produce reports that would inevitably lead to accurate assessment and therefore rational policy-making. Evaluation and planning were inextricably related. This meant that the Treasury Board Planning System was bound to be making arguments, based on its cost effectiveness reviews, that challenged the initiatives coming from the Privy Council Office — an indicator of the likelihood of friction.

68

Problems arose when particular departments' programs were selected for rigorous analysis. Programs in manpower training, direct job creation and youth employment, regional development subsidies, industrial research and development incentives, dairy price supports and so on were subjected to careful and critical analysis. Hartle's team was able and enthusiastic, and was buoyed up by the success of its analytical techniques. Now, with hindsight, it is clear that some of the analysis was questionable, as inevitably it must have been. However, "Hartle's brilliance and determination . . . threatened and intimidated vested bureaucratic interests at almost every turn."[14] Not only were the departmental managers concerned, whose programs were threatened, but also officials in the central agencies felt threatened and resented what they saw as invasion of their turf. The fact is that vested interests were frightened, and a feeling of alarm was spread in many comfortable bureaucratic corners. In addition, the character of politicians refused to change. The ministers continued to defend programs that were politically popular even though they could be shown objectively to be inefficient.

There is one budget control innovation from this period that has proven lasting and valuable: the introduction of the "A" and "B" budgets. This exercise involves dividing the expenditure proposals into two categories: the "A" Budget (for programs already in place) and the "B" Budget (for new programs). This division facilitates the process of examination of expenditure proposals in order to keep costs under control and prevent overruns.

Originally the staff of the Treasury Board was within the Department of Finance. The board is the agency that must approve expenditures by all departments and agencies of government each year and thus controls abuses in public spending. It was separated from the Department of Finance to allow the latter to concentrate on economic and tax policy matters without being unduly influenced by problems relating to expenditures. This permits the expenditure-planning process to be longer term, and it allows the Department of Finance to concern itself with the fiscal capacity of the economy.

Between the planning activities of the Privy Council Office, the Treasury Board Secretariat and the Department of Finance, the system had overloaded the capacity of the ministers and bureaucracy to respond. There was inevitable incompatibility between the first two of these, and a tendency for both of them to be resented by the venerable Department of Finance.

The Canadian government has had a bitter and largely unsuccessful experience with planning, not by doing too little but by doing too much, and by failing to integrate the various planning activities into a harmonious whole. The existence of several planning bodies persisted when integration was needed. The division of the planning function among several agencies meant that there was no effective control over the ministerial free-for-all in pursuit of resources, which always occurs in cabinet when ministers seek to augment the financial means of their own departments.

The Department of Finance

The oldest and most solidly based of the central agencies is the Department of Finance. In the past it had a virtual monopoly over the levers of control of the economy. It gave the expert advice, initiated policy and evaluated it for future action. Its major instruments have been the traditional fiscal and monetary policies, and its aim has been to stabilize the economy, while maximizing economic growth, employment, a favourable balance of international payments and a reasonable level of distribution of benefits among the regions and classes of Canadian society. This means that its major concerns have been: "1. economic analysis, fiscal policy, and international finance; 2. tax policy and federal-provincial relations; 3. tariffs, trade and aid; 4. economic programmes, government finance and capital markets; and 5. long range economic planning."[15]

To do these things the department has had to develop strategies for influencing other government departments and agencies. The department works closely with the departments of National Health and Welfare, Energy, Mines and Resources, Industry, Trade and Commerce, and Labour because the areas of economic policy are highly interrelated and often defy agency designation. There has been an ongoing debate as to whether the role of the Department of Finance in policy coordination should be strengthened by the adoption of a more formal planning approach or be reduced by further delegation of some of its responsibilities.[16] In the past there has usually been one major concern facing the economy of the country, and the department has undertaken responsibility for that. For example, in the 1940s the problem of stabilizing the economy through the war and reconstruction periods was followed by the problem of managing demand in the economy and eliminating cyclical fluctuations. In the Sixties things became more complex, and the department had to face the question of maintaining equilibrium in international balance of payments at the same time as it sought to attain full employment, the maintenance of economic growth and the beginning of a fight against inflation. With substantial immigration there was great concern about labour supply. In the 1970s with the energy crisis, emphasis was placed on making more natural resources available, and now in the 1980s, with the general worldwide economic crisis, the department has had to concern itself with serious inflation, growing unemployment and the problem of interest rates. The old term "fine tuning" to refer to the efforts of the department to stabilize the economy now seems grotesquely inappropriate, as the mounting crisis seems to defy the efforts of government to manage.

It is not surprising that policy conflicts have emerged, and debate on the appropriate role for the department has intensified. Some would have it take on more of a planning approach, while others would prefer to see its functions delegated and reduced. The creation of new departments such as Manpower and Immigration, Consumer and Corporate Affairs, and Regional Economic Expansion have all given rise to vested interests laying claim to some of the traditional functions of the Department of Finance.

The department's main objective, of course, has been to decide upon and implement major financial and other economic policies. Great emphasis is placed upon analysis and the monitoring of developments both in Canada and abroad. This involves the use of sophisticated econometric models, as well as more prosaic analyses and studies. These equipped the department to advise on fiscal and other economic policies and measures, and to recommend action on expenditure, lending, taxation, borrowing, et cetera. Also it advises on the balance of payments, exchange reserves and international monetary and financial arrangements. It participates in international economic negotiations, and it also advises on policies relating to federal-provincial fiscal and economic relations, and conducts discussions with the provinces on an ongoing basis.

Central to all this is the management of demand through fiscal, monetary and debt-management policies. This affects the level of taxes and of government expenditure, especially on social programs. This in turn involves mediating between groups in society, and therefore the minister has to consult the relevant interests. When the conventional fiscal and monetary instruments proved insufficient and consultations with labour and business did not produce appropriate results, the department was the government's instrument in implementing wage and price controls in the fall of 1975. Throughout all of this, of course, it has had to deal continuously with the provinces, particularly on such questions as energy policy, manpower policy and social policy. In the field of monetary policy, it works closely with the Bank of Canada on questions of the money supply and the rate of interest.

Within the government the Department of Finance finds itself acting as a kind of internal opposition to vet and monitor economic programs carried out by other departments. It gives an opinion on proposals put forward by other departments and agencies for new programs; it participates in the deliberation of the cabinet committees in which these programs are discussed; and it is ultimately responsible for the annual budget, which lays out aggregate expenditure and deficit levels for the forthcoming year. This means that it must analyze and appraise the economic proposals brought forward by other departments and help the government to decide which of these should be adopted and what changes if any should be made.

As economic questions have become increasingly controversial and in a sense complex, there has been concern to have more of a planning capacity in the government and greater availability of competent long-term economic advice. The Economic Council of Canada was created in 1963 to make such advice available to government and to the general public openly so that citizens would be informed as to the options available to government and a debate could be conducted in the light of relevant data and sound analysis. Within the Finance Department there has been a tendency since the 1960s to build up a staff of econometricians and other economics specialists to facilitate the capacity of the department to plan and monitor the economy. A Long-range Economic Planning Branch was established in the early Seventies. As noted above, there has been an ongoing discussion as to whether the department should be further strengthened analytically, or whether it would be better to simply strengthen the economic-intelligence process external to the department. In fact, both of these things have been done.[17]

A key part of the department is the Tax Policy and Federal-Provincial Relations Branch, which has the responsibility for formulating changes in tax policy. It maintains an ongoing relationship with the provinces, undertakes technical analysis and gives practical advice on the development of fiscal federalism in Canada. This relates to matters such as the joint occupancy of tax fields, fiscal transfers to the provinces and through them to the municipalities, shared-cost programs, opting-out provisions, and also mechanisms for intergovernmental cooperation in fiscal and economic matters.

A critical area in the early Eighties is the cooperative effort with the

Bank of Canada in order to fight inflation and defend the external value of the Canadian dollar. To do this the government has been seeking to reduce public expenditure since the fall of 1978, and to reduce demand by such devices as maintaining high interest rates. The Department of Finance has been led to adopt many differently oriented policies in order to maintain a simultaneous attack on inflation, unemployment and recession, and to cope with energy problems. The potential for conflict between policies working towards so many competing goals makes problems unavoidable and adds enormously to the complexity of policy planning and development. This complexity naturally leads to a search for greater sophistication and general capacity. This new situation has brought about attempts to develop a more long-term approach to planning of expenditures. In addition, the need for energy policies has led to long-term investment strategies. These policies can come very easily into conflict with short-term decisions to stabilize the economy, especially on the revenue side. These are difficult tasks and must be worked out in close collaboration with the other central agencies such as the Privy Council Office, the Treasury Board, and the Prime Minister's Office.

Generally the department has relied heavily on its stabilization instruments and is disposed towards an anti-interventionist policy, which places confidence in the allocation of resources by the market. The conservatism of the Department of Finance, however, has not been shared by the other central agencies noted above. Spending has increased substantially, and enormous budgetary deficits have been the order of the day, occasioned by costly social programs and the substantial expenditure to maintain the artificially low Canadian price for petroleum products through subsidizing imports. Richard French points out: "The Finance approach constituted a separate version of planning resistant to the collegiality of the Trudeau cabinet committee system with respect to the Department's prerogative in budgetary development."[18]

The old discipline of the belief in a balanced budget was not maintained in the postwar period, with the result that the government, despite the urgings of the Department of Finance, has allowed budget deficits to mount. The Department of Finance consistently produced restrictive and conservative fiscal frameworks, but it was never able to link its efforts in a common and overall plan with those of the Privy Council Office and the Treasury Board Secretariat. The rise of these new agencies inevitably led the department to feel threatened. Failure to unite with these other agencies meant that in the ministerial

73

free-for-all in pursuit of resources, effective resistance could not be mounted and deficits increased. After the first oil shock of 1973–74, followed by rising unemployment, social programs and petroleum subsidies mounted, and it became impossible to control increasing deficits. Fine tuning was no longer possible and the department had to implement the policy of controls in 1975. By 1978 it became clear that more restraint was necessary; so after the international economic summit in Bonn the prime minister returned to announce reductions of $2.5 billion from Canadian government spending. This was a unilateral prime ministerial initiative to impose discipline on the system, which seemed to be moving out of control, since the government was criticized for causing inflation through mounting public spending. The Lambert Royal Commission on Financial Management and Accountability, which reported in 1979, was severe in its comments on government financial management. It noted "a failure to plan thoroughly at the top. Accepted, instead, is a planning process too often dependent on trying too many uncoordinated proposals coming up from the bottom." It went on: "This has led to incremental budgeting, poorly conceived *ad hoc* solutions to problems, and excessive flexibility in program management."[19]

Federal Line Departments

7

In a sense all the departments of government are related to economic policy, but we shall examine only those with a specific commitment to it as their major concern, namely, Industry, Trade and Commerce (IT&C), and Regional Economic Expansion (DREE). (The departments are titled here as they were known before the reallocation of their titles and functions of 1982. At the time of writing the changes made in that year were not yet clear. Indeed one had little cause to be confident that the new structure would last, given the depth of the economic crisis and the likelihood of an abrupt change in policy direction. The nature of the changes are discussed in chapter 9.)

The Department of Industry, Trade and Commerce (IT&C)

The Department of Industry, Trade and Commerce is a clientele department devoted to the interests of business, mostly manufacturing, in Canada. It has the role of monitoring the wishes of the business community and articulating them in government circles, and also of being the instrument of government policy initiatives vis-à-vis business, especially such policies as incentive programs, grants programs and general government-business cooperative arrangements. It is the agency that offers business positive rewards but may at times impose negative sanctions. It is the major department to affect the industry-government interpenetration that is so typical of the Western capitalist system.

The department monitors the activities of other countries, especially their policies in support of business, so as to be in a position to imitate them or to counteract them. It is the instrument whereby the Canadian government supports its business community to meet the challenge of other governments supporting theirs. This leads it into all sorts of promotional activities in support of Canadian business: training programs, research support programs, sales undertakings for Canadian

75

businesses abroad, to name a few. The department undertakes to get government activities and policies synchronized with the objectives of the private sector. This means attempting to gain the cooperation and support of the business community for the goals established by government. It seeks to make the government play the role of top coordinator, but if it needs the cooperation of business, it must move significantly to accommodate the desires and demands of business.

This particular style of clientele relationship goes back to C. D. Howe, the wartime czar of business in Canada who occupied the key economic portfolios in the King and St. Laurent governments. It was Howe's policy to use governments to facilitate the growth and expansion of Canadian industry, to enable it to supply the armaments and munitions needed during the war. Leading businessmen were brought to Ottawa to act as wartime directors of production. This inevitably brought Canadian government and business closer together, with leading businessmen playing key roles in the governmental process, especially in the regulation of their own industries. This "government-business cooperation" was a major innovation of Howe's and was widely perceived as an effective means of encouraging the growth of industry, to expand production and increase employment. The fact that much of this increase in Canadian productive capacity was undertaken by foreign-controlled multinational corporations did not, at the time, appear to be an important consideration. Afterwards Howe wanted to see these facilities converted to peacetime production in an atmosphere of dynamic expansion. The trade commissioner service was developed to facilitate the sales of Canadian products abroad.

After the defeat of the St. Laurent government in 1957, attempts to support business and maintain employment were continued. Diefenbaker set up the National Productivity Council in 1961, and the Economic Council was set up in 1963. The Department of Industry was established at the same time, to facilitate the growth of manufacturing industry in Canada to supply more jobs. In 1969 the two departments of Industry, and Trade and Commerce were combined. Since 1972, the department has been working on an industrial strategy for Canada.

The major interest of the department centres on manufacturing and processing industries, tourism and the furthering of export trade. Since most of the processing industry is located in central Canada, the department has been most active in the central provinces. Consequently, some critics in the Atlantic provinces have referred to it as

76

"Ontario's DREE." To meet this kind of criticism, there has been considerable departmental decentralization, with regional offices devoted to local problems. There are ten such offices, each working closely with the provincial departments of industry. This is not always harmonious, however, because provincial objectives often conflict with federal ones. Every attempt has been made to establish good relations with the provinces, and the regional offices have concentrated on aid to small business, counselling them and helping them to qualify for government assistance.

The department operates through a series of major programs to assist business. For example, there is the Defence Industry Productivity Program (DIPP) to encourage companies to develop new products, the Industrial Design Assistance Program (IDAP), the Industrial Research and Development Incentive Act (IRDIA) and the Program for the Advancement of Industrial Technology (PAIT). The government provides operational and administrative costs (on a nonrepayable basis) to pay for new industrial designs; it gives tax-free grants for research when operating on a shared-cost program with business in its research efforts. Beginning in the late Seventies, there has been particular concern with technological innovation, which reflects similar policies of support undertaken in other major industrial countries. Similarly, efforts have been made to improve industrial efficiency in Canada to assist in meeting foreign competition.

The department has been interested in encouraging greater investment in Canada, incorporating new scientific developments in production. This involves it in studying the implications of foreign investment in Canada. It has prepared a survey of investment intentions, first begun with the cooperation of the Economic Council and now the sole responsibility of the department.

These activities to improve the structure of Canadian industry are, of course, somewhat unpopular with some business leaders, who would prefer government to play a purely supportive role. So far IT&C has worked virtually exclusively on the basis of persuasion and incentives, rather than relying on sanctions to enforce compliance. The result is that the government has been none too effective in inducing business to comply with its policy strategies.

In 1972 Jean-Luc Pépin attempted to formulate a comprehensive industrial strategy based on several sector strategies — "automotive, tourism, textiles, electronics, footwear, food products, book publishing and grain."[1] His successor, Alastair Gillespie, moved away from this relatively *dirigiste* position in favour of emphasizing consultation with industry. The department became involved in an elaborate exercise with the provinces and private business in analyzing the problems of Canadian industry (the ''Tier 1'' and ''Tier 2'' exercises are referred to in chapter 13).

The department inevitably encounters a certain amount of internal role conflict in that some of its policies are designed to support greater competition while others have the object of protecting Canadian industry from mainly foreign competition. Tariff barriers in one case contrast with incentive grants in another, and policies towards the weaker industries are different from those towards the stronger, internationally competitive ones.

There are also problems of maintaining interdepartmental coordination within the federal government. This is mainly achieved through interdepartmental committees. IT&C must work closely with the Department of Regional Economic Expansion whenever incentive grants are being provided to an industry. The department plays a major role in the Regional Development Incentives Board (RDIB) to advise on the larger grants for regional development. There is always a problem with conflicting objectives between IT&C and DREE in that the former is concerned with the competitive position of Canadian industry and its long-term survival vis-à-vis international competition, whereas DREE is concerned with creating jobs in depressed areas within Canada.

The major problem, however, is industry-government relations. There is considerable difficulty in coordinating the various activities scattered through the major departments of government, particularly in the area of integrating regional development with national growth. There is always a conflict of objectives when inherently inefficient industries receive support in order to create employment in under-developed areas of the country. This raises the question of the decentralization of industry, which some of the provinces have been anxious to foster in order to encourage employment. But decentralization in turn creates problems in federal-provincial relationships. Then there is the problem of small business and how to assist it. The current solution here is in the appointment of a special minister to look after the concerns of small business.

Tradeoffs always have to be faced. If a country is to develop some kind of industrial strategy, it must reconcile the need for developing the depressed areas and decentralizing industry, against the need to maximize productivity at the national level. Industrial incentives and development programs have been organized on a regional basis as the federal government has attempted to be more responsive to the demands of provincial governments and organizations. Regional development has now been approached on a more decentralized basis since 1973, in response to provincial demands.

A central problem is that of foreign ownership of major industrial undertakings in Canada. This has been generally criticized in the media and in public opinion polls, but various elites have taken a much more hedged position. The most ambivalent has been the Ontario government, which has come to accept the reality of substantial foreign control but has emphasized the Canadianization of management. The less developed provinces have been even less critical of foreign control because they are anxious to receive investment from whatever source.

Then, of course, there is the strong position taken by Canadian business and the public generally in favour of an open economy despite widely held reservations about the overly great role played by foreign capital in Canada. The federal government finds itself caught in the midst of disagreements on this question. Provinces differ drastically with each other on positions to be taken, and the result has been a resort to a posture of relative incrementalism. Indeed there is considerable disagreement within the various departments of the federal government. In terms of actual policy there has been a tendency towards product specialization as an attractive means of dealing with the problem. The best example of this is the Auto Pact, which led to the integration of the North American automobile industry and, of course, initially saved a considerable number of Canadian jobs in the assembly part of this industry. Mergers have also been countenanced in order to improve international competitiveness, particularly in the electrical industries — despite the generally negative attitude expressed in the antimonopoly legislation. Most important in this area is the Foreign Investment Review Agency, which acts as a screening mechanism. It negotiates with foreign firms proposing to locate in Canada in order to induce them to follow courses of action perceived to be in Canada's interest.

The upshot of these different attitudes and tactics has been a general posture of incrementalism, with IT&C favouring a series of "sector strategies." The attempt has been made to improve the level of sophistication of Canadian industries and create jobs where this can be accomplished. The department also has sought to diversify Canada's trade relationships and foster trade with overseas countries in order to lessen the heavy dependence upon the United States as a trading partner. This of course involves greater readiness to undertake risks and to plan aggressive industrial policies.

79

The main problem with IT&C is that over the years it has become a vast sprawling empire, accumulating sometimes contradictory programs; it has lacked an overall philosophical thrust. This is traceable partly to the fact that the department is a marriage of two somewhat contradictory parts: the old Department of Trade and Commerce, which was mainly concerned with developing overseas markets, and the newer Department of Industry, which attempted to build up manufacturing in Canada. In addition, the department's posture as the client of business meant that it had to attempt to respond to the varying demands of the business community. The department suffered from the fact that there was no imposition of a consistent policy framework upon it, to define its objectives and those of the government in the area of industrial development.

The Department of Regional Economic Expansion (DREE)

This department is often thought of as typical of the early years of Trudeau's prime ministership. While its programs were often inherited from the past, it represented a conspicuous attempt to use the political and economic power of the federal government to try to correct to some extent the regional inequalities within Canada. Its first minister was Jean Marchand, one of the "three wise men" who formed the core of the new leadership of the Liberal party in the late Sixties. The first deputy minister was Tom Kent, the dynamic British intellectual who became one of the main components of the Trudeau "brain trust" in the early years. He was a very fast-moving, blunt and effective person whose dynamism sometimes provoked resentment.

The early nucleus of the department was made up of some programs that had been scattered throughout the public service, but were consolidated with the setting up of DREE. From the Department of Industry came the Area Development Agency (ADA) — a program of industrial incentives for investment in industry. Related to it was the Area Development Incentives Act (ADIA) and the Atlantic Development Board (ADB). These provided the nucleus for work in special areas. The Agricultural Rehabilitation Development Agency (ARDA) goes back to the Diefenbaker government in 1961. It was Alvin Hamilton, then minister of agriculture, who first initiated this program, by which the federal government made agreements with the provinces concerning projects for alternative land use to improve incomes and employment opportunities in areas experiencing economic difficulties. ARDA was involved in making payments to provinces, doing research and establishing advisory committees drawn from the community. In the late Sixties ARDA was run by Paul Sauvé in an innovative manner. The agency consisted of a group of young and ethusiastic civil servants who worked out in the field and reported back every week or two to the minister to map further strategy. It was a loose, dynamic organization, setting an example for the new Department of Regional Economic Expansion to which it was attached in the late Sixties. This program really extended some of the operations of the Prairie Farm Rehabilitation Act (PFRA) — a program precious to the Prairie farmers — which had been put in place in the aftermath of the Depression to prevent a recurrence of the dust bowl conditions of the Thirties. It was mainly concerned with land use and the development of agricultural soil and water resources.

Related to these programs was the Fund for Rural Economic Development (FRED) and the Atlantic Development Board. These were very infrastructure oriented, with a mandate for conducting economic planning and research activities. While the ministers changed quickly, the guiding light of DREE was Ernest Weeks, one of the young dynamic economist civil servants of the day.

The original legislation setting up DREE gave immense discretionary authority to the minister, who had the power to designate special areas to receive preferred treatment. This involved the setting up of a plan of development in collaboration with the relevant provincial government. Costs were to be shared between the two levels of government, on a fifty-fifty basis in the case of the richer provinces but with the federal government paying a larger part in the case of the poorer ones. This free-wheeling operation with a large budget was obviously likely to draw the fire of the parliamentary opposition. The Industrial Incentives Program in particular was subject to very severe criticism mainly because of the large discretionary element involved in its operation. The Conservatives were inclined to see the department as an example of "the three wise men" building up the power of the Liberal party in Quebec. This line of criticism was particularly resented by the minister, Jean Marchand, who saw the role of the department as "defining issues for public debate." To do this, of course, meant being provocative in discussing the objectives of the department, and thereby inviting parliamentary debate.

Tom Kent, the deputy minister, was inclined to move quickly in order to achieve results, and this led him to adopt a "take it or leave it" attitude towards the provinces, one which drew their criticism. The attacks by the provincial politicians, in turn, were grist for the mill of the opposition parties in the House of Commons.

When Marchand was succeeded by Don Jamieson, there was an abrupt change in ministerial conduct. Jamieson saw his role as pouring oil on troubled waters and trying to facilitate the harmonious implementation of the department's policies. He saw himself as a friend of members of Parliament, and he handled criticism with patience and discretion. The department needed this conciliating approach because it was under severe attack. The NDP was riding high on its "corporate welfare bums" issue and was inclined to see patronage in everything the department did. The Conservatives too were extremely critical of what they saw as Liberal party patronage.

The department presented a rather vulnerable target in that its organizational structure was somewhat weak and overly large amounts of discretion were granted to public servants. The general strategy of the department up to about 1973 involved mainly industrial incentives, infrastructure assistance, social adjustments and rural development. The object was to make investment in viable industry more attractive in the slow-growing parts of the country. Authority tended to be concentrated in the headquarters at Ottawa, and this created some problems in relations with the provinces and the regional offices. For these reasons, it was decided in 1974 that DREE should adopt a new structure and a new strategy.

Four regional offices were created, in Montreal, Moncton, Toronto and Saskatoon, each under an assistant deputy minister, so that initiative could be taken at the regional level. The new concept was introduced in the form of the General Development Agreements (GDA) — contracts signed between the department and a provincial government. These could be broad and philosophical in nature as indicated in the *Annexes* to each GDA, listing the long-term development objectives agreed upon and showing how these were to be accomplished. The details were filled in on a more short-run basis through subsidiary agreements, which contained the precise details and financial information. This strategy confirmed a shift from the previous emphasis on rural development strategy to one on urban growth. This new policy represented extensive consultation between the federal government and the provinces, and also represented considerable cooperation with other departments of government — notably Finance; Industry, Trade and Commerce; Transport; and Energy, Mines and Resources.

More of the initiative was shifted to the provinces, and this may have involved less emphasis on the attainment of a coherent national development policy. It constituted a kind of multidimensional approach to regional development, utilizing the skills of several academic disciplines, in particular economics, geography, political science and sociology. The policy output of the new arrangement reflected provincial priorities, and these often involved developmental problems which were both political and structural, and, in the view of those involved, not soluble by purely economic analysis. It is clear that the implications of locating industry in the less developed areas has serious political and social consequences, as well as economic ones.

Alongside this relatively decentralized and flexible development strategy, the department developed considerable planning capability. The creation of the Atlantic Development Board in 1962 signalled the beginning of this. It performed three vital functions: the development of an integrated overall plan for the promotion of the economic growth of the Atlantic region in collaboration with the Economic Council of Canada; the coordination of measures agreed upon between different departments of government dealing with the Atlantic region; and to act as a vehicle for administering various special assistance programs.[2] Like the ADB many of these development agencies were taken over from previous departments and brought their planning capabilities with them to DREE. For example, the Economic Council of Canada was one of the major government planning agencies, and it became involved in cooperative arrangements with DREE to assist in its planning activities.[3]

Trudeau became extremely concerned with the problems of national unity and considered regional underdevelopment to be a major cause of discord. The government therefore favoured a politically oriented strategy of trying to correct regional disparities by encouraging development through government financial support. This policy reached its high point with the introduction of General Development Agreements in 1974, which met many provincial demands for development assistance. This was somewhat of a departure from the more economics-oriented development approach favoured by the Economic Council of Canada. This new strategy was made possible by the decentralization of the department under the regional ADMs (assistant deputy ministers) in the field, who in turn were backed up by sub-offices in all the provincial capitals and some other places besides. Consequently, there was great capacity for dialogue with the provinces. They took the General Development Agreements seriously and put the implementation of them under the control of one of their senior ministers. In New Brunswick it was the premier himself, in

Ontario the treasurer, and in all cases a senior and important minister. This meant that the provincial civil servants who dealt with the question were all senior and generally competent.

However, this reconciliation with the provinces and decentralization of the department drew fire in Ottawa itself. The Department of Finance in particular was critical.

The provinces most supportive of the DREE program were naturally the ones who received the most generous assistance, notably the Atlantic provinces. There the cost-sharing ratio went up to 90 per cent of costs paid by the federal government; whereas in the richer provinces it was much less. The major objection to the decentralization of the department was in the senior ranks of the civil service, particularly in such departments as Finance and Industry, Trade and Commerce. Politicians, on the other hand, tended to view decentralization favourably. It offered them considerable flexibility, and the possibility of doing things for their own home regions. The example of DREE in decentralization has been followed by others, notably the Department of Industry, Trade and Commerce itself, which has now established regional sub-offices. Decentralization brings the activities of the federal government closer to the people in the outlying parts of the country, thereby diminishing regional discontent and bringing the government closer to the people.

Another advantage of the General Development Agreements approach is that it has improved the analytic resources of the department with respect to the various regions of the country. All areas have been analyzed through the work of twenty-four community data desks. The data base used has been extremely broad, involving the usual federal government statistical material, plus material generated in the regional analytical groups and from other sources in the private sector and elsewhere.

The development of the constitutional issue in the late Seventies, which divided the federal government and the provinces, has had its effect on DREE. The posture of close collaboration with the provinces symbolized by the General Development Agreements, has become less popular in senior government circles because it appears to represent too broad a concession to the provinces. The federal government considers that many of its activities funded through DREE are not being properly credited to the federal government, which is paying the major share of the costs. It is now undertaking to perform its activities directly, rather than in collaboration with the provinces through joint programs. The minister, Pierre De Bané, commented in August of 1981 when the premiers were meeting in Victoria that the federal government is no longer content to develop national policies and let provincial governments look after their own specific needs. Instead, he said, Ottawa will develop its own programs in the various provinces, and it will be up to the provincial governments to reconcile their programs with the federal ones. He said, "The federal government must look after the specific needs of the people in each province." He referred to the program to develop fisheries in Nova Scotia: "Instead of Ottawa supplying the funds and that province administering the program as in the past, the program was divided into twelve components. The province will pay for four components and deliver the services; the federal government will pay for eight components and deliver the services itself."[4] Mr. De Bané went on:

> Up until now the federal government discharged its responsibility by giving money to the provinces. That will no longer suffice. It was acceptable ten years ago for Ottawa to develop national policies, and for the provinces to develop their own provincial policies because the provinces had little strength. Today the provinces are more mature and have more power. National programs applied across the country from Newfoundland to British Columbia — leaving the provinces to develop tailor-made programs for their own people — have been disastrous. . . . They have created balkanization and trade barriers that are worse than the common market.

As examples he cited the province-first purchasing policies of the Ontario and Quebec governments, the Quebec decision to give Quebeckers priority on construction sites, and the Newfoundland decision to give Newfoundlanders job priority on offshore drilling rigs. Therefore, "it is no longer enough for the federal government to develop national policies for the provinces to administer. . . . if the federal government is to remain relevant, it will have to design specific programs."[5] This statement represents a substantial change in the posture of DREE. Instead of collaborating closely with the provinces, it appears now that the department will render direct services to prevent the provinces from claiming most of the political credit and, more important, to prevent the provinces from undertaking policies that divide the country without the federal government being able to counteract these by policies of its own calculated to contribute to national unity.

Federal Advisory Bodies 8

Here we shall forcus on the Economic Council of Canada and the Science Council, the two bodies most relevant to the area of advising on economic development strategy.

The Economic Council of Canada

In the 1960s the government became aware of the need to equip itself with independent specialist advice, especially with respect to economic policy. Accordingly, in 1963 it set up the Economic Council of Canada with a very general mandate to look into the economic affairs of the country, prepare studies and give public advice. This represents a kind of permanent royal commission. Also it was as far as Canada could then go towards the planning commissions that were appearing in some other developed countries, such as France. Clearly, the Canadian government thought it could not go so far, given the general climate of opinion opposing government interference in the marketplace. However, the government at least could equip itself with the kind of academic and intellectual advice and analysis that more *dirigiste* governments were setting up. There was to be a permanent chairman and two directors, who would be professional economists and work full time. In collaboration with them would be twenty-five other members appointed from representative sectors of the economy, and of society in general, in order to achieve both legitimacy and authority.

The statute which set up the council gave it a very broad assignment: to advise the government and general public on how to achieve optimum employment, production and growth. To do this it was to assess the medium-term and long-term prospects of the economy, and to recommend policies that would achieve the stated objectives. It should consider means of strengthening Canada's international financial and trading position, and study how to increase Canadian participation in the ownership, control and management of industry.

86

Furthermore, it was to examine the implications of technological change and of international economic developments for employment and income in Canada.[1] The first chairman of the council was Dr. John J. Deutsch, a highly respected public servant, academic and statesman. Under his leadership the council laid down ambitious goals for the Canadian economy, including a high rate of employment (97 per cent) and a commitment to maintain price stability.

In its early years the council recommended expansionary policies to generate adequate levels of demand. It undertook a kind of educational program to focus attention on certain societal values. It favoured giving a high priority to general education and training, and recommended that new government departments be created in the field of manpower and immigration, consumer and corporate affairs, and regional economic expansion. It favoured consultative mechanisms between industry and government, and concentrated on particular industrial sectors.

Essentially the council has three roles: advisory, research and information. It gives policy advice to the government through consensus of its own members, which is tendered in public, so that it may have some impact on public opinion. It holds meetings with government departments and agencies to discuss problems and to give advice.

There are approximately half a dozen groups linked to specific research objectives. The range is very broad, including microeconomic growth studies of specific firms and industries, looking at innovation, the flow of ideas, technology transfer and the like. Also, there have been studies of labour market imbalances. Other studies have been of regional problems, natural resources, and the effect on growth and productivity of intergovernment transfers. The council has examined the question of government financial intermediation through the making of loans to get new development projects off the ground. It has examined the efficiency of the banking system, the pensions question, and government programs for housing and for lending to business and to agriculture to finance exports.

The council has its own econometric model (called Candide). This is a tool for reviewing the economic performance of the Canadian economy and for analyzing changes that are taking place within it. In writing up these results, of course, the council is involved in making general assessments and policy recommendations. It recommended, for example, higher energy prices when the government was involved in the heavy subsidization of petroleum before the agreement between

Ottawa and Alberta in September 1981 on energy pricing — an agreement strongly advocated by the council. About the same time it recommended five new megaprojects in order to bring about self-sufficiency in oil. In the process of making its findings public, the full-time members of council often appear before Senate or House of Commons committees to be questioned by members of these bodies.

The information function of the council is often achieved through holding conferences, publishing its consensus documents and setting up press kits to help media people write up its activities and the findings from its monographs and discussion papers. Its quarterly bulletin, *au Courant*, gives a rundown of recent activities.

From time to time the government will make a special request of the council for services; for example, in March of 1978 the prime minister asked it to undertake a special study of Newfoundland, concentrating on its low productivity level. This set off forty-two separate studies looking at the various aspects of the provincial economy. Another example is the request made by the prime minister for an investigation into the regulation of industry, which is leading to seventy different studies in the fields of agriculture, transportation, energy, fisheries, health, safety and so on.

The council communicates its findings and policy advice in a form reflecting a consensus judgement of the council. The original research workers' results are assembled into a draft that goes to the council for discussion. Since the members of the council represent various interests, differences of opinion arise and immediate publication of the findings is unusual. Revisions are made to meet the points raised by members. Sometimes recommendations are altered to obtain consensus. This consensus will be sufficiently broad that it may be accepted by government as policy.

Appointments to the council are political. It is not surprising then that most are supporters of the government party but reflect different positions. On the other hand, the government has not been prone to act on recommendations of the council, probably because of the strong opinions held by members of the cabinet and senior public service, who are closer to the exercise of power. Furthermore, cabinet members are more concerned about short-term questions, whereas the council looks at the medium and long term. Thus, even within the ideologically compatible circle of members of the council, the cabinet and the higher public service, strong differences of opinion develop. Philosophically, the Economic Council generally reflects prevailing positions in the field of economics.[2]

While the establishment of the council was Canada's attempt to respond to the popularity of royal commissions of enquiry and to indicative planning arrangements in other Western countries, the general idea of planning has not by and large been supported in the council. In the earlier period under the chairmanships of John Deutsch and Arthur Smith, the idea was fairly popular, and it was particularly so under André Raynauld when a serious attempt to give the council the mandate to undertake planning was made, unsuccessfully. Opinion both in political and business circles in Canada was unsympathetic to the idea, since it leaned to the "free market."

Once government economic policies proved unable to contain inflation, the government resorted to the imposition of wage and price controls in 1975. Any idea of indicative planning was abandoned (a position well received by both government and business), and a new concept of a social partnership (referring to the association of business, labour and government along the lines followed in Sweden and the Netherlands) became popular.

The labour movement was unsympathetic to any kind of planning, perhaps because it thought it was being treated as a junior partner. With the announcement of wage and price controls, the labour movement withdrew its cooperation and, as part of this, refused to allow its participation in the council to continue. The council then became essentially an instrument for doing in-depth research on policy questions with some participation by citizens. It also offered a link with the provinces, with whom it maintained good relations by undertaking assignments of interest to them, often with their participation, such as the reference studies of Newfoundland and the study of regulation.

The general posture of the Economic Council has been a liberal one, favouring competition for goods and services, and a low tariff. It has not been sympathetic to a sectoral, interventionist policy on the part of government. After being rebuffed, under the chairmanship of André Raynauld, in its attempt to "pick the winners" with reference to industry, the council moved with prevailing opinion in the economics profession and business in favour of a more macroeconomic approach, although it has shown some sympathy for the idea of an industrial strategy. With experience the council has become increasingly hesitant to make strong policy recommendations, since it has had no great success in having its ideas adopted.

The council has fallen short of the hopes of the people who originally established it, who looked to it as a kind of authoritative source of policy recommendations that would be sound and generally acceptable. No doubt these views were naive and failed to take account of the strong opinions of ministers and senior public servants, and of the effective role of interest groups in advising them. The council finds itself at some remove therefore from the actual decision-makers. One means of shortening this distance has been the recent policy of exchanging personnel with the Department of Finance and with other parts of the government. Thus a greater community of opinions should develop between the council staff and members of the higher public service. There is another suggestion that the council build up an open discussion of the fiscal framework drawn up by the Department of Finance. However, governments are generally very cautious and draw back from publishing estimates of future performance because they are often attacked in the House of Commons if predictions do not hold. An exception was in the budget of the Clark government in which substantial financial data were supplied as an appendix. The current approach to the problem is for the Economic Council to publish a medium-term projection and policy analysis with actual numbers. This means that the government itself cannot be blamed for the projections; yet a sophisticated discussion of current economic problems can take place within a parliamentary committee.

The council has generally been perceived as differing with the Science Council, although relations between the two bodies are good, if somewhat distant.

The Science Council of Canada

The Science Council, founded in 1966, is an agency, like the Economic Council, created by the government to give external advice. However, its brief was a much broader one and included giving advice on the following areas: the adequacy of the scientific and technological research going on in Canada; the priority that should be assigned to specific areas of scientific and technological research; the development of scientific and technological manpower; long-term planning for scientific and technological research; the responsibilities of government departments and agencies in relation to the universities and private corporations in furthering science and technology; the adequacy of statistical and other information; and the best means of developing and maintaining cooperation between the Science Council and other organizations.[3]

From the beginning the council faced problems. It was working in an area of public policy in which there was great uncertainty and unpredictability; there was little consensus on science policy and few sophisticated concepts to employ. Also the Science Council had to work through the Science Secretariat, which was located in the Privy Council Office. Since this body had its own ideas and initiatives, and its own staff, the independence of the Science Council was somewhat qualified. The council was supposed to be independent and open; yet it had to work through a body which was enshrouded in the attitudes of official secrecy and loyalty to the government peculiar to the Privy Council Office. As a newcomer to the world of bureaucratic structures, the Science Council had to earn its own legitimacy in the eyes of the internal bureaucracy whom it appeared to be challenging. These problems led the government in 1968 to give the council its own secretariat and research staff so that it could carry out its work independent of government. The council itself, not the government, determines what issues and subjects to investigate.

Since the creation of the Ministry of State for Science and Technology in 1971, the council has sent its reports to the ministry, which in turn has always tabled them on the day of their release by council. Therefore, almost all of its work and advice is in the public domain. The council consisted of twenty-five, later thirty, members appointed for three-year terms, chosen by the governor-in-council from persons knowledgeable about science and technology. Initially there were four associate members drawn from federal government departments, but these positions have been dropped. However, the secretary of the Ministry of State for Science and Technology and a senior member of the Economic Council have standing invitations to attend council meetings. All members of the council, except the present chairman, Stuart Smith, are part-time appointees; so there has been less likelihood of firm leadership than is the case with the Economic Council, which has always had a permanent full-time chairman. At first the members were drawn almost equally from the governmental, industrial and academic sectors. Now all members are from business or academic life. This has meant a preference for mission-oriented approaches, which does not sit well with the National Research Council, which is generally unsympathetic.

From the beginning the council developed a highly rationalistic conception of the policy process, and set out boldly to state how it thought societies ought to be steered. It frankly discussed what it thought Canada's social goals ought to be: national prosperity, physical and mental health and high life expectancy, a high, rising standard of education readily available to all, personal freedom, justice and security for all in a united Canada, increasing availability of leisure and enhancement of the opportunities for personal development, and world peace. This all-encompassing set of goals suggested that the council was prepared to articulate national goals somewhat independent of the political process, revealing a certain innocence about the way that process works and what its role in Canada is. To achieve these goals the Science Council recommended programs covering the major areas of infrastructure in which government might be expected to play a role.[4] The council suggested the creation of a ministry of science policy, a suggestion that in fact was implemented with the creation of the Ministry of State for Science and Technology.

The Science Council's relationship to the rest of the governmental structure has been quite uneasy. There has been some resistance to its tendency to make *ex cathedra* recommendations over a very wide area of public concern. This breadth of mandate has led the council to perceive the relationship of "everything to everything else," and has taken its recommendations into the long run. As a result, it is viewed by some as remote from the day-to-day concerns of government. On the other hand, it has taken positions on industrial policy largely because it could not usefully discuss the public policy implications of science and technology without addressing the structural and behavioural characteristics of Canadian industry. It has found that scientific and technological problems are, by their very nature, embedded in broader economic or political circumstances. Therefore, it has been somewhat difficult for the Science Council to be influential in day-to-day government policy-making. It does not have a mandate to represent the scientific community and thus finds it difficult to speak with very much authority. It plays the role of policy scanner, but its role extends over such a wide area and its reliance upon several intellectual disciplines gives it such a wide breadth of commitment that it also exposes itself to considerable criticism. This in turn affects the authority and legitimacy of the council's pronouncements.

Most controversial was its report, *The Weakest Link: A Technological Perspective on Canadian Industrial Underdevelopment* published in 1978. Six months later it published *Forging the Links*, which was its formal position on technology policy. This study was a plea for Canada to undertake a policy of technological sovereignty, that is, to emphasize the development in Canada, through research and development, of technological innovation in order to put the country in the forefront of industrial development, thereby claiming a more important role in the search for markets for high-technology products.

This, of course, would involve the government in an active program to "pick the winners." These would have to be supported by research and development grants, special government procurement arrangements to build a market, export sales initiatives and so on. The study ended with the words "the very foundations of industrial Canada are threatened. We are entirely convinced that only fundamental change directed by a coherent strategy can prevent collapse and begin the process of reconstruction."[5]

This approach challenged much of the doctrine accepted in the Canadian bureaucracy and particularly the Department of Finance, which favoured Canada following the doctrine of comparative advantage, that is, allowing the free market to determine to a considerable extent what Canada should produce and export, and what it should import. The challenge of the Science Council's position led to a spirited debate involving some of the country's leading economists and policy experts. *Canadian Public Policy* carried two lead articles by prominent economists, Donald J. Daly and A. E. Safarian, analyzing this policy.[6] Commenting on the conclusions of Safarian and Daly, the editor of the journal wrote:

> Daly is critical of the arguments presented by Britton and Gilmour which link the declining share in manufacturing employment to lack of technological competence, and to foreign ownership. He claims that the comparative performance of manufacturing industries in Canada is better than for most industrialized countries, and that the productivity gap between Canada and the U.S. has been narrowing in recent decades. . . . The Science Council's policy prescriptions with their emphasis on high technology manufacturing and technological sovereignty, are termed nationalistic and against Canada's comparative advantage. Subsidized home-grown technology would make our industries less competitive and would do little to close the productivity gap between Canadian and U.S. manufacturing industries. . . . The Britton and Gilmour policy proposals are essentially inwardlooking and would require massive government intervention. Moreover, such interventionist policies would be based on the difficult premise that government can pick the technological winners of the future.[7]

Safarian describes the policy recommendations as "key-sector protection precisely in areas where multinationals have been strongest, and where the opportunity cost of developing substitutes may be high."[8]

Even more critical was the study by Kristian Palda, *The Science Council's Weakest Link.*[9] This study perceived *The Weakest Link* "as a lobbying effort on behalf of the economic interests the Science Council has come to represent."[10] Palda argued that "the Council's set of duties does not include recommendations on the formulation of national industrial policies."[11] He perceived the study to be an exercise in economic nationalism that would have the effect of advantaging the Canadian scientific community, possibly at the expense of the community as a whole.[12]

It was obvious that the Science Council had struck a nerve in its publication of *The Weakest Link*. It had the effect of making the council much better known to the general public than it had ever been before, as a result of extensive editorial comment. On the other hand, it exposed it to the severe criticism of the policy-making establishment and of many prominent economists.

In general the Science Council has stuck to its guns. In its 1980 report its chairman, Dr. Claude Fortier, speaking for himself but with the general support of the council, continued the discussion on Canada's secondary manufacturing industry, which he designated as "a failing competitor in a fiercely competitive world."[13] While regretting Canada's deteriorating international payments position, with a $17 billion deficit in end-products in 1979 — six times greater than in the early Seventies — he considered that the best way out would be found through increasing research and development, more innovation, and more emphasis on effective marketing of Canadian manufactured goods. Also he advocated public procurement policies that would create demand for Canadian high-technology goods. He saw advanced countries as facing an alternative between "a carefully engineered withdrawal from threatened industries toward dynamic industries, or an attempt to hold the line." He advocated that Canada seek "a shift towards product novelty, quality and reliability, and automated assembly in durable consumer goods, towards high value added." He commented:

> The significant problem faced by Canada is an increasing difficulty, because of high wage rates, to compete on the basis of price in an ever growing range of standard products. Also, Canada's weakness in innovative capacity will hinder movement of human and financial resources into product markets where technical quality is at a premium. Without cuts in real wages, the threat of unemployment will be great. Without innovative firms and industries, the prospect of a declining standard of living is real. . . . Why has Canada reached this sorry state? The explanation usually offered is structural weakness. . .: small firms with production volumes too small to capture economies of scale; a high

degree of foreign control; low levels of R&D activity and product design and engineering. These related characteristics stem from the same historical causes. Long-standing government policies encouraged subsidiaries of foreign firms to supply the domestic market from behind Canadian tariff walls. . . . The high level of foreign ownership, accompanied by a proliferation of small Canadian-owned firms, has fostered technological dependence. By and large foreign subsidiaries have been technologically dependent upon their parent firm, and the Canadian-owned firms have relied heavily on licensed technology. . . .

Our basic position has been consistent: Only an industrial strategy with particular emphasis on the development of indigenous innovative and technological capacity will suffice for the creation of the competitive manufacturing industry that Canada so badly needs. . . . Canada's supportive measures lag seriously behind those of many other countries. . . . At present Canada is geared to react to problems in soft sectors, and to cushion the impacts of excessively rapid change, but still lacks sufficient coordination and preparation to act quickly and with a suitable battery of measures to grasp the industrial opportunities of the 1980s. . . . We must seek ways to reduce the current emphasis on protecting the weaker sectors and propping up those with few, if any, prospects for adjusting satisfactorily to the changing conditions of international trade. Our interests would be better served by policies designed to restructure our industry and to encourage mobility of both labour and capital into new or growing productive sectors.[14]

Dr. Fortier emphasized the importance of product design and engineering to bridge the gap between research on the one hand and production on the other. He pointed out that "firms without a product design and engineering capability can never be innovative. This is an area in which Canada is even more stunted than in R&D."

About foreign-owned subsidiaries Dr. Fortier argued that "measures must be taken to encourage significant changes." He pointed out that Canada could not afford to lose these subsidiaries in the short and medium term, and therefore they should be wooed away from purely branch-plant-type operations through encouraging them to obtain a "world product mandate" from their principals in order to develop an export capacity. To achieve this he advocated guidelines published by the government and the development of public sector procurement policies. In addition, more information should be obtained so that the government knows the nature of the situation, so that it can effectively encourage innovation, new research design and engineering, new product tooling, marketing and exporting.[15] From the above it is clear that the major preoccupation of the Science Council is with the reinvigoration of the Canadian economy through an industrial strategy.

Another indication of the thrust of the Science Council in the early 1980s can be seen in its research programs. The Industrial Policies Committee is following up on the earlier report *Forging the Links: A Technology Policy for Canada.* Studies are being done of the commercial and business environment confronting innovative firms in Canada, and of the policy options open to government. There was a standing committee on research in Canada that monitored research in progress and developed policy recommendations. Some other areas of study were food assistance to the world's poorest nations, science and the various aspects of the law, computers and communication (including computer-aided learning), intercity passenger transportation, elementary and high school science, and biotechnology. In addition, the council has completed a study of public awareness of science and technology in Canada, and one could go on. The breadth of activities is impressive, but it may indeed be too extensive for there to be effective marshalling of resources in key areas. There appears to be no question but that the issue of technological strategy is the key one to which the Science Council is devoting its attention, with the subsidiary issue of world product mandating a subject of current interest.

As events have developed, it is apparent that while formal relations may be correct, there is a considerably widening difference of perspective between the Science Council and the economics-oriented parts of the Canadian bureaucracy, notably the Economic Council and the Department of Finance. There is inevitably a certain sensitivity concerning the Science Council's brash invasion of the field of economics and its undertaking of policies which are out of step with the revealed doctrine of the economics-oriented ministries. Compared to the latter the Science Council is somewhat removed from central decision-making. Also, the fact that the Science Council is more influenced by such disciplines as geography and engineering tends to give it a different perspective than that of the Department of Finance and the Economic Council, which are mainly informed by economics. The internal disagreements within the profession of economics over such questions as monetarism, appear not to have touched the Science Council.

Federal Policy Integration: The Ministry of State for Economic Development

The Ministry of State for Economic Development (MSED)[1]

We have so far been tracing many different instruments for developing economic policy: the central agencies, the line departments, the Economic Council of Canada and the Science Council of Canada. Each of these bodies develops its own ideas and its own policies, producing a large number of conflicting thrusts and initiatives. Moreover, there was general disenchantment with the lack of success of Canadian government economic policy, seen in increasing inflation, unemployment and slow economic growth. The government responded in October of 1975 with the establishment of the Anti-Inflation Board to control wages and prices and thereby combat inflation.

The relative lack of success of Canadian economic policy has inevitably created many differences of opinion in the various departments and agencies of government, and has led to different policy initiatives. Prior to 1975 minimally coercive measures were preferred so as to enlist as much cooperation and goodwill as possible. However, the traditional levers of fiscal and monetary policy did not appear to produce sufficient results, and therefore it was decided to embark upon the controls experiment. It, however, did not end the differing thrusts of the various departments in the field of economic affairs.

The question of how to coordinate and integrate the various government initiatives remained an important and pressing question throughout the whole postwar period. The Department of Finance was most concerned with price levels and inflation, even at the cost of higher unemployment. Industry, Trade and Commerce sought to develop a so-called national "industrial strategy," and this in turn brought it into conflict with the Department of Regional Economic Expansion, which wanted to see that the less developed parts of the country receive support, even when not justifiable on rational grounds of economic efficiency. Other departments such as Manpower and Immigration and National Health and Welfare were concerned about unemployment insurance and the proposal for a guaranteed annual income. One could see that various economic values were becoming institutionalized in the different departments of government, as each agency has been awarded custody over certain goals and certain instruments and, in a sense, certain values. As the number of departments with an economic commitment increased, tension mounted between them, since their jurisdictions tended to overlap and their goals to conflict with each other.

The Department of Finance in particular found itself challenged by these newcomer departments. Finance had always been perceived as a government within the government, as a kind of economic affairs department. To do this job, it built up an analytical capability to monitor and analyze the economic developments in which the government was involved. This preoccupation was essentially in the short term. The department lost the major control over managing government expenditure when the Treasury Board was separated from the department. The Treasury Board on the other hand has not been able to devote itself to expenditure and program management because of the distractions of language policy and collective-bargaining difficulties within the public service. The result is that economic management has become increasingly pluralistic and unintegrated.

In the cabinet shuffle of 1978, Prime Minister Trudeau grasped the nettle by establishing the Board of Economic Development Ministers (BEDM). This board, chaired by Robert Andras, the former president of the Treasury Board, consisted of a committee of senior ministers with economic portfolios, and was charged with the responsibility of developing concerted and harmonious economic policies to help the country recover from its economic difficulties.

It was hoped that this new instrument would succeed in getting the various departments to cooperate in the development of a coherent economic policy for the government. This of course might require departments to alter their own policies. When the Lambert Royal Commission on Financial Management and Accountability reported in 1979, it was so critical of government ineffectiveness in controlling its own expenditures and economic affairs that the inevitable result was a greater emphasis being placed on the new board. Its objectives, and those of the Ministry of State for Economic Development, which acted as its secretariat, were:

- to improve the control of allocations and expenditures in the economic development area (a response to the Lambert Commission's criticisms);

- to develop a new and improved decision-making process, which would also control and assure commitments over future years (this became the "envelope system" discussed below); and
- to articulate a coherent approach to economic development, within which the constituent departments of the board could develop their own policies and programs.

Coherence would be achieved by establishing a common environmental setting on which each department could base its policy assumptions. There would be no coercion to achieve harmony; rather a consensus would be worked out as to what the problems and opportunities were.

Meanwhile economic conditions worsened. Canada's growing budgetary and balance-of-payments deficits led Prime Minister Trudeau, after his participation in the economic summit at Bonn in the summer of 1978, suddenly to declare that $2.5 billion would have to be eliminated from federal expenditures — this was the so-called guns of August! This dramatic act enhanced the authority of the new board, which began its work in January of 1979. Its first three months were very productive, following as they did the twenty-three sector task forces, which had reported on conditions in these key sectors of the Canadian economy, and when the overarching "Tier II" report was being prepared (see chapter 13). Its key recommendation was for the investment of substantial sums for the modernization of the pulp and paper industry. This led to a cooperative federal-provincial program on a national basis, involving collaboration among various government departments at both federal and provincial levels. The Department of Regional Economic Expansion worked out agreements with the provinces to accomplish the objective. This became a prototype for other initiatives to improve the delivery of government programs. The report laid out 450 different programs, all of which are detailed in the publication *ABC: Assistance to Business in Canada*.[2]

This apparently promising beginning suffered an abrupt shock with the defeat of the Trudeau government in the 1979 election. However, the new Clark government made no significant changes in the structure of this aspect of government machinery. The so-called envelope system, which was being considered before the defeat of the Trudeau government, was implemented. This was an arrangement that had been introduced into the New Brunswick government, which consisted, as mentioned previously, in grouping together several government departments' budgetary arrangements for a given fiscal year.

Allocations would be controlled by a committee of the relevant ministers, but the total expenditure of the departments grouped in the envelope could not go beyond the allocation made by the Department of Finance. Therefore, if it was decided to expand certain programs, economies would have to be found in other activities that were part of that same envelope. Prime Minister Clark also introduced a two-tiered cabinet system in which the inner cabinet was the real centre of power and decision. It did not differ so much from the Trudeau arrangement in an important sense, since the Priorities and Planning Committee of the Trudeau government had been in fact acting as a kind of inner cabinet anyway. Clark also introduced a Ministry of State for Social Development and continued the Ministry of State for Economic Development. Senator Robert R. de Cotret, the Conservatives' economic expert, became the minister in charge of the new department under the title minister of economic development and trade. This was a further utilization of the ministry-of-state idea inaugurated by the Trudeau government when it introduced the Ministry of State for Urban Affairs and the Ministry of State for Science and Technology. The idea was to have the ministries responsible for elaborating policies and integrating functions, rather than having to control a large bureaucracy and deliver programs.

After nine months the Clark government was defeated, and the Liberals came back to power. This did not involve substantial changes for the new department. While the inner-cabinet term was dropped, the Priorities and Planning Committee resumed its function as the inner cabinet, and the Cabinet Committee on Economic Development became the crucial decision-maker in the field related to the Ministry of State for Economic Development. Ministers who have proposals before this committee have a right to carry them to the Priorities and Planning Committee, but in fact they tend not to do so. Their proposals are made to the Cabinet Committee on Economic Development, which consists of eighteen ministers. It is a very large envelope, carried over from the Clark government. Committee decisions are virtually final, although disappointed ministers do have the right to appeal to the Priorities and Planning Committee, which has the last word. All provinces except Prince Edward Island are represented on this committee.

In 1980–81 the energy question became the key economic matter before the government. The prime minister played the key role, advised by the Priorities and Planning Committee of Cabinet on policy questions, and on energy expenditures by the Committee of Deputy

Ministers known as the Mirror Committee. The latter is chaired by the deputy minister in the Ministry of State for Economic Development, and meets weekly over lunch. Essentially, it consists of the deputy ministers of the departments whose ministers are concerned with economic development. Within this is a smaller committee, the Committee of Energy Deputies, chaired by the secretary of the MSED. This group identifies the program of work for the Ministers' Committee, which has the final word. This then is the process that drives the machine of the MSED. Once decisions are taken they are communicated to the departments and are followed up by the officials in the MSED. This system articulates the framework and sees that the decisions are carried out in an atmosphere of cooperation and consultation.

The Committee of Deputy Ministers has two separate opportunities for discussing questions, and therefore gets adequate opportunity for the deputies to consult their colleagues and take advice fairly broadly. In this process the Treasury Board must be satisfied that the financial aspects of the proposals are acceptable, and the Department of Finance must have an opportunity to perform the economic analysis to its satisfaction.

After all these processes have been gone through, the MSED prepares a briefing for the Cabinet Committee on Economic Development. This is a three-page summary of the proposals. Its brevity means that only three or four of the major factors can be discussed. The Cabinet Committee then considers the question, and only if it approves does a mandate exist for going to the provinces, or to business and to the trade unions, to enlist collaboration and endorsement. The analysis in this statement is synthesized from material that comes up from the participating departments after several rounds of consultation, with consideration to the general agenda. The issue is assessed against a policy framework, and the ministers make their decisions on the basis of these submissions. The material goes to all ministers and all deputy ministers for information. The MSED does not itself make recommendations, but simply raises issues which the Cabinet Committee may wish to discuss.

Occasionally there are exceptions. If the secretary believes a valid policy option exists that was not put forward by the line departments, then that option could be advanced, sometimes as a recommendation. The secretary might, in the assessment vote, put forward his recommendation to the ministers for their consideration.

And what are the programs that emerge from this process? Instead of

101

being judged purely by the criterion of economic efficiency, these are essentially economic decisions weighted by the political considerations of the ministers on the committee. It is they who must make the final tradeoffs and make the policies coherent in the political as well as the economic sense. They must ultimately do the final rationing of the capital involved. This means, therefore, that judgements have to be made between purely economic-analysis considerations and other criteria, such as regional equity and income-equality considerations. For example, in the case of fisheries the interests of the economically efficient offshore fishery have to be weighed against those of the inshore fishery, which employs a large number of marginal fishermen in relatively poor communities. The objective is to move towards productive investments and get away from subsidizing inefficiency, while at the same time being conscious of the political imperatives of caring for the interests of the local populations. The aim is to encourage economic modernization and improvement — to get enterprises to jump hurdles.

Fine judgements have to be made. For example, one never knows when an investment tax credit gives support to proposals that would have gone ahead without it. It is impossible to be certain what amount of support business requires to do certain things. It is impossible to know the corporate decision-making process, especially in the case of a multinational corporation where even its Canadian chief executive officer may himself not be fully aware of the considerations that motivate decisions in the head office in the United States or elsewhere.

Basically the Canadian government is in the position of trying to persuade and influence businesses to undertake decisions which are perceived to be in the national interest. This often involves tailoring government programs to appeal to business leaders. For example, a common application form is being produced for thirty-five of the government programs calculated to aid business. Clearly this is in response to business complaints about the bureaucratic complexity involved in dealing with government.

The Ministry of State for Economic Development is relatively new, and therefore its role is not yet fully understood. It tries to develop a coherent economic policy, but this is an extremely difficult objective to achieve. Given the current economic crisis, the major concern is to maintain an element of financial control and restraint in expenditure, as well as the inevitable need to find policy coherence where possible. A major problem for the department is finding an acceptable policy, since the points of view and policy preferences of the different departments

102

in the federal government vary so much. This is reflected in the difficulty of getting a sense of direction from the cabinet. Further confusion has resulted with government changing hands twice within a year (1979–80). Newly elected governments seldom have a clear perception of the economic conditions as revealed by government indicators, and they also tend not to have very well defined policy preferences of their own. Add to this the inevitable apprehension about the bureaucracy that had been the handmaiden of the previous government, and one can understand a certain incapacity of a new government to function harmoniously and with trust at the very beginning of its term.

The Conservatives in their short period of government decided to cope with the problem by calling a national economic development conference. However, the party was defeated before the conference met. The civil servants in this circumstance attempted to work out some kind of game plan so that there would be something to be discussed by the ministers. Naturally, however, they were somewhat hesitant to be too specific, lest they appear to be usurping the function of the responsible ministers. They sought, therefore, to give them a set of options spanning views from left to right.

When, after the 1980 election, the Liberals returned to office, they too had no clear policy orientation worked out, although they could fall back upon the economic strategy they had developed in 1972. The conditions in 1980, however, were very different from what they had been in the earlier period, when economic growth was satisfactory and such questions as the environment and foreign ownership were less salient. Then there had been a greater willingness to let the private sector take the lead, with the government playing a kind of facilitating role by maintaining a fairly open immigration policy so that a sufficient pool of labour would be available. The concern had been to guarantee an elastic supply of the factors of production.

By the late Seventies cracks began to appear in this idyllic picture. The limits-of-growth thesis became a preoccupation of many policy-makers. The American presence in Canada became less benign after the Nixon economic measures of 1971. This was followed by the oil shocks and the publication of the Gray Report on foreign ownership. Environmentalism too became an important concern of both the electorate and politicians. Unequal rates of economic growth in the different parts of the country were producing bitterness, and this in turn became an important political issue. The general consensus became more fractured than it had ever been. With increasing complexity and also with growing wealth and expectations, it becomes increasingly difficult to maintain consensus; governments find it increasingly difficult to govern because decisions seem to reflect minority positions, and therefore mobilize opposition against them. This situation produces a search for some strategy and a certain nostalgia for a simpler past.

This situation places the public servants in a difficult position. They do not have any analytical machinery to make the appropriate tradeoffs between the different policy preferences, and they also have no way of knowing whether to prefer primary industry or secondary manufacturing in the inevitable policy tradeoffs. The simple approach in the Sixties of maximizing growth everywhere is no longer possible. New constraints have appeared, and choices have to be made. The greatest difficulty is that of making choices between sectors. There is, at least, a recognition of the need for adequate statistical information that will make comparisons possible between one sector and another. Steps are being made to produce these data now. In other words, the government is equipping itself to make these kinds of choices through the preparation of statistical and analytical means. However, the big choices still remain essentially "political." To carry the planning process further would involve indicative planning with all the problems of securing agreement of the provinces and business leaders.

In the face of this situation the position of the Ministry of State for Economic Development is a difficult one. Bud Olson, then MSED's minister, in an address to the Canadian Export Association in Ottawa on 20 October 1980 stated its priorities.[3] He identified eight key areas which he considered must be developed if an appropriate economic development result is to be obtained:

- Human resources. Here he favoured upgrading Canadian workers' skills and a program to encourage workers to be as mobile as possible.
- Capital investment. Growth, he said, must be led by investment. This means the government must provide a favourable climate for investment by reducing the inflation rate. He favoured the federal government making productive investments rather than subsidizing unproductive sectors, and reducing the barriers preventing capital going where it is most needed. This means a willingness to accept investment from outside Canada, provided it is used to the country's greatest advantage. Key aspects of development therefore must remain in Canadian hands.

104

- Energy. Here the emphasis must be on maintaining security of supply, acting to conserve energy resources and maximizing employment.
- Natural resources. He favoured a policy of restoring renewable resource bases so that they will be more productive in future.
- Technology. The federal government here must be prepared to increase its real spending on research and development, and also induce the private sector to be more active in this area.
- Infrastructure. Improvement in transportation, communications and the elimination of bottlenecks in the national distribution system.
- Institutions. Here the minister was concerned to reduce administrative complexity and inefficiency, with closer and secure relations with ''partners in the economy'' — business and government at other levels.
- Market development. He favoured the development of a national Canadian market, and therefore the elimination of restrictions on interprovincial trade, also a further extension of the government's efforts to finance Canadian exports to be competitive in the international marketplace.

The emphasis placed by the minister of industry, trade and commerce, later president of the Treasury Board, Herb Gray, has been considerably more nationalistic than this. One can see then that there is no clearly defined government policy in this area. What seems to be emerging from the Priorities and Planning Committee of Cabinet (as reported by some senior public servants) is a general set of directions that could change at any time. However, they do take comfort in the fact that the government has now made clear that it intends to take over and dominate the energy supply, to impose heavier taxes on corporations and encourage them to carry out more investments, to build up a proper transportation infrastructure in the country, to encourage more private research and development, and to engage in more export promotion, so that Canada can develop a larger scale of production and therefore achieve economies. Furthermore, there appears to be a desire to simplify regulations in the hope of achieving greater efficiency. In the area of training workers in new skills, there is the problem of provincial government cooperation, since the provincial jurisdiction is greater than the federal. Also, provincial politicians are inclined to resist the export of labour from their jurisdictions, as this suggests the erosion of a politician's political base.

As has been noted earlier, the basic attitude of politicians leads to their approval of the policies undertaken by DREE, to try to build up employment possibilities in the less developed parts of the country. Economists, however, are often critical of this, tending to see it as against the national interest if it involves keeping people in relatively unproductive employment rather than moving them to more efficient lines of activity. There is coming to be considerable discussion of the effects on the behaviour of working people of such government programs as the various DREE initiatives, unemployment insurance, family allowances and so on. These programs, some economists argue, encourage people to remain where they are, and therefore make them less likely to move to more productive employment. The policies of DREE tend to bring the federal government closer to the position of the poorer outlying provinces, and in that sense may facilitate harmonious relationships between the two levels of government. On the other hand, this is not a situation that is favoured in the richer provinces. One of the implications of the DREE program, of course, is the fact that by enlisting a large level of provincial cooperation, the federal government has in some ways lost control of the programs. Since the area of jurisdiction covered is often largely provincial, the federal government has had to leave much of the definition of the policy in the hands of the provincial governments.

Under these conditions MSED has not been free to formulate and advance a coherent policy of economic development. Rather it has been trying to work out some sort of harmonious understanding with the other departments of government, and to build up a kind of framework for ready comprehension and analysis of the problems at issue. This means formulating an economic development policy to maximize the growth of the gross national product, in accord with the political and social values of the country.

An initial approach was to analyze the numerous programs of economic development that the government already had. There were between four and five hundred such programs, divided into sectors: resources, energy, manufacturing and services. On this basis the department attempted to build a framework for economic development, exemplified in Figure 9-1 (pages 108-109), which was published by the department. The object is to lay out the various areas which the department is seeking to integrate into an overall policy mechanism. The means of intervention are provided in the eight circles. The various policy fields are perceived in two ways: horizontal and sectoral. The horizontal ones immediately under the circles represent specific policies that can be and are being undertaken. The four sectoral policy fields consist of the various component industries of each sector. There are about eighty of these horizontal policies undertaken by the government. These policies are intended to accomplish the objectives listed in the circles at the top. Figure 9-2 (pages 110-111) shows the department's representation of the inputs and constraints facing it in its effort to deal with the Canadian economy.

The MSED examines the overall policy area sector by sector, and attempts to aggregate the various economic development policies into an overall governmental program. It tries to take into account the various constraints that are operative in relation to these policies.

The purpose, therefore, is to avoid undue concentration on a particular aspect, such as technological sovereignty or protective tariffs — and to consider the whole overall policy structure. The concern, of course, goes beyond industrial development policy to cover economic development generally, including the primary sector as well as secondary industry. This is particularly important in Canada because the primary industries are mainly located in the outlying provinces, and secondary manufacturing in central Canada. The aim is to achieve an all-inclusive policy that deals with all of the basic inputs to the economy. The search is for a strategy for the eight circles at the top of the chart, the reasons for intervention.

Since the MSED's task is essentially integrative, it invites the other departments to provide policy inputs. Because there is no general agreement to proceed with economic planning, it is content to erect the guideposts to show the way towards achievement of the chosen policies. There are obvious constraints in the self-willed interests of the various participants, particularly industry, and in the policy decisions of the provincial governments. They were not prepared to accept dominant leadership from the federal government. The MSED, therefore, is compelled to work within these constraints and in an incremental, step-by-step way.

Generally the contention, and therefore the discussion, is not on the overall objectives, but at the more tactical level where specific programs with specific industries are directly concerned. Some government agencies have become the articulators of particular policies. Here one thinks of the Science Council's enthusiasm for the policy of technological sovereignty, and of its emphasis upon research and development. The Economic Council also is perceived as reflecting the point of view of the economics profession, although it is not identified with any particular interest. DREE provides the political

FIGURE 9-1: FEDERAL POLICY FIELDS, PROGRAMS AND INSTRUMENTS RELEVANT TO ECONOMIC DEVELOPMENT

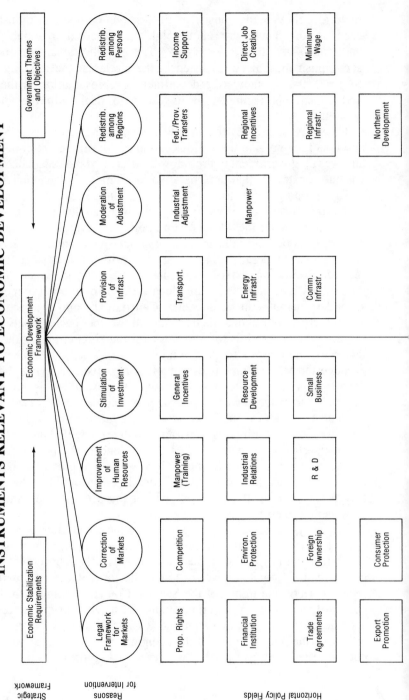

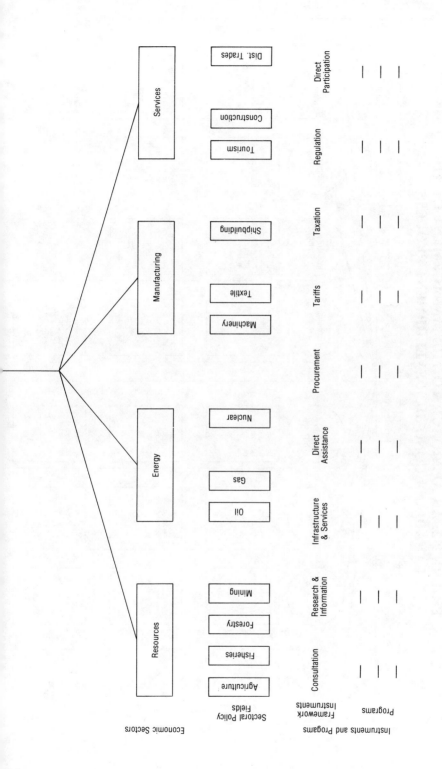

Source: Ministry of State for Economic Development

FIGURE 9-2: AN APPROACH TO THE MANAGEMENT OF THE CANADIAN ECONOMIC DEVELOPMENT PROCESS

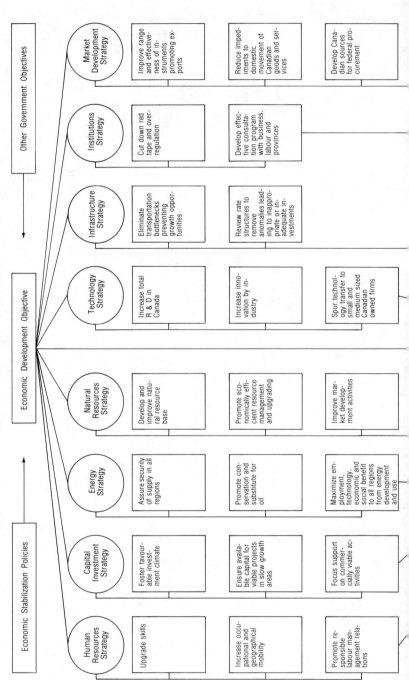

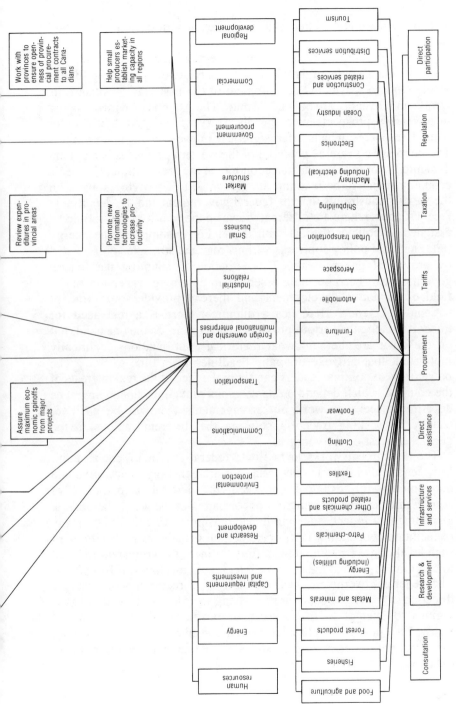

Work with provinces to ensure openness of provincial procurement contracts to all Canadians

Help small producers establish marketing capacity in all regions

Review expenditures in provincial areas

Promote new information technologies to increase productivity

Assure maximum economic spinoffs from major projects

Regional development

Commercial

Government procurement

Market structure

Small business

Industrial relations

Foreign ownership and multinational enterprises

Transportation

Communications

Environmental protection

Research and development

Capital requirements and investments

Energy

Human resources

Tourism

Distribution services

Construction and related services

Ocean industry

Electronics

Machinery (including electrical)

Shipbuilding

Urban transportation

Aerospace

Automobile

Furniture

Footwear

Clothing

Textiles

Other chemicals and related products

Petro-chemicals

Energy (including utilities)

Metals and minerals

Forest products

Fisheries

Food and agriculture

Direct participation

Regulation

Taxation

Tariffs

Procurement

Direct assistance

Infrastructure and services

Research & development

Consultation

Source: Ministry of State for Economic Development

and social reasons for intervention, particularly in the less developed parts of the country.

There is coming to be a general perception that, once the present crisis is past, all parts of the country face a relatively promising future. While Ontario's dynamic development of the past may be stalled, its wealth and diversity are beyond dispute. The Atlantic provinces appear to have new prospects with the discovery of oil, potash and other natural resources which offer significant development opportunites. The impressive resource potential of the western provinces is the main dynamic factor in the Canadian economy at the present time. Quebec's economy seems to be retaining its vigour. All the provinces agree on the various constraints that the federal government and the department face. Of course there are different views on the priorities that should be assigned to policies to deal with these. For example, in the energy field, national policy confronts various regional strategies propounded by provincial governments. This situation is tempting the federal government to become more assertive in assuming leadership in the field of economic development and thereby provide some kind of national coherence. Here lies a dilemma: there is a real need for tradeoffs among the various provinces and regions on the one hand, but on the other are the somewhat rhetorical confrontations, politically motivated, that provoke dramatic headlines from time to time. The power trips of political leaders can fly in the face of the real interests of the country, which depend on harmonious mutual understanding. The department seeks to work out arrangements that will be positive, usually by seeking tradeoffs between the different regions in the general interest of the country.

The department works to facilitate federal-provincial cooperation. Between parallel departments, relations are generally cooperative and harmonious: for example, between the federal Department of Agriculture and its provincial counterparts, or between the federal Department of Finance and provincial treasurers' offices. The best way to facilitate cooperation is to make certain that the responsibilities of each level of government are carefully defined, the grey areas reduced to a minimum, so that the need for intervening mechanisms is reduced. The federal government has the task of forecasting the strategic direction in which the economy is moving in order to allow the various regions to attempt to maximize their positions within this overall thrust. This process emphasizes mutual consultation and cooperation, but does not necessarily halt so as to obtain consensus on given policies.

The MSED's posture has been to work within existing institutions and not to seek to elaborate new ones or to impose any kind of planning arrangement. There is no disposition to move in the direction of the French indicative planning secretariat. There is greater respect for the consultative and cooperative approach undertaken within the Federal Republic of Germany, perceived as more relevant because it involves a federal country. It also emphasizes certain qualities that are viewed as necessary, such as an attitude of self-discipline and cooperation. The MSED seeks above all else to prevent the provinces and regions from engaging in "beggar my neighbour" policies, and to achieve as much candour and cooperation as possible. The department is convinced that Canadian political and social values are not disposed to favour a planned economy. Certainly the Canadian business community has shown itself unsympathetic, and the provinces too wish to preserve their freedom of action as much as possible. When one comes to consider any particular plan, it almost always involves a particular region of the country. This means that most of the provinces find themselves unaffected by or excluded from it, and therefore tend to oppose it. The diversity of Canada makes acceptance of overall plans extremely difficult. Policies that deal with the entire country have a much greater chance of being accepted by the various provincial governments.

The importance of the members of the cabinet in Canada emphasizes the great reliance upon informal accommodation between political actors. They do not believe in a master plan, but rely heavily on the process at which they themselves are expert: the making of political tradeoffs between competing interests. They are prepared to go as far as medium-term objectives. This imposes a certain kind of limitation on how far the government can go, at least within the current political reality as seen at the apex of the bureaucratic and political power structure.

Another factor is the United States, whose enormous investments in Canada give it an actual and potential power within the country. Americans are generally firm believers in the free market economy, and the Reagan administration holds this view with greater conviction than most of those that preceded it. Since Canada requires good relations with the United States, it seeks to avoid provocation to maintain these. However, the rather sharp U.S. reaction to the adoption of the National Energy Policy suggests that Canada cannot take American non-interference for granted.

Another concern of the department is to maintain good relations with other departments of government, in particular the Department of Finance and the Treasury Board. Since the Ministry of State for Economic Development is a relatively new department and a small one, it inevitably feels somewhat vulnerable. Furthermore, its mandate is broad, and it might be perceived as a threat to the other departments. To date relations have been good, but the existence of the other departments imposes a kind of moderation on the MSED, lest it appear to pose a threat to the other departments or the general tranquility of the policy-making community. The department has passed its major tests since its creation. It has weathered the storm of two changes of government and the introduction of the new envelope system for controlling spending allocation within the government. It has carried on the general approach introduced in 1978 with the creation of the Board of Economic Development Ministers. It appears that this innovation is now perceived as an ongoing one in the Canadian government, as an accepted player to participate along with the Treasury Board and the Department of Finance in the field of formulating a macroeconomic policy. In addition to these essentially planning functions, the MSED is concerned with resource allocation within the federal government through manipulating the envelope system. This is part of its role in integrating the economic activities of government and strengthening its planning power. This is an important function, the details of which are beyond the scope of this study.

The Organizational Changes of 1982

Since 1978 with the creation of the Board of Economic Development Ministers, the government has been moving towards more centralization in the field of economic policy-making. The Ministry of State for Economic Development was its secretariat and inherited its functions after the changes of government in 1979 and 1980. Its task has been to coordinate federal economic policy between the departments. The next major step came in January 1982 with the announcement of a major reorganization of government departments, but without changing the statutory basis of the existing departments. The previous Ministry of State for Economic Development was expanded to encompass some of the development functions of the Department of Regional Economic Expansion, such as the negotiation of the General Development Agreements with the provinces. The enlarged department would be called the Ministry of State for Economic and Regional Development (MSERD). It would help to integrate the regional orientation of DREE into the nationwide preoccupations of the MSED.

Parallel to this was the splitting of the Department of Industry, Trade and Commerce. The trade commissioner service was attached to the Department of External Affairs under a new Ministry for International Trade, to form an enlarged foreign service including both diplomatic and trade promotion aspects. The programs for support of industrial development (notably the Enterprise Development Program [EDP]) and the Defence Industry Productivity Program were combined with most of the Department of Regional Economic Expansion and the Ministry of State to Assist Small Business and Tourism to form the new Department of Regional Industrial Expansion (DRIE). This reflected the centralization bias by combining the central-Canada-oriented IT&C with the concerns of DREE for the outlying provinces. Policy-making henceforth should be pan-Canadian, without the regional biases of the previous organizational structure. More attention can be paid to the overall efficiency of the Canadian economy in the face of foreign competition. The emphasis will be on support of a noninterventionist kind for individual targeted industries where the best opportunities were perceived to lie, no matter whether they are Canadian owned and controlled or not. The aim is to induce good corporate behaviour: that is, that the firms act in Canada's interest and become autonomous rather than be subsidiaries taking orders from distant corporate head offices; that they do their own research and development; and that they claim a world mandate for given product lines.

Another aspect of the new centralization orientation of the federal government is the FEDCs (pronounced fed-cees), the federal economic development coordinators. These are senior civil servants (just below the deputy minister level) sent out to the regions of Canada to coordinate federal economic programs and work out relationships with their provincial opposite numbers. They report back to MSERD. Naturally there was apprehension in the provinces, since this development accompanied the departmental reorganization that saw DREE merge into DRIE. On the other hand, the merger is bringing the different federal departments and programs together and harmonizing them, as well as bringing intelligence to Ottawa from the provinces, and thereby preparing the way for closer federal-provincial collaboration in industrial policy, perhaps even culminating in collaborative regional plans for economic development. Since the FEDCs are senior and able people, they have succeeded in engaging the provincial governments in discussions and winning trust for the federal government. The seriousness of the economic crisis has improved the willingness to collaborate between the two levels of government.

On the other hand the disruption of bureaucratic routine that has been continuous since the creation of the Board of Economic Development Ministers in 1978, the two changes of government and the subsequent governmental reorganization have created an atmosphere of exhaustion in the public service. There is need for a settling-down period, to make the new structures work, and for a higher level of consensus to develop between the two levels of government and between government and the private sector. However, the proliferation of organized interests pressing governments in their own cause is an inevitable drag on the making and carrying out of rational policy in the general interest.

The Provinces: 1 **10**

When the British North American provinces were united in 1867, the object of the enterprise was economic development. The individual colonies were encountering difficulty after the abrogation by the United States of the Reciprocity Treaty, and after the decline of the economy of the Maritime provinces because of the shift from the wooden sailing vessel to the steel-hulled steamship. These problems were accentuated by the British decision to end preferences on colonial exports in favour of free trade. Confederation seemed to offer a way out of the economic dilemmas of the provinces through a policy of mutual help based on improved railway communication. Therefore, the building of the Inter-Colonial Railway was part of the Confederation settlement, and to entice British Columbia, a railway to the Pacific was also promised. To make all of this viable, the National Policy was introduced a decade later to protect infant Canadian industry and produce revenues for the support of further capital expenditures. Clearly, it was the federal government that was responsible for directing the economic development policy in the early years, through railways and the tariff to support the development of a Canadian manufacturing industry and commercial activity. In all of this the provinces were expected to take a back seat and to look after local problems, cultural questions, education and so forth.

Under the British North America Act (BNA Act) the provinces were given control over public lands, which came to mean control over the vast natural resources of Canada. These were very unevenly distributed, and some provinces were encouraged to pursue economic development policies based on particular resources. Around the turn of the century Sir Adam Beck pioneered the development of a publicly owned hydroelectric system in Ontario, which would constitute a significant enticement to the establishment of secondary industry in that province.

It is difficult to generalize about early provincial activity because of the vastly differing resource endowments of the provinces. Mineral and forestry developments on a significant scale developed in British Columbia, Ontario and Quebec quite early, and these called into existence interest groups, which worked in close partnership with provincial governments. Canada's early policy "may be summed up as a national program expressed in terms of staples and transportation, tariffs and railways, land and immigration policies, and the buttressing of enterprise by government ownership and support."[1] This was a period dominated by federal government policies looking to the creation of an east-west economy oriented toward the markets of Europe for Canadian staple products and toward local consumption of the products of the secondary manufacturing industry.

This phase was followed by a more regionalized pattern of development beginning after the First World War, based upon the natural resource wealth of the regions, as they developed in relation to adjacent areas in the United States. Base metal mining, the pulp and paper industry, and a new subsidiary secondary manufacturing industry were established. In the latter case, large American producers established branch plants in order to gain access to the Canadian and British Empire markets. These more regional industries developed close relations with provincial governments, which depended upon them for employing their labour forces and for taxation revenue. The result was close clientele relationships with a considerable amount of direct state intervention to protect industry located within the province. This meant growing rivalry between provinces, and great inequality, as the natural resource endowments differed vastly from one province to another. For example, by 1975 about 45 per cent of Canada's total mineral production value came from the single province of Alberta.[2] This has meant very substantial revenues for that province, making it possible for it to encourage industrial diversification and reinvestment in new resource development, such as the Syncrude project.[3] This regionalization of the Canadian economy and the new-found role of the provincial governments have created regional rivalries and protectionist policies conducted by provincial governments in the interests of the industries located within their borders. Both the inequalities and the rivalries have been accentuated as a result of the spiralling prices for hydrocarbons, which have greatly benefited the producer provinces (Alberta, British Columbia and Saskatchewan) and disadvantaged the consumer provinces in eastern Canada.

These rivalries have produced the adoption of a pattern of

protectionist policies by provincial governments against products of other provinces. While the BNA Act does not permit provinces to erect customs duties, the newer technique of nontariff barriers has given provincial governments the capacity to protect their own producers in many different ways. For example, government procurement policies have been formulated to entice or direct government departments to favour local suppliers of goods and services. These have even spilled over in attempts to influence the private sector to favour provincial sources of supply, hire residents of the province, or locate or relocate plants there. Subsidies have been used to attract capital and/or to prevent labour outflow. For example, Alberta has imposed regulations regarding the use of energy in industry by requiring an industrial development permit.

Governments have struggled one with another to protect markets for their products in other provinces. The "chicken and egg war" of the early Seventies was an outcome of provincial attempts to raise and stabilize incomes for chicken and egg producers in Quebec and Manitoba. Provincial governments have even intervened in the private purchase of productive facilities: for example, Quebec and British Columbia blocked attempts by capital interests in other provinces to buy up local corporations.

Provincial governments have also restricted labour mobility by using their licensing and certification powers to restrict certain types of jobs to residents of the province. A similar objective has been achieved by imposing regulations on professionals such as lawyers and account-ants, obliging those moving into the province to take additional training. The same effect has been secured by denying the portability of certain types of private pensions. Provincial or municipal income support plans often have residency requirements, and the provinces have imposed restrictions on professional faculties at universities by putting quotas on the enrolment of out-of-province students. Particu-larly obvious have been the discriminatory policies of the provincial liquor "control" boards whose pricing policies discriminate strongly in favour of items produced within the province.

All of these discriminatory policies have done substantial damage to the national market within Canada. The result has been a pattern of provincial protectionism that has diminished efficiency within the country, as each province seeks to protect its own against the others. These policies raise the costs of transacting business within Canada and involve a permanent subsidy for certain types of industry that must be borne by the taxpayer. The cumulative effect is self-defeating, as each reduces the markets of the others, and the stimulus to private investment declines, as overall efficiency is reduced.[4]

Each province, in short, has been led to follow policies calculated to bring development to the province and avoid out-migration. This has counteracted the natural adjustment process by which movements of people and capital would take place in response to variations in wages, job opportunities, production costs and so on. The result was the creation of ten provincial economies rather than one Canadian economy. Each province seeks to enhance the processing of its own natural resources and to maximize local decision-making. The prohibition against the imposition of tariffs has been bypassed by the erection of nontariff barriers, by subsidies to local businesses, tax concessions, loans and other incentives. Add to this discriminatory purchasing policies to complete the picture.[5]

Another problem is the very great economic inequality between the provinces of Canada. Generally speaking, the farther west one goes the wealthier the community in terms of per capita income. The Atlantic provinces are the poorest, Quebec is in an intermediate position, and Ontario and the western provinces are generally in a comparable position one with another, although Alberta is clearly the leader at the present time, given its substantial natural resource income. Therefore, the services rendered by provincial governments would be vastly different if each province had to rely exclusively on its own tax base. The federal policy of equalization payments has not only made it possible for Canadians living in the poorer provinces to receive a general level of services up to the Canadian average, but it has also enabled provincial governments, even in the poorer provinces, to pay for the improvement of their provincial bureaucracies, enabling them to undertake policies that challenge the federal government itself in certain areas. For example, the Maritime provinces have developed a costly system of fisheries services that has led them to champion inshore fisheries at the same time as the federal government has favoured the more capital-intensive offshore fishery. In short, the improved financial capacity of the provinces may well have served to accentuate the rivalries between provinces, and between federal and provincial authorities, because it has made possible a level of provincial intervention that could not have occurred without such improved financial capacity.

Each province has developed its own planning and economic staffs, which have elaborated complex and sophisticated programs for economic development to improve the competitive position of one

120

province in relation to the others and to the federal government. The federal government is coming to the conclusion, somewhat late in the day, that it would be better off to render services directly to citizens rather than to support provincial government activity, because the latter course permits provincial politicians to claim credit for federal expenditures and to challenge the federal authority while relying in part on federal funds.

Let us examine the activity of these provincial governments on a regional basis. For purposes of our analysis we will divide the provinces into four categories: the western provinces, Quebec, the Atlantic provinces and Ontario.

The Western Provinces

Cooperation between the four western provinces in a formal sense began in 1965 with the meeting of the Prairie Economic Council — a committee of the three Prairie premiers — with a view to coordinating economic development policies and reducing conflict. At first the discussions were related to narrow topics, such as specific transportation questions. However, in the Seventies, attention shifted to the place of the western provinces in Confederation. In 1973 the Prairie Economic Council was expanded to include British Columbia in the new Western Economic Council. This first meeting led to the preparation of a common western submission to the federal government. The Western Economic Opportunities Conference, which was held in 1973 under federal auspices, did much to induce the western provincial governments to work together to present their common position to the federal government. It inspired the provinces to continue this sort of interprovincial cooperation from then on. For example, the Committee of Western Industry Ministers was formed; it presented a western position to the federal government on the trade negotiations under GATT, coordinated a joint trade mission to Latin America, and has conducted a study of the purchasing policies of the federal government and of their own governments.

There has been informal cooperation in the field of transportation by establishing Westac (the Western Transportation Advisory Council) in 1973. Also, the Prairie Agricultural Machinery Institute was set up in 1974, funded by the three Prairie provinces to review prices and quality of farm implements available for purchase. Similarly, there was a Western Canada Fertilizer Prices Review Panel set up at the same time to review supplies and prices of fertilizers.

These were cooperative efforts of an informal kind, and did not

121

involve formal institutionalization. Indeed, the Western Economic Council does not even have a permanent secretariat like its Maritime equivalent. It has been known as the Western Premiers Conference since 1974. The provinces develop papers for these conferences jointly. The practice is to strike western provincial task forces at the ministerial level, to study and report back to the premiers on specific questions, such as federal intrusions into provincial jurisdiction. The bias, therefore, is towards preparing a united western provincial stance.

However, cooperation has been more effective in some areas than others. Clearly transportation is the major question, although industrial and resource development matters have been important. Efforts have been made to encourage interprovincial trade and to enhance the western share in Canada's export of manufactured goods. In the field of agriculture, there has been considerable cooperation relating to crop insurance, farm machinery testing, product marketing, research, stabilization programs, and on developing common attitudes towards federal policy.

There has been concern about developing a common western position on cost-sharing programs; the western provinces find that speaking with a single voice enhances their strength in dealing with the federal government. The premiers issue a common communiqué stating an agreed-upon western position. On the other hand, the premiers have failed to agree on social questions reflecting different philosophical positions and party stances. Therefore, the essential content of the premiers' meetings has stressed the development of common policies on economic questions.[6]

During the decade of the 1970s, the value of hydrocarbon deposits has increased to the point that they are much the most valuable Canadian resource; the provinces in which these are located are in an entirely different class economically from the others. We shall begin our analysis by looking at Alberta where the bulk of the resource is located, and then shift to British Columbia and Saskatchewan — the two other provinces that have benefited substantially from natural resource development. Manitoba, which lacks the rich resource endowment of its three western neighbours, completes the discussion.

Alberta
The province of Alberta currently exercises extraordinary power within the Canadian federal system because of its extensive supplies of depleting, nonrenewable natural resources. The problem for the

government of Alberta, therefore, is to make the best of this "window of opportunity" that affords the province a high level of surplus that can be devoted to stimulating and diversifying the economy. The provincial government has been the agent that has formulated a policy based on provincial ownership of the resource, and is currently attempting to implement this policy in the interests of the local residents. This poses a challenge to the federal government, which must attempt to recover some of the rents to alleviate distress and support development in less well endowed parts of the country. This intergovernmental rivalry is further complicated by the important role played by the privately owned industries, particularly the multinational oil companies. Indeed, much of the government action, both provincial and federal, has been to prevent them from capturing most of the rents as windfall profits, which they could use either to buy up vast holdings of economic properties in Canada, thereby using Canadian resources as a device to take over an ever-increasing part of Canadian industry, or to export the profits to the United States or other countries, thereby denying benefits to the Canadian people and destabilizing Canadian currency in international markets. The amounts involved have been so large that whatever happens it is bound to have a disequilibrating effect on the overall Canadian economy.

The federal-provincial rivalry over the resource rents has seriously undermined the legitimacy of the federal government in western Canada — a fact eloquently attested to by the failure of the Liberals to elect any member of Parliament west of Winnipeg in the 1980 federal election. This rejection reflects an alienation of those with superior wealth who are apprehensive at the efforts of the federal government to appropriate what appears to them as an inordinate share of the benefits of western Canada's resources. This attitude is epitomized in the new middle class, which has made its fortune in the resource sector in partnership with the large foreign-dominated oil and gas corporations.

The struggle of the government of Ontario and the federal government to keep prices low was perceived in the West as an attempt to claim an excessive share of the resource rents. The feeling of resentment in the West has been translated into the raising of a separatist option.

This situation has led the government of Alberta to maximize its capacity to monitor and analyze the complex economic circumstances involved, and to formulate effective policies to meet them. In particular it wishes to protect Alberta's interests in intergovernmental negotiations. Its key agency in this respect is the Ministry of Federal

123

and Inter-Governmental Affairs (FIGA). Another agency is the Department of Economic Development, which monitors and seeks to influence the rapid economic growth that has been occurring within the province in recent years. It is composed of three sections: the International Structures Unit, the Domestic Structures Unit and the Priorities Unit, whose titles indicate their functions. Its Strategic Planning Branch is an example of the government's attempt to maximize its analytical knowledge by developing sophisticated policy research agencies.

The rapid growth of the provincial economy because of the boom in the petroleum industry created substantial structural changes, which had some harmful effects on other provincial sectors. Some of the traditional industries have been seriously disadvantaged (for example, the feedlot industry in southern Alberta). The petroleum industry has drawn to it a disproportionate share of the province's labour supply and bidded up the prices for factors of production so that other industries are no longer able to compete. This has tended to heighten the trend towards dependency upon a single industry, and is the reason for the government's strategy of diversification based on the long-term strong points in the economy.

Much of the economic activity of the province is dependent upon investment, particularly in the resource sector, and relatively little upon consumption. This means that investment decisions of a few major economic actors have an inordinate effect on the provincial economy. Therefore, for the sake of the stability of the provincial economy, it is necessary for the timing of these substantial investment projects to be carefully managed so that severe dislocations do not occur. The government has attempted to do this by regulating private sector investment through a permit system. It has funnelled substantial surpluses from the hydrocarbons industry for investment in the Heritage Fund in order to maintain economic stability.

Despite the exceptional wealth of the provincial government, the pattern of services rendered by it are not unlike those prevailing in other provinces. Government departments provide financial assistance, technical research and market information services to assist economic development. This enables the government to compete effectively with other regions of Canada for the benefit of corporate investment. In addition, there are crown corporations to provide financial assistance in housing, agriculture and small business.

Because of the enormous revenues from the sale of nonrenewable resources, the province enjoys a revenue base radically different from

124

all other provinces. Indeed, one might have said before the recession that the other taxes were exacted more for their policy impact than for the revenue they yielded. Corporate and income taxes existed mainly for the purpose of preventing the grossly anomalous shifts in labour and capital that would ensue if Alberta's tax structure were significantly out of step with other provinces'. Also, one must keep a conventional tax regime in place, looking to the day when the greater revenues from nonrenewable resources will no longer be flowing.

The current problem, however, is to find ways to invest the excess revenue to prevent it from being wasted or from upsetting the stability of the provincial economy. The strategy has been to invest heavily in capital and other projects that it is hoped will provide a return to the provincial treasury in the longer term, or which can be justified as in the long-term interest of the people of Alberta.

Another tactic has been to cancel municipal debts by paying them off out of the provincial treasury. This has allowed local governments to take on new debt obligations for additions to the economic and social infrastructure, which is also a means of decentralizing governmental decision-making. The major instrument, however, for recycling government surpluses is the Alberta Heritage Savings Trust Fund, which contained in excess of $12 billion in 1983. There has been a progression in investment in this fund from the safest types of investments — government debentures, high-quality corporate bonds and other marketable securities (which comprised 51.9 per cent of the fund's total assets as of 31 March 1979) — to more high-risk and speculative ventures.

There are three divisions that administer the Heritage Fund, in addition to the routine tasks of looking after the low-risk investments. The Alberta Investment Division holds the debt for the housing, agriculture and development corporations, for Alberta's share of Syncrude, as well as a variety of other investments, which may be either equity or debt. This portion of the fund has no limits imposed upon it and comprises over a third of the total investment. The second division is the Canada Investments Division, which has made loans to Maritime provinces and Manitoba at preferred rates. This part of the fund is not permitted to exceed 20 per cent of total investments by an amendment enacted by the legislature in 1980. The Capital Projects Division funds projects deemed to "provide long-term economic or social benefit to Albertans" and "will not yield a return of capital or income to the Heritage Fund."[7] In this division there is a trust fund of some $300 million, which pays for a wide variety of grants for medical research, the construction of health care facilities, irrigation and land development projects and so on. Airport terminals, educational resources and other items are included, which cannot be calculated in a short-term balance sheet. They could have significant long-term effect on the provincial community.

The Heritage Fund, as a silent shareholder, also holds the province's share (44 per cent) of the Alberta Energy Company (AEC), and through it holdings of Pan-Alberta Gas, Steel Alberta and AEC Power. The Alberta Energy Company and, in a less direct sense, Nova (formerly Alberta Gas Trunk Line Company) were encouraged by the Alberta government in becoming established, but maintain an arm's-length relationship with the government. The government does not retain a significant amount of stock in AEC, but it has the right to nominate two members to the Board of Directors.[8] The company thus provides basic infrastructure for the oil and gas industry and the government.

Another important aspect of the government of Alberta's approach to economic development can be seen in its power to affect the extent, speed and nature of private sector activity. The provincial government has an unusual level of influence because of its legal position with respect to resources. The convivial state of government-business relations in Alberta and the fast rate of economic growth have favoured government influence. In the licensing of exploration and development, the government has used its legal control over resources to maximize the benefit that accrues to it. There is the well-known Alberta-first policy that obliges corporations to procure materials and services from Alberta suppliers, provided they are competitive. The expenditures for major projects are often made outside of Canada because heavy machinery and major engineering facilities do not exist in Canada in many cases. To carry out such a policy, the government has had to monitor the operations of large corporations within Alberta, develop the expertise and capacity to analyze the minutiae of procurement schedules, and relate this information to existing and potential productive capacity of the province or country over the longer term.

British Columbia
Like Alberta, British Columbia's economy is overwhelmingly committed to the production of resource commodities for export: 86 per cent of exports originating in B.C. are from the forestry and mining sectors; tourism and fisheries are third and fourth in importance. While the United States is still the major market, it is much less important to

British Columbia than to eastern Canada. The countries of the Pacific rim and in particular Japan are an important and growing market. This has led to a substantial market in British Columbia for Japanese manufactured goods. The result is a situation in which the interests of eastern Canada and of B.C. in foreign trade are somewhat contradictory. British Columbia is heavily dependent on the Japanese market, and therefore is favourable to the import of Japanese goods in order to keep this market open. Eastern Canada, on the other hand, is threatened by the invasion of Japanese manufactures, and seeks to slow it down. This in turn threatens to provoke retaliation by Japan, which would of course fall most heavily on exports from British Columbia. Clearly this is a very difficult contradiction to resolve in the overall Canadian interest.[9]

The major industry in British Columbia is forestry, which has been experiencing increasing concentration of ownership and control and growing difficulties as the housing market in North America has been declining due to the downturn in both demographic demand and economic conditions. By far the largest corporate interest in the forestry industry is MacMillan Bloedel. The central position of this corporation was amply demonstrated by the intervention of the government of British Columbia to prevent its purchase by Canadian Pacific Investments. Premier Bennett announced that "British Columbia is not for sale," and warned off this attempted purchase, although subsequently when it passed to Noranda, the provincial government did not protest. At the same time there are substantial American-controlled and now Japanese-controlled industries in the province. No doubt this illustrates an attitude in British Columbia towards interests outside the province in economic affairs that does not bode well for Canadian national unity.

The major concerns of the British Columbia government are, first, to diversify its industry by expanding the range of spin-off activities conducted within the province related to the forestry sector, thus encouraging the maximum processing of these primary commodities within the province; and second, to attempt to induce the industry to undertake policies for forest management so that the resource will be renewed in the future to maintain sustained yields. The federal government has shared modestly (less than 10 per cent) with the province the financial burden of supporting scientific management of the British Columbia forest.

The mining industry of course has been a volatile but important factor in the provincial economy, dramatized by the substantial rise and then fall in the price of copper. On the other hand, the petroleum industry rose steadily in importance to about half of the value of mineral production only to subside to about 30 per cent in 1981. The rise of coal has been even more dramatic, from 2 per cent of the total in 1968 to 19 per cent in 1978.[10] While petroleum was long dominated by the multinational giants, Petro-Canada is now the largest single firm. The production of other minerals has involved a profusion of smaller "junior" resource companies. These have experienced problems of financing, which has led the British Columbia government to complain about the difficulty of securing high-risk capital in Canadian capital markets. This has produced an undue concentration in some industries and a substantial degree of foreign ownership. The Social Credit government has responded to the problem in three ways:

- It has pressed for constitutional revision to institutionalize federal sensitivity to regional problems.
- It created the British Columbia Resources Investment Corporation (BRIC) to take over many of the crown corporations established by the previous administration. This corporation was a means of "privatizing" these government operations by giving five free shares to each British Columbia resident qualifying, and then raising $400 million in a public stock issue.
- The government has developed a new regulatory framework to govern the trading of junior resource stocks on the Vancouver Stock Exchange.[11]

British Columbia has been a latecomer in the development of sophisticated bureaucratic mechanisms to assist the cabinet's decision-making processes. When the NDP succeeded the highly personalized government of W.A.C. Bennett in 1972, it tried to superimpose its own agenda of social and economic priorities. However, with a civil service not yet modernized to facilitate effective economic policy-making, it lacked administrative skills. The NDP government, which was defeated in 1975, failed to make the necessary reforms and therefore was largely unsuccessful in bringing about the changes it had wished.

Saskatchewan
The postwar period has seen Saskatchewan emerge from its one-crop economy, which with its boom-and-bust cycles had carried it from general prosperity to a level of impoverishment during the Depression below all other Canadian provinces. This economic volatility led the

128

farmers to cooperative action to protect their economic interests. It manifested itself politically in the election of a CCF (Co-operative Commonwealth Federation) government in 1944 — the first socialist government in Canada. Since then, the party has been the main holder of political power in the province, although it had to give up to Ross Thatcher's Liberals in the Sixties and in 1982 was again defeated, this time by Grant Devine's Conservatives. Therefore, what we shall be describing is essentially the institutions and arrangements for economic development that have been put in place by CCF-NDP governments.

Since the war, the Saskatchewan economy has been greatly diversified by the development of new staple products: uranium, potash, petroleum, and pulp and paper. These have posed problems for the government — how are they to be managed? This was largely determined by the experiences of the CCF governments with nationalized industry. The early CCF governments had been enthusiastic supporters of government-owned business, and therefore were readily led to "save" faltering industries by public takeovers. This resulted in the government's early business failures in such unlikely ventures as a shoe factory, a woollens mill, a box factory and a brick plant. If judged in comparison with much of the private sector, these experiments were not particularly grim. However, they were politically embarrassing and were exploited by the opposition parties.[12] This led the government to eschew government involvement in business, and to carry on a policy in the field of natural resources parallel to that of other provinces from 1948 until 1973. The government opted for the role of rentier rather than that of enterpriser, and the royalties charged were generally as low as in other provinces with old-line party governments.

The experience of the potash industry is particularly important for the development of Saskatchewan government attitudes. During the Liberal Thatcher government years, a drastic decline in potash prices and a threat of U.S. government protective tariff action led Premier Thatcher to agree on a prorationing system in 1969, in which the price was fixed at an artificially high level and the production rationed among producers. The result was that the Saskatchewan mines were held to about half of their capacity, whereas those in New Mexico produced at 80 per cent capacity. However, with increasing demand and greater prosperity, and with the CCF-NDP back in power, the province began to increase taxes on natural resources to recover a larger share of the economic rents. When the companies resisted through political pressure and legal action, the government responded

129

in 1976 with a policy of nationalizing some of the potash mines in the province.[13] This was a significant departure from the posture of conservative rentier to that of profit-maximizing entrepreneur. After facing a series of court challenges over its resource policies, this policy was undertaken as a matter of principle. It also offered a means of excluding the federal government from regulating and taxing the Saskatchewan industry, and presented the government with an issue for electoral purposes.[14]

All of this suggests the Saskatchewan government's concern with economic planning. It was the first provincial government to experiment with the organization of the cabinet into committees, with the formation of an Economic Advisory and Planning Board (EAPB) in 1945. The board was chaired by a civil servant and consisted of six cabinet ministers and two professional advisors. Its task was to develop an economic plan for the province, evaluate policy in relation to the cabinet's objectives, and bring crown corporations under government control.[15] Later the Budget Bureau was established as a policy instrument of the planning board. It was later moved to become a branch of the Department of Finance.

The EAPB passed through several phases. At first it worked on various *ad hoc* projects directed by the cabinet, assisting various departments. It published the annual *Economic Review*, and experimented with a "fiscal framework" and a five-year plan during the 1950s. Then its role was more restricted, leaving room for planning by the individual departments. With the election of the Thatcher Liberal government in 1965, the board was abolished, and the roles of the Budget Bureau and Government Finance Office, which, as the central agency relating to the crown corporations, had been a key instrument of economic planning, were greatly reduced. However, with the return of the NDP in 1972, the planning structure was revived. The Budget Bureau and Government Finance Office received more resources, and the new Planning Bureau was made part of the executive council secretariat. The Planning Bureau, however, found that the departments had by this time developed adequate planning capacity of their own, and therefore it became a kind of coordinator for the various departments of government.

In 1979 the Intergovernmental Affairs Branch, over the objections of the Finance Department, was split off to become a distinct department responsible to a minister. The Planning Bureau was divided into three branches: the Social Planning Unit, a Resource and Industrial Policy Unit, and an Economic Analysis Unit. The Planning

130

Bureau acted as secretariat to the cabinet planning committee, with its chief planning officer acting as secretary to the committee.

The Planning Bureau in 1976 began to develop what became by 1979 the only economic model of a provincial economy that was based on provincial economic accounts and was used regularly in the economic planning and budgetary cycles. Presentations of one-, five- and ten-year economic forecasts were made to cabinet three times a year, and were used to coordinate the economic forecasts used by departments and crown corporations in their planning. The NDP's views of the way private corporations function has led to a suspicion of the resource companies, resulting in a fairly aggressive posture (for Canada), involving a determination to recover substantial economic rents from rich natural resources.

On the other hand, in relation to manufacturing, the government is much more tolerant of a profit maximization attitude on the part of industry, and has welcomed investment from whatever source in manufacturing.

The government has established by act of the legislature a Crown Investments Corporation to act as a holding corporation to administer crown assets. It is controlled by a board of directors drawn from the cabinet. The chief executive officer is a career civil servant. It also supplies legal, accounting, personnel and industrial relations assistance to the corporations, and is responsible for its overall capital budget. In turn a minister of the crown is chairman of the board of each of the seventeen crown corporations.

This positive approach towards planning has not, however, involved much close collaboration with neighbouring provinces. Provincial rivalries often appear even when attempts to cooperate are undertaken. For example, the cooperative Prairie provinces' steel industry, IPSCO, was planned in both Alberta and Saskatchewan, and 20 per cent share capital is owned by each government. There have been difficulties in this relationship, and Alberta went off on its own Steel Alberta initiative. The two provinces are now cooperating once more, as the difference in philosophies regarding the accountability to the government of publicly supported corporations no longer exists since the NDP defeat in 1982.

In intergovernmental negotiation the Department of Finance in Saskatchewan has retained a dominant role, relying on its own Tax and Fiscal Policy Branch for policy analysis and formulation. The Ministry of Intergovernmental Affairs was the key player on the constitutional question.

The government of Saskatchewan has undertaken the conventional role of supporting the private sector with a range of services. In addition, however, there are new roles, such as initiating new activities and attracting new high-technology industries to the province. This has led the government to "slice off" various activities that have been traditionally those of the private sector for government activity by a cautiously incremental process, with each new project justified on its own merits. Thus, there is government participation in joint ventures in uranium exploration activity and in the setting up of a fibre optics industry on contract with Northern Telecom. Clearly, without government participation there would be no electronics industry located in Saskatchewan. On the other hand, when it comes to the exploitation of natural resources, the goverment seeks to recover a large share of the economic rents for the people of the province, rather than allow them to be creamed off by large resource companies, most of which are foreign based. As the government in its own documentation commented, "It wants the 'starring role' in the control, development and extraction of non-agricultural raw materials."[16] In the area of renewable resources the government is usually only a regulator; in manufacturing it no longer participates directly, neither does it impose conditions on the nationality of ownership. "Saskatchewan welcomes foreign investment" is an accurate slogan in the manufacturing sector.[17]

The election of April 1982 saw the defeat of the Blakeney government, and the election of the Devine Conservatives. While it is premature to make a general assessment of the significance of the change, press reports suggest substantial terminations of policy-level public servants. Whether this represents a change in policy or merely the substitution of Conservatives for public servants whom the new government associated with the NDP, is not yet clear. If the Thatcher experience in the 1960s is a fair precedent, it is more likely to be the latter than the former, but this time the numbers are greater. A year into the Conservatives' mandate has seen few structural changes made in the provincial administration. The twenty-five crown corporations are still in place. Sask Oil, the government firm, has seen its expansion frozen, and the Potash Corporation of Saskatchewan is not permitted to sell its own product and is obliged to remain a partner in Canpotex, a private-industry-dominated agency. The recession has taken its toll, but the government has honoured its promise of cheap gasoline, mortgages and farm loans.[18]

Manitoba

Manitoba is in many ways a half-way house between East and West. It was the first Prairie province to be established and settled. Winnipeg became the gateway to the West, the major staging and distribution centre. In terms of natural resources, apart from its great agricultural lands, it shares more with northwestern Ontario than with Alberta and Saskatchewan. Its reserves of petroleum and potash are tiny compared to its western neighbours; yet its industrial development is not great. Therefore, Manitoba is less fortunate than either of its neighbours, east or west.

In recent years the province has oscillated between the New Democrats with their penchant for planning and the Progressive Conservatives, who have favoured a more noninterventionist, free enterprise approach to government. The Liberals have largely been destroyed in the polarization and in the general anti-Trudeau wave.

In the early 1970s the New Democrats under Ed Schreyer set up a planning commission, with McGill University economist J. C. Weldon as its secretary.[19] It was an empirical "rolling" plan with a six-year horizon. It involved the cabinet in the planning process in a unique arrangement. The cabinet was divided in two: half spent their time planning, while the other half tended to day-to-day administration. The two parts would alternate so that all ministers were involved in the planning process. The planning themes were few and were largely politically determined.

A major theme was the "stay option," that is, a plan to retain population and move jobs to people, instead of people to jobs, thereby to avoid wasting infrastructure. Plans were elaborated for individual towns, such as Leaf Rapids, a government-run mining town, and for marketing boards run by the government. The Kierans Royal Commission on the forest industry tied into the planning arrangements, although its strategy for recovering resource rents went beyond what the cautious NDP cabinet was prepared to do. The planners worked also in the medical field, suggesting a shift from provincial to regional control.

The government developed confidence in indicative planning at the provincial level. Its approach was practical and empirical, aimed at affecting employment by such methods as building houses. By involving the cabinet directly, it generated the political will to act — a unique experience in Canada.

However, this was not sustained. The NDP lost to Sterling Lyon's

Progressive Conservatives in 1977, a party committed to free enterprise and cutbacks of government involvement. The heady planning experience with full political backing came to an abrupt end in Manitoba. Some of its personnel and approaches moved next door to Saskatchewan, but at home it was dead. Premier Lyon considered it his mission to get government out of the economy as much as possible, and devote it to simple administration. Taxes were cut, civil servants dismissed, programs cancelled, government participation in mineral and petroleum exploration ended, government regulation cut back, the government deficit (in the early years, at least) reduced, and hydro rates fixed to encourage business. In short, in place of government involvement in economic planning, the Lyon government sought to let private business take the initiative, and to have government stand aside and reduce its costs. It did continue federally supported programs under the General Development Agreements, such as the Crops Production Agreement and the Industrial Development Agreement ("Enterprise Manitoba").[20]

The provincial election of 1981 brought the Lyon return to free enterprise to an end as abruptly as it had begun four years before. Howard Pawley, the new NDP leader, a man who had been deeply involved in the earlier planning effort, became premier. However, hard times ruled out a return to the earlier approaches. It is too early to discern the new directions of the Manitoba government — one that had charted its course more directly in favour of planning in the first instance, and against it in the other, than any other western province, despite its relatively poor economic underpinnings.

Quebec

The changes in perspective and outlook since 1945 in Quebec are greater than in any other province. They affect the nature of the problem of the economic organization of Canada profoundly. What are these changes?

Before the Second World War, French Canada had many of the characteristics of a traditional society: a high birth rate, a low capacity to assimilate immigrants, high status and authority for the Roman Catholic church, its priests and lay supporters, a small elite in the liberal professions leading a traditional, uneducated population, composed of workers and farmers, and patronage-oriented politics.

The English-speaking minority largely monopolized the executive and technical positions in the large industries and commercial establishments; so English was the language of the higher levels of business. Montreal was the major metropolitan centre, where the head offices of many large business organizations were located. The city and the province were home to the two solitudes, English and French speaking.

All this changed rapidly after 1960. After the death of Premier Duplessis, politics lurched out of the traditional rut. Jean Lesage's Liberals offered French Canadians a new order in which they would be masters in their own house. The educational system was overhauled to give young French Canadians the opportunity to acquire the technical and business skills that had been the preserve of the English. The civil service expanded and became more professional and technically competent, giving opportunities to the newly trained French Canadian graduates. It became the instrument for modernizing old Quebec. However, it could not itself offer enough career opportunities to the young French Canadians, who sought to enter the executive suites and technical offices of the private sector — the area traditionally occupied by anglophones. With government backing, they made great inroads: the English monopoly was broken.

This social transformation of French Canada had great momentum. Once in motion it could not be stopped or even slowed down. "Maîtres chez nous" led to demands for independence. In 1976 the Parti Québécois came to power pledged to lead the province to sovereignty, with or without an economic association with the other provinces. These developments were to have a profound effect on Canadian federalism, and the Canadian economy.

In 1961 the Lesage government set up the Conseil d' Orientation et de Développement Economique du Québec — an economic planning agency — to guide the provincial economy. The government recognized that the state is only one among many agents, and therefore cannot get its plans carried out unilaterally, and that in the Canadian federal system Ottawa has most of the power. However, the new agency still constituted a challenge to federal dominance of economic policy. Its second director-general, Roland Pronteau, put his mark on the organization, favouring a system of indicative planning on the French model. The name was changed in 1969 to the Office de Planification et Développement du Québec (OPDQ). It had the dual task of preparing studies for the economic development of Quebec and working with the federal officials on the DREE development contracts. The problem facing the provincial officials was great — to prepare plans for Quebec's development in the face of the federal government's overriding authority in economic matters.

After the failure of the regional planning attempt for the poor eastern area of the province (the Bureau de l'Aménagement de l'Est du Québec or BAEQ) under Guy Coulombe, based on the French indicative planning approach, the first integrated plan for Quebec on a large scale was the so-called Descoteaux Report in 1974 under the Liberals. It addressed such questions as export financing, research and innovation, control of foreign capital, the role of the Quebec government as economic innovator working through crown corporations and other agencies such as Hydro-Quebec, and government-funded financing institutions.

In addition to within the OPDQ, economic planning and research began in the Ministry of Industry and Commerce in the 1960s. Later, other departments began planning. To integrate these various efforts the Parti Québécois government decided to bring them together in the cabinet. Then to service it, they established a super-ministry (Ministry of State for Economic Development) under the dynamic minister Bernard Landry. This now defunct ministry was intended for coordination and planning only, without line operations. Naturally friction developed with operating departments that had their own ideas and programs. Landry decided that the best way to proceed would be to initiate a large, integrative study to produce a master plan for the province. All the agencies charged with planning were invited to submit their ideas and plans, and the team under Jean P. Vézina (the associate secretary-general of economic development) was charged with integrating the submissions into the master plan: *Bâtir le Québec*.[21]

It was a large undertaking that served to bring the various economic departments together in a common enterprise. The group of ministers who were joined in this effort is called the Committee for Economic Development. It built on the planning begun in the Sixties and owes much of its inspiration to French indicative planning. The French, at first, sent young conscripts who were fulfilling their military service obligations by voluntary work abroad, to serve as teachers and professional civil servants, and some gave advice in the early planning exercise. This connection has now waned in economic affairs, although it survives in cultural matters, and most of the professionals now are trained in North America. While the emphasis is very provincial, it is essentially capitalistic in nature. The civil servants, who are the professionals, are much the same people who served the Liberal and Union Nationale governments. Indeed the Parti Québécois encountered some resistance when it attempted to impose its social

136

democratic ideas on the planners, who succeeded in side-tracking much of this input.

The role of the state as entrepreneur is important. The Ministry of Industry and Commerce is organized to parallel the economy of the province, with each area of decision under an assistant deputy minister: one looks after industry, another services to companies, another research and planning, another international trade and so on. Essentially there are three means employed to encourage economic development: state actions of a supportive nature to encourage private initiative, financial assistance from the state, and the use of crown corporations.

In ongoing operations there is cooperation with agencies of the federal government, especially DREE and the inheritors of its programs, DRIE and MSERD. The modernization of the pulp and paper industry, for example, was effected on a cost-sharing basis with this federal department under the General Development Agreements. These efforts go on, despite the rivalry and even hostility between the two governments, although there are complaints about the different orientation of the other level of government, and of delays and strained relations, especially at higher levels, where political differences are more likely to surface.

Government procurement is carefully conducted to favour Quebec products and services. In cases where sufficient competition exists, usually only Quebec firms may tender. In other cases, producers whose products contain a high proportion of Quebec input are favoured.[22]

The thrust of Quebec government economic actions can best be seen as a long continuum from the 1960s on. The province pioneered in government involvement in the economy, motivated in the Sixties to reduce the control of non-Quebec interests over the economy. In the Seventies the government sought to ease the way for French Canadians to find their place in the management of the province's industry. This developed into a large role for provincial government institutions in shaping the economy — for example, Quebec-Hydro; Sidbec, in steel; Société Nationale de l'Amiante (SNA), in asbestos; Société de Développement Industriel (SDI), in financial aid; and Société Générale de Financement, a holding company. Also, the Caisse de Dépots et de Placement du Québec offers a government-sponsored fund in which authorized agencies can invest their savings in Quebec economic activity. It is autonomous legally, but reports to the minister of finance; it invests both in Quebec government bonds and in private industry —

and is a uniquely Quebec arrangement, channelling private savings into development projects favoured by the government.

The thrust has been aggressive and nationalistic (in a Quebec sense), but not socialistic. It has been an example as well for other provinces, who have come to follow Quebec, either out of self-preservation or to claim for themselves the powers and prerogatives that Quebec was assuming.

The provincial government, of whatever political stripe, has worked with business. The Parti Québécois government has held several "summits," or conferences, bringing together business executives, trade union leaders and government people, in order to bring about "concertation" — or cooperation — to make Quebec business more competitive. While Premier Lévesque has favoured the establishment of an economic and social council along French lines, this has not come about. Instead there is a Conseil d'Orientation Economique, which works with the OPDQ. However, the hopes for indicative planning for Quebec have not been fulfilled. After all, the federal government still holds the major economic levers, and in North America business holds much more power than in Europe, and governments correspondingly less. Nevertheless, extensive government studies are proceeding in preparation for future initiatives when the occasion presents itself.

Generally, the prevailing attitude among Quebec civil servants towards the federal government is one of reservation tinged with hostility. It is perceived as their rival and as the purveyor of policies that many see as favouring Ontario industry over Quebec's — manifested in aid to the automobile industry, for example. These feelings are stronger among the younger members of the public service than among their seniors.

In the third phase of the major planning document, *Bâtir le Québec*, called *Le Virage Technologique*, one notes the severe criticism of the federal government. It is blamed, because of the high interest rate policy of the Bank of Canada, for causing "losses of jobs by the thousand,"[23] and for policies which adversely affect the Quebec economy.[24] Reflecting the poor economic environment, the document concentrates on projects for job creation and maintenance, along with others for the support of industry, especially in high technology, such as hydrogen applications, biotechnology, new energy development, and the adaptation by the asbestos industry of chemical and metallergical techniques to replace the hazardous traditional mechanical extraction methods. It promises research centres and substantial

138

government investment in assistance projects for Quebec industry in financing exports, marketing, loan guarantees, and in providing easier access for smaller Quebec enterprises to existing government services.

The government proposes to encourage worker participation in the management of the firms for which they work.[25] It also proposes to involve more citizens in decision-making by devolving powers from Quebec City to the regions.[26] Along similar lines, it proposes the establishment of an economic and social council to maintain close contact with industry and labour between summit conferences.[27]

For the foreign investor it proposes a sectoral approach that would show him in advance which sectors are open to him.[28] Regulations would be simplified, and employer subsidies for job creation are proposed.[29] Of course, much of this is the familiar material of government rhetoric these days; full realization is prevented by shortages of funds and the weight of public debt, but there is no mistaking the more *dirigiste* and interventionist posture of the Quebec government when compared to the anglophone provinces, as well as its forthright, independent thrust.

To accomplish these ambitious objectives, the Quebec government has reorganized itself by making concerted use of the device of the minister of state, especially since the arrival of the Parti Québécois government to power in 1976. The purpose of a minister of state is to assure the coordination of several line departments behind a coherent government policy. There were five such ministers in the first Lévesque government who participated in the planning and priorities committee of the cabinet. This was carrying forward reforms initially undertaken by the previous Bourassa government.

These ministers of state had no administrative responsibility, thus permitting them to concentrate on planning and coordination. This, of course, risks the possibility of friction between the line departments and the ministries of state. However, since the latter were members of the priorities committee of the cabinet along with the minister of finance and the minister of intergovernmental affairs and the premier, they had considerable weight in decision-making; so line department ministers hesitated to cross them. This device has served to bring pressure to bear on the departments to live up to the government's electoral commitments and to adhere to the coherent policy program. The minister of state was considered a *"primus inter pares"* in his relationship with the line ministers; therefore, the premier, in deciding between possible disputants,[30] could determine who would be master. This enhanced his authority. However, in September 1982 the cabinet was reorganized and the minister-of-state experiment brought to an end. Line ministers were given the responsibility of presiding over cabinet committees covering the major functional areas.

Quebec has been the pathfinder province ever since the Second World War. It has been guided by its role as the defender of the interests of the French Canadian population to challenge the federal government and to seek to maximize provincial powers. Concessions have been made to it because of its peculiar position, but these concessions were immediately claimed in most cases by the other provinces on the ground that they had a right to the same treatment as Quebec. The process of developing provincial power has therefore been one that has moved on two legs: concessions to Quebec, and then the granting of similar rights to the other provinces. Since the rejection of the two nations theory and the perception of Quebec to be a province like the others, it has been extremely difficult to resist this process of province-building, leading to the balkanization of Canada. Probably if Quebec had been considered a spokesman for French Canada, and therefore given the kind of concessions appropriate to that status, it may have been possible to resist the tendency for the other provinces to claim similar powers. One can never know for certain, but there is no denying the fact that this process has indeed proceeded apace.

The Provinces: 2 **11**

The Atlantic Provinces

The four Atlantic provinces constitute that part of English Canada least affected by twentieth-century immigration. Their populations are largely descended from the eighteenth- and nineteenth-century British immigrants, and seventeenth-century French ones. Their economies are mixed; forestry, agriculture, fishing and small-scale manufacturing dominate, with the usual admixture of service industries. The small scale of operations, the sparseness of nature's endowment compared to the West (offshore oil may turn out to be an exception), and the relative isolation from major economic centres have produced economies that are less productive than in the rest of Canada. The region has become a deficit area, and is therefore the major beneficiary (on a per capita basis) of equalization payments, special aid programs and DREE's activities in Canada, all of which help make the government sector the most important single one in the regional economy. This has produced provincial government postures very different from those in the rest of Canada. Federal government spending activities occupy a central role in provincial priorities; so strategies to affect these are important. The provinces differ in this; Newfoundland, a recent arrival in the Canadian confederation, has taken a stronger, independent line towards the federal government, whereas the Maritimes are traditionally more accommodating and cooperative.

There are several arrangements for cooperation among the Atlantic provinces, although generally Newfoundland is much the least involved in these. This is partly because the province is geographically apart from the others and being the last to enter Confederation, didn't develop as close associations with the others. More important, however, are the different economy and prospects of Newfoundland, where the offshore dominates (oil and fish) and fires the imagination. The Maritimes, on the other hand, feel close to each other and have, on several occasions, considered union to form one province.

The best known of the instrumentalities of Maritime cooperation is the "summit" Council of Maritime Premiers, which grew out of the initiative undertaken in 1968 relating to Maritime union. The project, chaired by J. J. Deutsch, functioned like a royal commission, contracting for studies of various aspects of economic life, receiving briefs and stimulating discussion of the proposal. In its report it urged a full political union as a definite goal, and proposed the establishment of a Council of Maritime Premiers, a Maritime Provinces Commission and a joint legislative assembly.

After receiving this report the premiers decided to form the proposed Council of Maritime Premiers as an experiment. This agreement was confirmed by the legislature in identical acts.[1] When the accord was signed, the premiers agreed to establish the Maritime Provinces Industrial Research Council, to develop a centre for police training, to establish a central organization for mapping and surveying, and to develop a regional data bank and statistical service. They also decided to standardize regulations for the trucking industry. In addition, as a result of the five meetings within the first fifteen months of the council's existence, further cooperative measures were agreed upon, for example, a common building code, joint positions for first ministers' meetings, Maritime tendering and procurement practices, the establishment of the Maritime Resource Management Service, the Land Registration and Information Service, the Maritime Provinces Higher Education Commission and proposals for uniformity and harmonization in various legislative areas, a set of personnel policies, and procedures for the council as an employer. The statistical service did not come to be, but the council has provided a forum and has acted as a means of conveying joint positions to the federal government.

The council meets quarterly, and has developed a substantial secretariat, four operating agencies, a regional treasury board and a complex series of committees and agreements.[2]

The steering committee of the council meets eight times a year — when the premiers meet and once between their meetings. The council has worked out a common government purchasing policy. Realizing that the provinces on their own are often too small to support individual institutions, joint ones have been created, for example, joint dental and medical schools, the forestry school at the University of New Brunswick, the forest rangers school, the Atlantic Provinces Tourist Commission, the Maritime Lottery run from Moncton, New Brunswick, as well as the above-mentioned institutions established at the beginning. A common veterinary college is currently being proposed, probably for Charlottetown, P.E.I.

Another summit-type meeting is that of the Eastern Provincial Premiers and New England Governors, which discusses common problems. It has been meeting over a ten-year period, but has not been an effective body. It serves for contacts and lobbying.

Informally there are other forms of collaboration. Since New Brunswick has the largest staff working in federal-provincial relations, it often prepares most papers for such meetings for all three provinces. On the other hand, the provinces are rivals, competing for markets. They have no common development strategy, and parochial concerns often lead to deadlocks and bitterness, especially over jobs and other advantages.

Outside the formal government bodies stands the Atlantic Provinces Economic Council (APEC). It receives one-sixth of its revenues from the provincial governments, about half from memberships, and about one-third from research contracts. It is a nonuniversity think tank doing in-house research, with six professionals located in three offices (Halifax, Fredericton and Moncton).[3] Its activity relates mainly to the business community, but its frame of reference is limited to the Maritime provinces.

There are other examples of cooperation. Atlantic Canada Plus, an arrangement for publicity in the region, urges people to purchase products made there. The Newfoundland government chose not to participate in this initiative. The Eastern Spruce Budworm Council brings New Brunswick and Newfoundland representatives together to exchange research results relating to this pest. And one could go on.

Now we shall look at the provinces individually: Nova Scotia, New Brunswick, Prince Edward Island and, finally, Newfoundland.

Nova Scotia

Nova Scotia is the most populous, longest settled, and industrially the most developed of the Maritime provinces. Its capital, Halifax, is the largest city in the region, and is the only one that could pretend to metropolitan status. The province was a wealthy, thriving shipping centre before Confederation. The displacement of the wooden sailing vessel meant a serious economic depression for the province, and led it to consider union with other British North American colonies in the 1860s. Then followed the long stagnation of the provincial and regional economy. Migration tended to be out of the province, and the level of investment was low.

The stimulus of the federal DREE program prompted the province to develop a planning capacity in 1971 and 1972; this equipped the province to elaborate proposals leading to the signing of a series of sixteen sub-agreements under DREE's 1974 General Development Agreement with the province. The Department of Development was set up to prepare the development strategy. It prepared a green paper on development and worked out the proposals for the DREE sub-agreements dealing with shipyards, forestry, agricultural development, industry and so on.

Collaboration with the federal government has thus forced the province to plan. It has done so with the objective of escaping dependency upon the federal government by developing managerial and labour skills to increase productivity, improve education and upgrade resource management.

Nova Scotia hopes, too, that through planning it will attract new and more dynamic business activity such as electronics and plastics in place of the heavy industry that is in chronic difficulty. The success in attracting the Michelin tire company is an example of the newer effort.

In 1963 under Premier Robert Stanfield, it was decided to set up a cooperative board with the private sector called Voluntary Economic Planning. This was implemented by his successor, Ike Smith. The government provided the staff, and the business community organized itself on a voluntary basis by economic sector (fishery, agriculture, mining, etc.) to plan along with the government's Department of Development for its future. Its plans have tended to be general and long term rather than concrete and specific. The inspiration was the French system of indicative planning; but in Nova Scotia the chairman of the board was a businessman, and he therefore lacked the authority of government. As a result, the effects of the system are less impressive than they might have been.[4]

To accommodate this newer, hands-on planning approach, the government has improved its organization so as to avoid the situation where departments were autonomous of one another, and therefore rivals for funds and policy initiatives. Premier Buchanan set up a committee on government efficiency, which reported in 1979 in favour of a twofold structure. This was adopted. There was a Management Board, consisting of half the ministers in the cabinet and chaired by a minister. Its staff was drawn from the civil service commission and the treasury board. This body attends to day-to-day government business. The other half of the cabinet (about eight persons) constitutes the

Policy Board and is chaired by the premier. There is a deputy minister and two policy advisors to support the Policy Board. They keep contact with the departments and bring up policy suggestions for consideration. The decisions of both boards must be ratified by the whole cabinet, and ministers are free to attend meetings of both. In 1982 an Economic Investment Fund was created to be administered by a committee of the cabinet's Policy Board.

Another policy device consists of having government back-benchers chair committees of civil servants concerned with policy. Ideas and suggestions from these are passed up to the cabinet boards via the policy advisor for the Policy Board.

The emphasis in the Nova Scotia government is to work out a consensus among senior civil servants, ministers and the private sector, and the above policy devices are intended to contribute to this. The province has centralized its negotiating and implementation activity in the Federal-Provincial Development Agreements Branch of the Department of Development. This, along with strong representation in the federal cabinet and a generally good political climate in relation to Ottawa, exemplified in its agreement to federal demands for visibility and program control, has permitted Nova Scotia to do particularly well in attracting federal economic support on generous terms.

New Brunswick

New Brunswick, part of Nova Scotia until 1784, was separated to constitute a separate colony for the United Empire Loyalists fleeing the rebellious colonies to the south. It became a conservative, loyalist community on the Bay of Fundy and the Saint John River. To these settlers were added waves of Irish and English immigrants in the nineteenth century, who developed the rich forests of the Miramichi and Restigouche rivers and built the shipbuilding trade. In the north were the Acadian settlements, poor and isolated.

New Brunswick's development paralleled that of Nova Scotia: a long stagnation after Confederation, culminating in a general improvement after 1945, but at a level well below the Canadian average. The economy remains mainly primary: forestry, agriculture, fishing and mining, with a small and weak secondary manufacturing sector and the usual tertiary component. The province therefore welcomed the federal government's regional development policies from the Sixties on. Indeed they, especially the DREE programs, have

145

been the main engine of provincial economic development. Thus, the main concern of government has been to influence and if possible direct these initiatives.

The basic instrument, of course, is the General Development Agreement, which is the framework or enabling contract under which the specific sub-agreements are made. Many of these are essentially federal initiatives over which the province has little influence, given the fact that it wants the federal spending to take place. More of them, however, are a result of pressure from the province.[5] Most programs have related to natural resource industries: forest management, pulp and paper modernization, nurseries for trees, fish processing plants, plus tourism. There are seventeen such agreements with the province, representing a federal commitment exceeding $500 million. Much of the money has gone to hire experts, and more to create jobs, especially in construction.

The province has been in a vulnerable position in this relationship. When the federal government insisted on loading on the province the ongoing cost of a facility initially provided through federal funding, the province has had to accept these terms: for example, the program of shelter workshops and the Young Canada Works Program.

The province has thus found itself at odds with national priorities. It has always favoured more foreign investment to create jobs. Premier Hatfield has been the most outspoken opponent of the Foreign Investment Review Act, threatening to take the federal authority to court if it interfered with such investment intended for New Brunswick.

As a senior official commented: "Our main policy instrument is always DREE." It carries the weight, and gets the large-spending jobs done. Under it the province has a Department of Commerce and Development to work out policies relating to individual companies. It also had the New Brunswick Development Corporation to encourage industrial initiatives, but this has been phased out. Provincial Holdings Limited holds equity in various private corporations for the government. There is an Industrial Development Board to recommend government support to industry.

Beginning in the early 1980s, the federal DREE approach has been shifting away from a sectoral approach to a project approach — no doubt because it makes federal support more visible to the voters. As a receiver of largesse, New Brunswick cannot hold the federal government to deliver what it wants, when it wants.

In the Department of Commerce and Development's 1982 strategy document, greater diversification of industry was proposed, as well as continuing modernization, with federal help, of the pulp and paper industry. It recommended expanding secondary manufacturing through computer-aided design and manufacturing (CAD/CAM), but offered no new support programs. Rather it proposed adapting existing programs to the specific needs of individual industries.[6]

The nerve centre of the New Brunswick government is the Cabinet Secretariat — a small version of Ottawa' Privy Council Office. Each committee is served by five professionals to develop its general goals. New Brunswick first developed the much-vaunted envelope system in 1974–75, later adopted by Ottawa.

These groups operate under the general supervision of the Cabinet Committee on Economic Policy, although a committee of deputy ministers reviews all proposals of a policy nature. It in turn reports to the full cabinet. Much of the province's economic policy is made through negotiations with DREE, which culminate in further sub-agreements. The Cabinet Secretariat works in collaboration with the operating departments to maintain their support, and draws on the planning officers of these departments. The small scale of the government and the concentration of its central agencies, mainly in a single building, facilitate this close association.

Prince Edward Island
By far the smallest province in Canada, P.E.I. has just over 120,000 people. It merits close attention, however, because it is the province in which more planning and closer federal-provincial cooperation have occurred than in any other case. Public administration and the general service industries are the two largest single contributors to the provincial domestic product (19 and 24 per cent respectively in 1979). A full 72 per cent of the activities that contribute to the gross provincial product are involved in the service sector, as against a Canadian average of 61 per cent. The goods-producing part of the economy is fairly evenly divided among agriculture, manufacturing and construction. There is a small fishing component (1.6 per cent of the gross provincial product). The public sector over the past decade has increased enormously to the point where it is three times the national average (19 per cent in contrast to 6.8 per cent). In addition, a large part of the private economy is supported by public funds through various business assistance programs.

P.E.I.'s planned economic development began in 1969 with the introduction of the "Development Plan," authorized by the cabinets at both federal and provincial levels. The agreement was essentially a framework for institutional and fiscal cooperation between the two levels of government. The federal participation was coordinated by the Ministry of Forestry and Rural Development, later to become the Department of Regional Economic Expansion, which actually came into being the day after the plan was signed. A division of the department was established in Charlottetown with a director-general who was given substantial discretion to deal with his opposite numbers in the provincial government.

The provincial government created a new Department of Development to function as the secretariat to the Planning and Development Board of the Executive Council, and to administer the development policies. Its deputy minister became senior planner, and the department secretariat to the cabinet; so it became a very important central government agency, at least during the Liberal administration.[7] This meant that it tended to tower over the Budget Bureau because of the substantial input of federal funds, which naturally were accompanied by federal authority coming through the Department of Development. This influence even extended to the field of education, the most jealously guarded provincial area of jurisdiction, as a result of the Development Plan.

The plan was arranged at the end of the Pearson years, and imposed by the federal government in 1968. It was taken over by the Trudeau government whose approach was cybernetic and technocratic, favouring statistical and other quantitative systems of analysis. The Trudeau government favoured managing the economy through top-down imposition of policies designed to modify the infrastructure in which growth could take place. Virtually all of the province's economic development questions came under the plan. It was expected to mitigate the persistent high levels of unemployment that had plagued the province, and attract industries that would provide stable, year-round employment. Prince Edward Island became a kind of extreme example for this kind of planning operation, amply supported by substantial inputs of federal government money in a time of economic prosperity. Therefore, there were few concerns about the inevitable inefficiencies that accompany such a crash program.

The first stage involved the setting up of an infrastructure for an advanced industrial economy: improving roads, and building schools and technical institutes so that the province could meet the demands for skills that would be needed in the new industry. The plan phase was extended to 1975, when the second stage, involving the development of industrial parks and incentives geared to particular types of industries, would be put in place.

This phase was to have been completed by 1980, but because of difficulties encountered, its deadline has been extended. Meanwhile, the plan was considered "out of style" as a development instrument. The industrial parks were built, but have remained underutilized. Despite great efforts, unemployment remains persistent and high, and the industries that were attracted have proven to be volatile ones on the larger international market. An auto parts manufacturer has now gone bankrupt, and the electronics manufacturing firms are in deep financial difficulties. In short, P.E.I. has not accomplished successful deversification. This failure contributed to the defeat in 1979 of the provincial Liberal government and the return of the Conservatives under Angus MacLean, who sought to conserve much of the traditional economy of the province.

In fact, there was no great change of policy under the new government as far as development strategy was concerned, despite the Tories' preferences—no doubt, at least partly, because under the General Development Agreement the provincial government had very little power over the larger forces affecting the economy. Essentially they have done two things. They have renamed the Department of Development, the Department of Planning and Priorities, and replaced the deputy minister with a Conservative appointee. There has been some pulling back from the previous intervention in the economy, and a greater emphasis upon the primary industries under Jim Lee's Conservatives since his election in 1982.

This change, combined with the arrival of more difficult times, has resulted in a downgrading of the earlier technocratic bias. Since, for whatever reasons, the inducements to private capital have not been successful, the quantitative economists, who would stick to their econometic evaluation of economic development, have been somewhat abandoned by others who are more inclined to see the quality of life in P.E.I. as inherently worth preserving. There is, therefore, a process of re-evaluation going on as to how in fact to induce desired changes in industrial structures. The agricultural industry, on the other hand, has been successfully modernized.

One can identify three positions in this debate. First, the technocratic position from the 1960s argues that the government can step in and provide infrastructure and inducements, thereby attracting private capital. This in turn would mitigate regional economic disparities. A second even earlier position sees economic development as basically unfeasible in the Maritime provinces because of overpopulation. Those of this opinion would argue in favour of grants to assist people to relocate in more economically viable parts of the country. These people would favour income support and manpower training to permit the relocation of surplus population. A third school represented by Tom Kent, the previous deputy minister of the Department of Regional Economic Expansion, would prefer a qualitative evaluation of government programs, favouring cooperative economic development between government and industry rather than the supplying of inducements. This position would argue in favour of regional economic development strategies, but would also support the development of institutions to assist people to organize themselves to become self-sustaining. It is unfortunate that the economic crisis has come before these strategies could be sorted out and a firm policy put in place.

Newfoundland
Newfoundland is the last province to enter the Canadiar confederation (in 1949), after attempting unsuccessfully to be a separ.te dominion in the British Commonwealth. Because of the vicissitudes of the Great Depression of the 1930s, Newfoundland was compelled to turn to Great Britain and accept what amounted to a trusteeship under a Commission of Government. The Second World War involved greater contact with both Canada and the United States, mainly through the establishment of American and Canadian bases on the territory of Newfoundland. It seemed to be appropriate, in view of the reduced economic status of the United Kingdom, to end this system and seek association with Canada or the United States. After vigorous debate, it was finally decided by referendum in 1949 (by a narrow margin) to seek entry into the Canadian confederation as a separate province.

The union was to have profound effects upon Newfoundland. Canadian social security arrangements were much more generous than the slender resources the province could provide, and with their arrival profound changes in the lifestyle of Newfoundlanders ensued. The family allowance had a profound effect, as well as the other social programs that were administered via the provincial government. The new financial means encouraged the provincial government to undertake substantial programs intended to bring about social betterment, such as the improvement of the educational system and communications, and the movement of population from poor and isolated outports to larger communities. This meant profound changes

150

in the fishery, the development of the forestry sector, especially the pulp and paper industry, and the expansion of mining operations. Such substantial changes could not be brought about without profound social friction and the inevitable blunders that are bound to occur under such conditions. An inexperienced provincial government was gulled by several fast-talking promoters into making substantial concessions of natural resource wealth for prolonged periods of time. The one that rankles most with present-day Newfoundlanders is the Churchill Falls power development, which permitted the province of Quebec to receive the lion's share of the power produced by this development at what, since the oil shocks of the Seventies, is an absurdly low price.

If one looks back upon the years since the province entered Confederation, there can be no doubt that it is now a much richer community, with greater industrial development, and that it is looking forward to a much brighter future because of these industries and the promise of offshore oil. However, it is not a community with the humble expectations of the 1940s; rather it is an optimistic community that expects further improvements in its future. Its rising expectations have largely outrun its actual progress, and it is coming to perceive the federal government as an obstacle to its betterment rather than as the source of its advance.

Newfoundland is somewhat removed from the Maritime provinces, not only geographically, but with regard to its stand on policy questions. Newfoundland's problems are very different from those of the Maritime provinces. Its economy is less stable and, in some aspects, less developed. There are serious problems of poverty and chronic unemployment, which are more acute than those of the Maritimes. On the other hand, Newfoundland has greater cause for optimism about the future because of the substantial benefits expected to flow from offshore oil, in greater quantity than that expected in Nova Scotia. In addition, there are substantial expectations from further development of the hydroelectric power potential of the province, and also for the forestry sector, the fishery and mining. The result is a much more aggressive attitude in Newfoundland towards economic development in general, and towards the federal government in particular; this contrasts with the more patient cooperative attitude that has long been characteristic of the Maritime provinces.

Government spokesmen in Newfoundland are quick to assert that the province has its own philosophy of development, with some clearly articulated principles. The government is determined not to repeat the mistakes of the past, such as signing agreements with outside interests that did not give the province its fair share of benefits. The province is determined not to engage in a further cooperative development of hydro resources with the province of Quebec until that province agrees to renegotiate the Churchill Falls arrangement. There is a willingness to wait and negotiate hard in order to receive just compensation, rather than to make agreements just to get the economic activity started.

There is concern to see the substantial oil reserves offshore developed at a deliberate pace so that there will be no undue disruption of the fishery and other economic activities in the province. There is hope that spin-offs from the oil industry will create additional jobs, to help meet the chronic unemployment of the province. The oil industry is expected to stimulate subsidiary employment, such as the manufacture of drilling platforms and other drilling equipment in the province. This can only happen if the development is slow enough to be carefully planned. The government has set up its Manpower Needs Committee, which was to conduct training programs in the College of Fisheries and the College of Trades and Technology. The fishery is looked to as a major employer, and also as a stimulator of jobs in the processing industry.

The government has undertaken to protect its resources by issuing regulations, such as those proclaimed in 1977 giving preference to local people and calling for the use of local materials in the development of the oil and gas industry. The government monitors the purchases made by the oil companies to make certain that they are adhering to these regulations.

The government has a Department of Development, which employs professional economists, engineers, business administration graduates, et cetera. Here policies are prepared for the economic development of the province. Relations are maintained with the federal Department of Regional Economic Expansion through the Intergovernmental Affairs Secretariat, which provides substantial federal support for projects. For federal-provincial programs to be legally binding, the provincial government requires that they be approved by this agency. The province has been pressing for unconditional federal payments, and has not favoured shared-cost programs that involve federal participation in the formulation and administration of programs. The Newfoundland and Labrador Development Corporation funds development projects. The department advises businessmen about funding through this corporation and through DREE. The Cabinet Secretariat has prepared a five-year plan for the economic development of the province entitled "Managing All Our Resources" (St. John's, 1980), which lays out a strategy based on processing resources and industrialization that builds on "upstream" linkages, such as manufacturing fishing equipment and oil drilling platforms. This emphasizes more local procurement.

One discerns in these development plans a considerable desire to maximize the freedom of action and independence of the Newfoundland government vis-à-vis the federal government. Philosophically the government is not interventionist and is disposed to move away from the crown corporation instrument, which was a favourite of the Smallwood government in the Fifties and Sixties. It is actually trying to sell off the government real estate holdings, such as the Holiday Inn property and the Marystown shipyard. The Come-by-Chance oil refinery has been sold to Petro-Canada. The government would prefer to influence industry through legislation and regulations rather than through direct ownership.

The government has been very concerned not to become dependent on large outside business organizations or on the federal government. In seeking federal assistance, the province's condition has obliged it to make demands for federal support beyond those made by its sister provinces for the Trans-Canada Highway, the ferry service and so on. These encounters have tended to isolate Newfoundland, since the Maritime provinces have been willing to settle with the federal government on less generous terms than Newfoundland required. In more recent years when Newfoundlanders think of interprovincial cooperation, they are as likely to think of association with Alberta or Ontario as of association with their Maritime neighbours. This is partly because the optimism inspired by resource riches has led Newfoundland politicians to think in terms similar to those of the richer provinces. There is an impatience with the generally cooperative attitude of the Maritimes towards Ottawa.

The government's policy instruments focus on the Cabinet Secretariat, which has absorbed the Planning and Priorities Secretariat and the Newfoundland Statistics Agency (which reworks Statistics Canada data and originates some local information for planning purposes). The premier chairs the Planning and Priorities Committee, on which the minister of finance, the president of the Executive Council, the minister of fisheries, the chairman of the Social Policy Committee, and the Resource Policy Committee sit. These few men, backed up by professional specialists, have initiated the policies of the government, and have articulated the independent development strategy of the province.

Ontario

As the great central province, Ontario occupies a position like no other in the country. Since it produces over half of the country's gross manufactured product, is its major commercial centre, and is the province wherein the national capital is located, Ontario occupies a kind of pre-eminent position in relation to the rest of the country. From shortly after the time of Confederation, Ontario became the major industrial centre of Canada, and therefore it has developed a more national perspective than the other provinces. Ontario, along with Quebec, was the major beneficiary of the National Policy of tariff protection for Canadian manufactured goods against foreign competition. Therefore, it developed an attachment to the Canadian national market as its own preserve. This was the fulfilment of the hopes of the Fathers of Confederation from the United Province of Canada who looked to the establishment of a commercial empire based on the St. Lawrence Valley. This involved selling the processed goods manufactured there to the rest of the country and developing a system of east-west communication by rail that would make possible this internal system of trade. Whereas the rest of Canada was mainly export oriented, relying largely on the sale of primary products overseas and to the United States, Ontario's economy, roughly from the turn of the century, was primarily industrial, although it also had a substantial component of export-oriented primary industry. It is not surprising, therefore, that Ontario has never boasted a separatist movement such as has occurred in western Canada, Quebec and the Atlantic provinces. There has never been any doubt in Ontario that Confederation was beneficial, even if other parts of the country have from time to time had second thoughts.

The early industrialization of Ontario was largely based upon the advantages of a protective tariff combined with a central location for the development of industry. There Canada was able to supply much of its own manufactured products, although this meant that consumers had to pay a substantial premium because of the protective tariff. The early industrialization involved the development of small-scale and largely Canadian-owned industry. However, after the First World War and the development of the large, consumer-product industries in the United States, a considerable number of these concerns looked northward to establish branch plants. There they could produce their

154

consumer products for sale both in Canada and in the British Empire trading system, which involved lower tariffs for members of the Commonwealth and empire than for others. This was the period during which the automotive industry, the consumer durables industry, the pulp and paper industry on a large scale, and much of the mining industry were established. Ontario, therefore, developed a very close association with the United States and particularly with the headquarters of these large corporations, many of which were located in states adjacent to the province: Michigan, Illinois, Ohio and New York. Most of these industries were essentially branch plants that concentrated on the assembly of products from imported components.

This was a rather vulnerable industrial structure; Canada became a somewhat marginal processor for American industry. The country was hard hit by the Great Depression and subsequent recessions, which saw substantial unemployment in these branch plants and left the Canadian government in a position in which it was difficult to exercise effective control over these undertakings.

After the Second World War the branch-plant operations were renewed with greater success. There was general prosperity during the Forties and Fifties, and these manufacturing operations tended to enlarge their activities. However, with the general reduction in protective tariffs, which was a part of the General Agreement on Tariffs and Trade, the advantages accruing to these branch plants became of lesser importance. In some cases companies reduced their manufacturing operations in Canada in favour of a simple warehousing operation, importing the finished goods from the United States, Japan or other countries. This process of "de-industrialization" has greatly alarmed Canadian political leaders. They do not know how to respond to it. There have been cries for global product mandating. It is hoped that if firms agree to this the Canadian manufacturing industry can be preserved and will be able to develop a large export market for goods produced on a large scale in Canada that are now replicated abroad. So far this strategy has not attracted much interest from the multinational corporations, who have not generally found this proposal particularly advantageous to themselves. There are, however, exceptions, and some of these have been highly successful.

With the decline of tariff protection, countries have tended to rely on other means to protect their own industries, such as nontariff barriers and the use of government procurement on a highly selective basis. These approaches have been employed in Canada, but since Canada is a federal country, provincial governments as well as the federal

155

government have undertaken to use these devices. The Constitution does not permit the application of protective tariffs between provinces; however, it is silent on the question of nontariff barriers and procurement policies. Therefore, provincial governments have moved into these areas as a means of self-defence and province-building. This has been a particularly unfortunate development for Ontario. With the GATT agreements, the province has had to give up the highly effective protection of the tariff in favour of a situation in which other provinces are able to employ these new devices in order to protect themselves against products from Ontario so as to develop their own industrial structures. This latter involves competition with the industrial structure of the old imperial province. Imports from Japan, the U.S. and the EEC have flooded the Canadian market. Canada has experienced the bitter consequences of this development in the very severe unemployment during the recession of the early Eighties, which has seen the unusual development of Ontario having unemployment levels close to the Canadian average.

Beginning as far back as 1971, the organizational and decision-making structure of the government was modernized. A cabinet committee system was adopted, with a Policy and Priorities Board chaired by the premier to determine both long- and short-term objectives, and a Management Board to succeed the Treasury Board, plus three functional committees. The twenty-two departments were recombined into seventeen ministries.[8]

On 27 January 1981, a few weeks before the provincial election of that year, Premier Davis elaborated a strategy called "BILD," the Board of Industrial Leadership and Development, a committee of the provincial cabinet, chaired by the provincial treasurer and minister of economics, with the minister of industry and tourism as vice-chairman. The members consisted of six ministers in economically oriented portfolios.[9] This body was created in November 1980 as successor to the Employment Development Board, which decided on provincial grants to firms. The glossy publication *Building Ontario in the 1980s* laid out the strategy of government to be carried out by BILD, consisting of spending programs for the major sectors of Ontario industry: agriculture, forestry, mining, transportation, manufacturing, energy and tourism. The major commitments included $400 million for energy-saving urban transportation systems, a similar amount for primary industry, $300 million for research and development, $200 million for tourism and infrastructure, $200 million for job-skills training. The heavy emphasis on high technology was reflected in a commitment by the government to take the risk of buying shares in corporations up to $300 million over a five-year period, and to establish the IDEA Corporation[10] to fund research centres, monitor research programs and coordinate research between universities, the research centres and industry. Research centres were promised for microelectronics, biotechnology, automotive parts, robotics, in addition to existing facilities, such as the Urban Transportation Development Corporation. Marketing services abroad, including export financing, were promised.

Some of the ideas and proposals in the program were highly experimental and futuristic. A Canadian Hydrogen Technology Centre was promised to investigate the storing of hydrogen for energy purposes. Also, plans were announced for reducing the use of coal for energy generating by undertaking a program of small-scale hydraulic generation to provide electricity in remote communities, to be supplemented by upgraded transmission facilities. The Ontario Research Foundation is to be expanded, with the IDEA Corporation empowered to purchase patents and licence rights and to enter into joint research and development ventures with private business.

These plans must be seen as a continuation on a more ambitious scale of programs already in place. For example, the province has already a Technological Assessment and Planning Program (TAP) under which the Ontario government, with federal assistance, pays up to 90 per cent of the cost of research and development and technical assessment work performed by the Ontario Research Foundation for small businesses. An Ontario interministerial task force has been studying other ways to use procurement policy to promote industrial development.[11] There is a research and production facility at Malton in the first stage of production of a ten-year, $100 million investment program in support of high technology. The province will contribute $30 million, of which $5 million is "up front" investment in the joint venture with private business. Ten million dollars will be lent to finance a research facility, and $15 million to support ongoing research costs. A substantial program is proceeding to support research into opportunities for the application of research findings to manufacturing. The purpose is to foster the development of specialized technology and manpower in the province, and to develop new Canadian firms able to compete internationally. Also, efforts are being made to prevent costly duplication of government assistance.[12]

Ontario lent financial support to the federal mission to the 1980 Paris air show, where preliminary sales from twenty-nine Canadian firms included twelve offers to buy the De Havilland Dash-8. The provincial government itself has already paid for the first two copies of this aircraft in order to assist the firm's cash flow.[13] The province has mounted an $11 million hardware and software program for diffusion of Telidon technology by cooperating with private firms in this program. The government will buy two thousand Telidon units, and thereby stimulate the sales of videotex terminals in Canada. Other aids to industry include the bringing together of firms that can export complementary product lines, and the setting up of an office of policy to help Ontario firms that encounter unfair practices in international trade. The province undertakes to double financial assistance for export through development corporations and the BILD program.[14]

About the same time as Premier Davis was extending the BILD program, Larry Grossman, minister of industry and tourism, released a study, *Interprovincial Economic Co-operation: Towards the Development of a Canadian Common Market*.[15] This was an analysis of the effects of the balkanization of the Canadian market by nontariff barriers and preferential provincial government procurement policies. It discussed the failure of Canada to respond to the challenge of foreign industrial penetration of the Canadian market. There was a plea for a common response by the provinces and federal government through a cooperative program to work out tradeoffs. In this way effective Canadian challenges could be mounted to the foreign producers who are capturing a growing portion of the Canadian market, even for the items purchased by the provincial governments.

Ontario admitted that as the province with by far the most manufacturing industry, it has the most to gain by cooperation, but made the point that by failing to work out a common strategy, all parts of Canada are losing out to foreign producers. It proposed concerted Canada-first programs in areas where the governments are the major purchasers, such as in health care products. Such a policy would produce economies of scale, allowing Canadian producers to become internationally competitive.

Ontario has the least protectionist policy of all provinces. In procurement it "offers a ten per cent preference for Canadian content,"[16] and it does not have a policy of preferential purchasing against products from other provinces. Many of the provinces (Quebec, British Columbia and Alberta) have preference policies, and one even excludes out-of-province tenders for certain products. Ontario, therefore, is making the argument for solidarity among provinces on the basis of the most nondiscriminatory policy of all

Canadian provinces. It has the most to gain from cooperation and stands to lose little or nothing. The substance of the proposal is for an agreement on specialization among the provinces to substitute for imports, thereby reducing unit costs, and possibly producing for the export market. Attention is drawn to the opportunities offered for machinery production for mining and tar sands projects — as well as for the megaprojects of the future. To this end, Ontario proposed a Canadian Domestic Market Development Agency, owned by all provincial governments, plus the federal government, to foster interprovincial trade and economic cooperation by working out procurement policies maximizing Canadian sourcing, identifying opportunities and doing analyses of interprovincial trade.

The structure proposed was a board of directors under a president, with three professionally staffed sections: one for policy analysis, another to link potential manufacturers with megaproject managers, and a financial section to provide concessionary financing to Canadian firms to meet foreign competition.

With the deepening recession, the provinces have, if any change can be seen, become increasingly protectionist. Grossman's visit to western Canada to propose the above policy produced no results (perhaps because the Ontario government failed to follow up the initiative). Press reports show a negative attitude towards Ontario, generally viewed as exploitative and unfairly advantaged. In short, recent experience shows Ontario's protected advantage at an end. Tariff liberalization has heralded the arrival of the nontariff barrier — an instrument that trading nations use against one another to replace the declining tariffs, and which provinces in their zeal for province-building can employ. They have shown some willingness to do so, although so far not to an alarming extent. Nonetheless, the Canadian economy is less competitive in international trade as a result.

Federal-Provincial Economic Relations

12

First we shall review two important federal-provincial cooperative programs to gain some insight into how these have operated; then we shall survey the economic relations between the two levels of government since the Second World War.

Federal-Provincial Cooperative Bodies

The number of federal-provincial programs operating in Canada has become substantial. For example, an inventory published by Alberta federal-provincial programs in the province listed 110.[1] While many of these are specific to local installations, such as the Canyon Creek Wharf Agreement, others are substantial and important programs relating to such vital matters as the Canada Assistance Plan, the Canada Manpower Industrial Training Program, Established Programs Financing, Fiscal Equalization Payments and Fiscal Stabilization Payments to Provinces. In short, there is a large network of cooperative federal-provincial programs, most of which operate unobtrusively and cooperatively and together form a network of government which enables the country to function through the maze of elaborate jurisdictional overlaps that have emerged as government activities have expanded in recent years. It is beyond the scope of this study to present a close analysis of these programs.

However, for purposes of illustration, it may be useful to look at one such program that has benefited from careful scholarly analysis. This is the Canadian Council of Resource and Environment Ministers (CCREM).[2] After the Resources for Tomorrow Conference in 1961 the minister for northern affairs and natural resources decided to involve the provincial governments in the process of planning and administering Canada's resources. A steering committee was formed with the provincial governments, and it was decided a permanent resources council would be created. The Canadian Council of Resource and

Environment Ministers was incorporated in 1964 under the Companies Act. All provinces and the federal government would be represented by their resource ministers. The chairmanship of the council would rotate annually, and a permanent office would be set up in Montreal. CCREM proceeded to organize conferences and seminars on resource and environmental questions.

The council operated by simple majority vote, but in fact substantive issues were settled by consensus. Its board of directors had three members, elected from council under the chairmanship of the president, with each having a three-year term. The board met infrequently and in effect delegated its powers to the secretary-general. In addition, there was the Committee of Coordinators consisting of senior civil servants nominated by the minister for each of the participating governments. This committee, in turn, set up *ad hoc* specialist committees, and served as the major communication link between the member governments. These were generally deputy ministers. As time went on, fewer senior civil servants tended to be appointed to the Committee of Coordinators. During the active period from 1964 to 1973, one person, Christian de Laet, was secretary-general, and much of the vitality of the organization can be traced to his activity. He had only the power to advise, but in practice he had considerable practical authority. He was the major intergovernmental liaison agent, as well as maintaining contact with the private sector. There were nine *ad hoc* committees, most of which served as steering committees for large conferences.

CCREM was confined to renewable resources and sought their orderly development. Its purpose was to facilitate federal-provincial coordination in order to develop better resource policies across Canada. It provided a means for ministers to consult with each other, and was essentially oriented towards immediate operational goals and problems. Environmental quality was at the core of its concerns, and often it served as a means whereby the provinces could resist pressure from the federal government. Its major problem was the fact that with the rapid turnover of ministers it was difficult to maintain continuity. The senior bureaucrats, however, considered it a useful facilitator for the exchange of policy ideas and personal contacts. It conducted many conferences and workshops, especially relating to pollution. It published a monthly resources-environment bulletin, which was distributed free to about eight thousand people and institutions, as well as an annual report, which went to members of government and "friends of the council."

The organization appeared to be generally supported and very active until 1973; then suddenly it became quite inactive, after holding the large Resources for Tomorrow Conference in that year. This reflected the federal government tendency to avoid dealing with the provinces as a group in favour of one-on-one relations, in order to prevent the provinces from "ganging up" on the federal government. Also, some of the more experienced people in the council staff retired, and some of the provinces reduced their contributions towards its operation. With a general decline in the popularity of ecological issues, the council found itself isolated. It became inactive and faded from public view.

This case illustrated how effective a federal-provincial body could be, provided it received support and strong leadership. It also showed that once these were withdrawn, it took very little time for only a shell to remain. Given the lack of an overall federal-provincial framework for cooperative activity, CCREM lived an isolated and precarious existence.

At the interprovincial level as well, there are numerous institutions of cooperation. An important and successful one is the Council of Ministers of Education of Canada (CMEC).[3] It is an agency created in 1967 by the ministers of education of the provinces to provide a mechanism for consultation. The annual meeting is held in September, and there are other regular meetings as well. While individual provinces retain full jurisdiction over their own policies, CMEC facilitates the exchange of information and the harmonization of policies. CMEC activities are funded by the provincial departments of education.

CMEC has three components: the Executive Committee, the Advisory Committee of Deputy Ministers of Education (ACDME) and the CMEC Secretariat. The Executive Committee consists of five ministers who act as a steering group for policy and finance questions. The members serve a one-year term. The Advisory Committee is composed of all the deputy ministers responsible for education. The CMEC Secretariat in Toronto is headed by an executive director with a staff of about twenty-five persons. Established in 1968, it supports activities jointly undertaken by the provinces through the council. The secretariat observes the council meetings and committees, preparing reports and documentation for their meetings.

The main issues considered have included financing arrangements for postsecondary education, the provision of adequate funding for the Bilingualism in Education Program, and also the educational use of satellites.

The secretariat organizes numerous meetings for council committees and subcommittees, including federal-provincial working groups with a total involvement of about two hundred provincial officials. The committees of council are established with specific objectives for stated time periods. Every province is normally represented on each committee, with a chairman selected from among the provincial officials. An officer of the secretariat is assigned to each group to provide administrative support. Emergency issues can be handled by council without recourse to a structured committee approach.

The council has offered the Summer Language Bursary Program, which has permitted 6,500 eligible postsecondary students to take part in a six-week course in English or French as a second language, offered at forty-five accredited institutions. The Official Language Monitor Program, like the Bursary Program, is funded by the federal government but administered by CMEC in liaison with the individual provinces. It assists certified teachers in the instruction of English or French as a second language. The council has also set up French-language education services to operate via radio and television. It has carried out studies on student assistance in order to propose a series of options for future government aid arrangements for students.

Economic Developments and Federal-Provincial Relations

As we have seen in chapter 6, the end of the Second World War gave the initiative in federal-provincial economic relations to the federal government. It extended the wartime tax rental arrangements by negotiating the tax rental agreements and the tax-sharing agreements with the provinces. Following the White Paper on Employment and Income, the federal government took charge of Canada's external economic relations by participating in the General Agreement on Tariffs and Trade, sending out the trade commissioner service, making the one-billion-dollar gift to the United Kingdom for its reconstruction and participating vigorously in international economic relations. At first the provinces made no serious objection to these federal initiatives, because they had neither the bureaucratic competence nor the experience to pursue vigorous economic policies beyond their borders. These were prosperous years when Canadians were confident of their future and saw their wealth and the demand for their products expanding.

Not surprisingly, the first significant challenge to the federal initiatives came from Quebec. This province had serious reservations about the federal government's right to take charge of the distribution of taxation revenue from the three major tax fields, income tax, corporation tax and succession duties. Premier Duplessis refused to sign these agreements, and thereby tested the initiative and inventiveness of the federal government, which would have to devise a scheme whereby Quebec would not suffer discrimination even if it did not sign an agreement. After the death of Premier Duplessis, and with the election of Jean Lesage's Liberal party in 1960, the Quebec challenge was intensified even though the government of that province was of the same political stripe as the federal Liberals. Lesage's modernization of Quebec inspired a new dynamic nationalism based on Quebec rather than Canada. This attitude accelerated under the premiership of Daniel Johnson of the Union Nationale, Robert Bourassa of the Liberals, and finally René Lévesque of the Parti Québécois.

The federal government found itself, at first, obliged to make concessions to Quebec in the hope of appeasing its nationalist ambitions and satisfying its appetite. This policy is identified with Prime Minister Lester Pearson (1963–68); it saw Quebec being permitted to opt out of the Canada Pension Plan, and make separate arrangements for the delivery of health services and for federal government transfer payments for social security. These concessions, of course, paved the way for other provinces to make similar demands, forcing the federal government to acquiesce in a situation in which it was supplying the funds for services delivered by the provincial governments.

The federal government was in effect carrying out the role prescribed for it by the Royal Commission on Dominion-Provincial Relations, which pointed out in 1940 that only the federal government could tax the pools of wealth that were concentrated in central Canada, and distribute them to the areas in need of government services. As long as relations between the two levels of government were good (as they tended to be during the Pearson years), and as long as the country was prosperous, this situation was acceptable to the federal government. It appeared to be the great equalizer — the honest broker between the different regions of Canada. The policy seemed to enjoy the support of the Canadian people, as they returned the Liberals to power continuously except for the 1957–63 Diefenbaker interlude. Even then, the federal government under the Conservatives continued the general thrust of federal-provincial economic relations.

During the postwar period, the provinces proceeded to build up their bureaucratic capacity, partly with federal funds and partly in response to the need to set up machinery to administer programs that were, in part at least, funded by the federal government. This produced provincial governments with a new-found competence to defend their own areas of jurisdiction and to develop sophisticated economic policies. They recruited skilled economists, statisticians and lawyers who assisted in formulating the provincial development strategies that we have come to refer to as province-building.

These were the years when the federal government set up the elaborate structure of equalization and stabilization of provincial revenues so that all provinces would be able to supply services to their citizens up to the Canadian average.

Considering the will of Quebec to assert its independent status, as well as the desire of the other provinces not to be left out of benefits that were going to one province, one can see the dynamic forming of the provinces embarking upon a course to maximize their autonomy and develop their own programs.

Given the rapid growth of economic activity in western Canada, particularly in Alberta with its oil wealth and in British Columbia with its base metals, timber and hydrocarbon reserves, it is not surprising that province-building led to vigorous challenges to the federal authority by provincial governments seeing themselves to be in opposition to the federal Liberals. As the western provinces prospered, they came to realize that they were providing substantial revenues to the federal government that were being used in part to finance the transfer payments to the have-not provinces. Consequently, they sought to develop their own economies under provincial government control, and this encouraged the economic balkanization of the country. As we saw earlier, provincial governments began using their power to license certain types of economic activity in order to protect their workers from competition from beyond their borders. Gradually, the Canadian common market was being fractured along provincial boundaries, producing rivalry and adding to the economic inefficiency of the Canadian economy, which was already high cost by international standards.

Differences in per capita income among the provinces and regions of Canada persisted despite attempts by the federal government to attenuate these differences by sponsoring economic development projects in the less developed parts of Canada. Knowledge of these variations created jealousies between regions and augmented tensions among them. Unemployment was generally higher in the less developed provinces in eastern Canada, while the western provinces and Ontario were prosperous.

There was little federal-provincial economic coordination, but during the 1950s the federal government tended to run budgetary surpluses, which acted as a hedge against inflation. These ceased in the Sixties, and the economic climate for Canada grew more sombre. Continuing foreign investment in Canada created a demand for the Canadian dollar, which pushed it above the American. It was allowed to float from 1950 on — watched over by the Bank of Canada. However, with lower GATT tariffs, Canadian exports were coming to experience serious competition, and some mines and factories began to close after 1957. Unemployment had become a significant problem by 1962.

By the late Sixties, the West was riding the crest of the wave of rising oil revenues and high wheat prices. Unemployment, however, was a serious problem in eastern Canada, and the funds of the Unemployment Insurance Commission were in such deficit after 1970 that the program became a form of welfare rather than insurance. The federal government moved in with substantial programs for regional development to offset the depressed economic conditions in eastern Canada. The Department of Regional Economic Expansion, as we have seen, was the major instrument here. The development of powerful lobby groups in Ottawa, along with the growing financial commitment to programs to relieve regional disparities and inequalities in income, added to the growing inefficiency of the Canadian economy. As costs rose, competitiveness in the international marketplace declined. The federal government came to the aid of Canadian industries in distress; for example, it implemented quotas against cheap textiles from the Orient and against shoes from there and Europe. It failed to deliver on its promises for substantial reform of its tax and competition policy, except for marginal changes. The government oil company Petro-Canada was set up at the end of 1973, and in 1974 the Foreign Investment Review Act was passed. Tensions began to develop between East and West over the pricing of oil after the first oil shock at the same time.

While the country had been experiencing increasing economic problems from the late Sixties, the government did not see these as serious. After the re-election of the Trudeau government in 1974, it undertook the priorities exercise; the cabinet retired to its Meach Lake retreat to determine these. They emerged with five themes with sixteen priority policy areas. The emphasis was on a more just, tolerant Canadian society, with a greater balance in the distribution of people and in the creation and distribution of wealth among regions.[4] These reflected the attitude that Canada was a rich society that could afford to concern itself more with internal redistribution and minority rights than with meeting foreign competition in the marketplace. This attitude was reinforced by the growing political saliency of regional disparities, and by problems in French-English relations in Canada. Furthermore, the interests of the prime minister and the commitments of the Liberal party centred on such questions as economic disparities and constitutional change as paramount government concerns. Real apprehension about the consequences of the growing economic balkanization of the country further emphasized the importance of the Constitution.

Despite the government's stated priorities, inflation became a growing concern. As the Prices and Incomes Commission guidelines of 1968 were ineffectual, the government set up the Food Prices Review Board in 1972. Lacking regulatory authority, it accomplished little beyond publicizing substantial price rises. In 1975 the government resorted to compulsory wage and price controls despite its stand against controls in the election campaign the year before. These severe measures did have an effect on prices, although they seriously alienated both the labour movement and elements in the business community.

By September 1976 the two major interest groups, the Canadian Labour Congress and the Business Council on National Issues, began a series of meetings with the economic committee of the federal cabinet to discuss the state of the Canadian economy after controls. These meetings lasted until the following July, and it was agreed to establish tripartite boards to facilitate decontrols. The government issued its paper, ''The Way Ahead,'' consisting of fourteen points for the reconstruction of industrial relations.[5] Subsequently the labour representatives withdrew in reaction to what they took to be the government's take-it-or-leave-it attitude; so the tripartite boards never were set up. Most premiers demanded an early end to the controls program, and the federal government refused, keeping it in effect until 1978, despite the withdrawal of Quebec, Saskatchewan and Alberta.

After the generally negative reception of the wage and price controls program, the government decided to try to mend its fences with the business community. From April to September 1977 it launched Enterprise 77 — an intensive program to court the business community. Teams of senior public servants drawn mainly from the Department of Industry, Trade and Commerce, with some from other departments and from the provincial governments invited in, went to

167

visit the offices of 5,500 businesses from coast to coast. In the security of their own offices, business leaders were asked to unburden themselves of their thoughts and complaints about government and its policies and services relating to business.

The public servants were exposed to a torrent of complaints relating to areas of federal, provincial and municipal jurisdiction indiscriminantly. There were four major themes. The government's unemployment insurance and other transfer payment programs were creating a labour shortage even in areas with high unemployment. Businessmen felt that workers were being encouraged to stay home and collect government benefits rather than accept humble employment. Small businesses in particular complained of the difficulties of securing adequate finance, and of the high cost involved because of high interest rates. Other businessmen complained of excessive government regulation slowing down and imposing obstacles to their plans for expansion and development. Municipal zoning by-laws were found irksome. Then there was a general complaint about the size of government, the expense burden, the demands it made in terms of reporting by corporations, and other demands that added to the costs of doing business.

Enterprise 77 was deliberately undirected so that the attitudes of the business community could be candidly expressed, thus both informing the government and permitting a catharsis that would clear the air for a more positive relationship between business and government. The government representatives were surprised at the vehemence of the negative reaction they received, and were convinced of the need to undertake positive measures to repair the damage.

When the tripartite meetings among government, labour and business broke down, mainly because of the estrangement of labour occasioned by the compulsory wage control program, the federal government sought to reach some kind of understanding with the provinces. It was receiving conflicting advice: the Economic Council pressed it to lower tariffs in order to control rising costs, while the Science Council launched its program for "technological sovereignty," that is, the policy of developing technology in Canada instead of importing it via multinational corporations. The government's own demand management policies were proving unsuccessful, inflation was picking up after the pause during the controls period, unemployment was growing more serious, and attention to the economy was becoming increasingly necessary.

The Federal-Provincial Conference on the Economy of 1978

In the pre-election atmosphere of 1978 the federal government called a first ministers' conference on the economy. The provinces took this matter seriously; they prepared a substantial number of studies and papers, and came to the conference with high expectations. In preparation for the meeting of the first ministers, the federal and provincial ministers responsible for various economic sectors came together. In addition, the federal government got all of its line departments whose mandates concerned the agenda of the conference to prepare background papers. It convened the Committee of Deputy Ministers from economically related departments (commonly known as "DM-10"), chaired by the deputy minister of finance, Thomas Shoyama.

Provincial suggestions included one from Ontario for a "National Council on the Economy," to be composed of the federal and provincial finance ministers and representatives of "business, labour and other groups in the private sector. It would be a forum on the economy in which all governments and the private sector would, after a full discussion, define the major economic issues of the day and offer policy alternatives for consideration by the First Ministers."[6] This very general suggestion was an indicator of a growing awareness, at least in Ontario where much of the country's industry was centred, of the need for the concertation of economic policy among the governments. Stillborn then, the proposal was to reappear in the future in varying forms.

The high expectations for the first ministers' conference were not realized. The first of the conferences took place in mid-February with full television and radio coverage by the CBC. There were 281 people participating, including 78 ministers and 203 officials. The agenda was divided into two categories, the horizontal items dealing with the framework of the economy as a whole and the vertical ones dealing with specific sectors of the economy. The meetings began in a collegial mood of cooperation, but on the second day when regional and transportation issues surfaced a more confrontational attitude developed. It was after this discussion that Premier Lévesque left the conference and denounced the entire event to the press as "a pre-election extravaganza."

The conference soldiered on and issued a communiqué on the third day consisting largely of platitudes and generalities. There was agreement to keep the growth of government expenditure below that of the GNP, to accept the Bank of Canada's tight monetary policy, and to

169

ensure that the level of compensation of public sector employees did not lead that of the private sector. Also, the communiqué asked the federal and provincial finance and resource ministers to review taxation of the mineral and petroleum industries. The first ministers favoured intergovernmental collaboration of various kinds. The conference ended, but the governments continued to act unilaterally.

As we have seen, the federal government showed its concern over the declining economic environment by setting up the Board of Economic Development Ministers, under the chairmanship of Robert Andras. The board included the ministers of Industry, Trade and Commerce, Employment and Immigration, Regional Economic Expansion, Energy, Mines and Resources, Labour, Small Business, Ministry of State for Science and Technology, and Revenue. The minister of finance and the chairman of the Treasury Board served *ex officio*. This body was to develop the economic strategy for the government on an emergency basis.

It was set up partly to meet an organizational need within the federal government. Each department had its own area of responsibility and had developed its own policy; it was therefore difficult for one department to induce the others to cooperate in its initiatives. Even the Department of Finance, the Treasury Board and the Privy Council Office could not be enlisted to support a line department's initiative. A new structure was needed to enable the government to unite behind a policy. This was the response to the complaints of the business community asking the government to "get its act together."

It was during this period between the February and November meetings of the conference on the economy that the twenty-three industry-sector task forces were set up, composed of business and labour representatives, with federal and provincial observers. Such teams were established in all major processing industries, to aid in the preparation of a general report that would guide Canada in developing an industrial strategy. This is discussed in detail below. There were other programs launched during the interim period: a federal-provincial mineral taxation review, the establishment of the Centre for the Study of Inflation and Productivity within the Economic Council of Canada, a study by the Economic Council to investigate the effects of government regulation on economic activity, federal-provincial meetings on public sector compensation, and a conference on the funding of research and development, plus meetings of officials of industry with ministers to discuss industrial development.

It was at this time that the federal government, as an anti-inflation measure, induced the provinces to reduce their sales taxes in exchange for federal compensation for a six-month period — a program which Quebec rejected as contrived to benefit Ontario's manufacturing industry, and which the western premiers sharply criticized for its unilateral and intrusive character.

Costly government programs and increasing demands upon the unemployment insurance fund pushed the government deeper into deficit. The federal government determined to reduce its deficit, and the prime minister made his famous "guns of August" speech, in which he committed the government to a $2 billion spending cut. Despite this effort the deficit soon mounted once again.

On 27 November 1978 the first ministers' conference reconvened. The prime minister stressed the inseparability of the constitutional and economic problems facing Canada — a position that did not enjoy much provincial support. The premiers, especially from the western provinces, were generally critical of the federal initiatives and of the general atmosphere of tension, which seemed to be exacerbated by the extensive television coverage. The interval between conferences had left time for the preparation of voluminous position papers by all of the parties, and these taken together swamped the conference. There were eighty-one separate documents distributed, thirty by the federal government, thirteen brought by Quebec, and ten by Ontario. In addition, the pre-election atmosphere and the open sparring between Trudeau and Lévesque spoiled any possibility of harmony.

Each government had its own objectives for the conference. The federal government had to be seen to be doing something about the economy before the election was held. Therefore, it wanted a highly publicized, open process. Also, it wanted to encourage as much federal-provincial cooperation as possible to restore the international competitiveness of the Canadian economy. Since the federal government itself was becoming increasingly broken up into several departments pursuing different courses in economic development, such a conference might encourage coordination among the federal agencies as well. In particular, it wanted to restore business confidence by showing that it was taking the initiative in putting its own house in order and bringing about collaboration with the provinces.

The provinces' objectives varied. Quebec was most critical and defensive of its own jurisdiction. It carried a watching brief to make certain that the federal activities carried on within the province would be in line with provincial priorities. At the other extreme was Ontario, which welcomed the prime minister's initiative and favoured extending federal-provincial consultation. Among its tabled documents was one in favour of protecting the "Canadian common market," which some saw as Ontario's market for processed products. The province was careful to include proposals in the interest of other provinces in order to secure their support. Ontario was closest to Ottawa in its concerns for cooperation and concerted action.

The western provinces, with their legacy of grievances and their new-found resource wealth, were less tractable. Most critical was Alberta, which did not want to be seen working in partnership with the federal Liberals; yet it was generally committed to the process of consultation. It wanted to prevent the federal government from profiting politically by its initiative.

Premier Sterling Lyon of Manitoba voiced a neoconservative position, favouring the pre-eminent role of the private sector and the need for government retrenchment. On the other hand, Saskatchewan shared the federal government's "medium-term" approach. It favoured proceeding with energy megaprojects to create jobs, and it endorsed the need for coordination of policy between governments.

British Columbia took the conference most seriously and presented a detailed and comprehensive statement on economic policy ("Towards an Economic Strategy for Canada"). This was a serious and detailed proposal that, unfortunately, in the haste of the conference, received much less attention than its proposers expected. The conference was not prepared to devote detailed consideration to a package coming from a single province.

The position of the Atlantic provinces was much more consistent than that of the western provinces. They had met beforehand to try to coordinate their presentation. Nova Scotia was primarily concerned with fisheries, energy and regional development issues. New Brunswick was also interested in the energy question. Newfoundland wanted a commitment on the further development of its hydroelectric potential. Generally, the Atlantic provinces were anxious to get as much federal support for their region as possible, and were inhibited by their dependent economic position from taking strongly divergent initiatives like Alberta and Quebec.

During the interval before the November conference, the participants had been acting unilaterally. The federal government's announced intention of reducing federal expenditures by $2 billion shocked the provinces, since it was bound to affect their revenues. The second conference, therefore, came together with somewhat diminished enthusiasm. While there was the usual interregional squabbling, the major thrust was the provincial premiers' criticism of federal economic policy. The agenda began with an economic overview, then turned to labour market and employment issues, a progress report by the prime minister, followed by a series of specific items, including industrial development, energy, minerals policy, fisheries, regional development and transportation. The conference failed to consider the economic coordination process because of the wearyness and discouragement of the participants, and their failure to agree on specific issues. It ended in considerable demoralization.[7]

The conference had come at a time when virtually all governments had armed themselves with new departments of intergovernmental relations, which sought to enhance their own roles, exercise their powers to set agendas and defend the jurisdictions to which they were responsible. Overly long agendas resulted in a highly charged political atmosphere. Antagonistic debates developed, especially over the fisheries, and soon the leading participants were unable to absorb all the information supplied. They simply could not read all the paper. In the void of federal leadership, consultation became a substitute for policy, and as it proceeded, exhaustion replaced agreement. The conference was in part an open one, which led participants to play to the gallery, posturing for their home constituents, and thereby making compromise and accommodation difficult, if not impossible. This killed the cooperative spirit of the conference; it failed despite an upbeat communiqué at its conclusion.

While the conference was not much worse than the usual federal-provincial meeting, it was becoming clear that the format of such conferences left much to be desired. The first ministers needed to show political gains, yet were exceptionally committed to their own parochial interests. In the glare and heat of the television cameras they were unable to establish the easy rapport from which compromise comes. The conference was too brief to permit the development of interpersonal relations.

The attempt to prepare the conference by preliminary meetings between federal and provincial public servants to identify the key outstanding issues did not work out as had been intended.[8] In some cases the federal line departments were reluctant to consult their provincial counterparts, and in others they simply failed to reach agreement (for example, on the question of support of the fisheries, the federal government leaned towards support of the inshore fishermen, while the province of Nova Scotia sought to direct support to the industrial and highly capitalized offshore fishery).

173

There was no mechanism that would have permitted the first ministers to digest the detailed issues presented to them. There simply was not time. This fact, plus the pressures of television, resulted in a growing negative attitude on the part of some of the participants, and in the excessive complexity and inappropriate nature of some of the issues. Moreover, there was a lack of direction because of the failure of the federal government to assume a leadership role. Individual provinces were in no position to do this. Consultation itself became a substitute for policy, and clear conclusions simply did not emerge. The exhaustion that overcame the participants added to the frustration.

However, despite the generally discouraging outcome of the conference, it remains the most serious federal-provincial meeting dealing with the economy since the Second World War. While in the end unsuccessful, much serious thinking went into the preparation of the submissions, and genuine efforts were made to deal with the economic questions facing the country.

This discouraging experience suggested that the sense of community in Canada was on the decline. It led to recriminations and an atmosphere of pessimism. Generally, the richer provinces shared a neoconservative attitude, favouring the reduction of government intervention in the economy in the interest of the less well off. They tended to prefer private sector initiatives and the cutting of federal spending and intervention. There was much vague talk about an expanded role for the private sector as the major impetus for growth in the economy. This kind of rhetoric, however, was no substitute for policy. No doubt it was an inevitable by-product of the fiscal crisis that the governments were facing, combined with the evidence of declining confidence being articulated by business spokesmen. It was a difficult atmosphere in which to discuss more positive government intervention, such as an "industrial strategy." There was not even agreement on whether to work towards horizontal policies relating to trade, tariff, energy and transportation, or whether to concentrate on sectoral or vertical policies for individual components, such as manufacturing, mining and fishing.

Some provinces had their own strategies that they were anxious to shelter from federal action; for example, Alberta's industrial development program, relying in part on the Alberta Heritage Savings Trust Fund. Saskatchewan also advocated an entrepreneurial role for government, and wished to be free to pursue this initiative.

Ontario, of course, wanted assistance for its manufacturing industry in making adjustments to the lower post-GATT tariff structure. It

wished, therefore, for federal government promotion of the modernization and rationalization of its industries, and assistance in international
marketing of its products. It also wanted the national common market
to be protected, to resist the fragmentation of the national economy.

Quebec's attitudes, on the other hand, were much more negative.
For it, the idea of a national economic policy in Canada was an
impossibility. It had taken its own position for a provincial economic
strategy in its white paper *Bâtir le Québec*. It was critical of the federal
government's policy of restraint as it affected Quebec, and argued in
favour of continued protection for the ''soft'' sectors of its economy.
Premier Lévesque advanced two cardinal principles: each government
should mind its own business, and occasions for federal-provincial
discussions should be reduced.

The Atlantic provinces supported trade liberalization, especially
with the eastern United States, and favoured the use of General
Development Agreements to support the weak economies of the
Atlantic region. This, of course, meant continued federal government
financial assistance.

The federal government avoided putting forward a comprehensive
plan, and adopted a strategy of reacting to provincial statements and of
mediating interregional disputes. For the federal government, consultation itself was important, and, as we have seen, became a substitute for
policy.[9] In a sense, Ottawa was on the defensive, and faced conflicting
demands from the provinces, with its own departments of government
often not in agreement on policy. The conference's failure to come to
significant agreement meant that no single national policy was then
workable; so some of the provinces were prepared to undertake their
own initiatives.

In short, the major contribution of the economic conferences of 1978
was to reveal the unsuitability of the federal-provincial conference
format for dealing with such a complex matter as the economy of
Canada. It was simply beyond human capability for first ministers and
their officials to deal with the myriad of complex problems involved in
federal-provincial economic relations in the format of a conference
lasting a few days. Either the governments would have to go their own
separate ways, or a better mechanism for concerted efforts would have
to be devised. In the general letdown after the frustrating experience of
the conference, however, there followed a period of exhaustion
exacerbated by recrimination. Constructive thoughts about new
mechanisms would have to wait.

In February of 1982 Prime Minister Trudeau called another

federal-provincial conference on the economy. There the governor of the Bank of Canada continued to maintain that his policy of high interest rates was necessary if Canada was to avoid a drain of capital to the United States. The premiers, on the other hand, were most concerned about growing unemployment, and clearly the majority of them favoured policies to stimulate job creation rather than the government's current policy mix calculated to reduce inflation.

At the conference the prime minister did not lay out any strategy but merely invited dialogue. The premiers also tended to speak in generalities, although there was mention of controls on wage increases in the public sector, advanced by the Alberta and Ontario leaders.

It was apparent that the conference had been called on fairly short notice, and that the premiers had been anxious to attend in order to show that they were concerned about the worsening economic conditions in the country. However, it was equally clear that none of the participants had any particular strategy or plan for dealing with the situation. The federal government was determined to reduce its transfer payments and deal with its serious budgetary problems; the provinces were equally resolved to prevent the erosion of federal transfers. When the dust had settled, nothing had been achieved. The nation's expectations had perhaps risen slightly (although the credibility of government by this point was sufficiently low that reference to higher expectations can easily be exaggerated).

After this disappointing meeting, the country continued to witness signs of growing and deepening economic malaise. Governments were trapped between insurmountably large deficits and the need for public expenditure to stimulate employment. Furthermore, they faced the problem of stubbornly high inflation, and therefore dared not depart from policies that keep interest rates high. At least one did begin to hear more reference to the need for greater intergovernmental cooperation and for more serious long-term planning. However, these general feelings were not followed by concrete suggestions or actions. With the deepening unemployment problem, the Bank of Canada was persuaded to relent somewhat on interest rates, which were allowed to decline in 1982. At this time, late 1983, the deeper problem of improving the machinery for coordination has not been resolved — or sufficiently addressed.

Consulting the Private Sector   13

The idyllic relationship between the federal government and the big business community that existed in the postwar C. D. Howe period had greatly changed by the mid-Seventies. Where previously there had been general agreement on the simple objectives of managing economic growth, now there were conflicting priorities. There was disagreement about the degree of foreign control of the economy; in any event foreign investment capital was becoming difficult to attract. Apprehension was growing about the social and ecological consequences of headlong economic growth, and the United States was coming to be looked upon as a less reliable and more controversial neighbour. The Canadian economy was experiencing deepening recessions often accompanied by more serious effects in the poorer regions of Canada. Also, the country began to be affected by trade imbalances; the government was beset by pressures to develop "an industrial strategy" — a kind of holy grail that would bring about a return to stability and prosperity. It became apparent in the Seventies that the old consensus of the postwar period was gone, and it was difficult to reach compromises among the various economic actors. Some provinces had undertaken province-building exercises, which involved erecting barriers against the free flow of people, capital and goods across provincial boundaries. These new adverse circumstances were affecting the attitude of the business community towards government.

When the Department of Industry, Trade and Commerce undertook its Enterprise 77 exercise, it discovered suspicion and hostility towards government. Businessmen complained about the growing size and cost of government and the impediments it created to the free movement of economic forces. Government regulations, they claimed, were getting in the way of business initiatives, the smaller businesses were having difficulty securing adequate financing, and government programs often created problems, such as causing labour shortages through overly generous employment benefits.

This experience led the government to try to deal with the mounting discontent. To do this, it decided to seek the guidance of the private sector in formulating economic policies. The Department of Industry, Trade and Commerce prepared "sector profiles" of twenty-three sectors of the manufacturing industry in Canada — descriptions with analyses of the problems they faced as perceived by the government officials, supported by statistical data.

The next stage was to consult the private sector, that is, business and labour leaders (despite the post-controls unpopularity of the idea of "tripartism"). The government decided to invite them to constitute study groups for each industry that would advise government on policy. The provincial governments were invited to send representatives. The federal officials served as resource persons who would be "on tap but not on top."

These twenty-three sector task forces drawn from business and labour constituted the first tier of a general consultation with the private sector.[1] Since there was to be a federal-provincial conference on the economy, the members of these task forces were assured that their advice would be taken seriously. It proved to be somewhat difficult to enlist the support of labour because it was, not surprisingly, somewhat suspicious of government after the controls exercise. Also, since most of the power in the trade union movement is held at the individual trade union level rather than at the level of the Canadian Labour Congress (CLC), it was difficult for the latter to respond quickly and coherently to the government's invitation. The government chose to act through the CLC in order to strengthen it in the hope that it would bring about a more coherent position in the labour movement. (Provision was made to represent non-CLC unions, especially from Quebec.)

The task forces, each with a government secretariat, met about four times. They began by revising the sector profiles prepared by IT&C officials, and they then made substantive recommendations affecting their sectors. On nine of the twenty-three task forces, at least one labour member dissented from the majority report. Generally, however, there was substantial agreement on the recommendations to be sent to government.

It was decided to send these "Tier I" reports to the "Tier II" committee, which was drawn from Tier I chairmen and labour representatives. The labour demand for parity on Tier II was accepted; so there were five labour and five business participants, a chairman drawn from the business community, plus one academic expert. Their job was to synthesize the Tier I reports into one omnibus document. The federal government prepared a response to the Tier II report, "Action for Industrial Growth: A First Response." There was a second government paper entitled "A Continuing Dialogue," which appeared in February 1979.

The Tier I exercise was an attempt to tap the grass roots of the private sector. The task forces consisted of equal numbers of senior labour and business representatives. Business *organizations*, however, such as the Canadian Chamber of Commerce and the Canadian Manufacturers Association, only participated as observers. Each task force consisted of between ten and fifteen people working with the assurance that their reports would go directly to the minister of industry, trade and commerce. The provincial governments (except for Alberta, which refused to participate) sent observers. Each task force had one academic participant to assist in the deliberations. The reports from both Tier I and Tier II were submitted to the government in July of 1978, with about 850 recommendations, 300 of which related to areas of provincial jurisdiction. Not surprisingly, they were largely self-serving pleas for government assistance, and many of them conflicted one with another.

This substantial effort by the federal government was expected to help win the confidence of the private sector. However, since this is not the only consultative exercise in recent years, and since the results obtained so far are slight, the burden carried by it was considerable. The reaction among the industrialists varied from one sector to another. The high-technology industries such as aerospace reacted quite positively, whereas such soft sectors as clothing, furniture and footwear remained generally disenchanted. Also, smaller firms found the burden of participating great because of the loss of time by key members of their organizations. The large business firms always participate in such exercises simply to keep informed; they can readily afford the lost executive time. Labour clearly was less supportive than business. Furthermore, there was the problem of disagreement between the Canadian Labour Congress and other union organizations outside it — most notably the Quebec-based Confédération des Syndicats Nationaux.

Provincial observers varied in their attitudes. Those from line departments were generally supportive, whereas there was a certain tendency among those from the central agencies to perceive the exercise as essentially "political." Alberta had decided to boycott the operation because it wanted to be free to pursue its own province-building operation. It argued that "federal and provincial governments should consult separately with the private sector." It saw the exercise as essentially publicity seeking by the Trudeau government. On the other hand, Quebec participated in the exercise, perceiving it as a continuation of the summits that it had initiated itself with its own private sector in 1977.

The task forces themselves, of course, constituted forums for special pleading in which the participants in a given industry could state their grievances and list the various forms in which government aid could be extended to them. Clearly they were not objective analyses of an industry, and taken together they could not, by themselves, form the basis for government policy. The government, of course, knew this when it initiated the process. However, there was doubt as to whether it was fully aware of the inevitable entrenchment of the status quo situation that mobilization of such groups would entail. There was no intention for the study groups to be ongoing consultative bodies that could respond to the government's reactions to their reports. There were some complaints from the outlying provinces that the exercise was essentially central-Canada based. This, of course, was inevitable because of the meetings' preoccupation with secondary manufacturing. Generally, the labour and business representatives worked well together in formulating statements that would serve the industry. The boycott by the Alberta government did not prevent representatives from Alberta's private sector from participating — and they did so seriously.

The Tier II committee digested the Tier I reports, summarized their conclusions and identified areas where joint recommendations by business and labour could be made. In the field of taxation, manpower, and labour relations, however, there was no general agreement. Points of agreement included: corporate taxation in Canada should not exceed that in the United States, and the recognition of the need for greater coordination of fiscal policy between Canadian governments. The committee favoured tax measures to stimulate manufacturing. On manpower, the Tier II report simply recommended "an autonomous body . . . to integrate sector inventories of manpower availability and needs, and to advise on manpower policy, training and educational requirements."[2] It also favoured on-the-job training for workers. On trade policy it urged Canada to negotiate reciprocity arrangements under GATT. Industries that are uncompetitive but vital should enjoy the same level of protection in Canada as do their counterparts in other developed countries. It favoured the establishment of export consortia supported by the federal government. The committee agreed on the rationalization of Canadian manufacturing, with government support for communities and individuals adversely affected by it, and on the use of government purchasing as a means of supporting Canadian industry. It disapproved of provincial restrictions reducing the mobility of manpower, and generally was sceptical of province-building as a misallocation of resources.

Undoubtedly a major contribution of the exercise was the improvement of relations between business and labour. Many of the senior officials on both sides met one another for the first time, and the meeting, of course, was not a confrontational one, but rather one for the consideration of questions of mutual concern.

In its reply, the federal government supplied detailed point-by-point answers. Provincial governments, on the whole, did not reply, and those that did gave only very general responses. The federal government made the point that it already had programs in place intended to meet the criticisms advanced by business and labour. It also pointed out that the cost to it of acceding to most of their requests would be beyond its current means.

It is somewhat difficult to assess the contribution of the Tier I and Tier II operation. Clearly, it built up expectations for improvement beyond what the straitened circumstances facing the government would permit. The inevitable result, therefore, was disenchantment and a renewal of the hostile attitude to governments that had preceded the operation. By their very nature, governments are slow to make decisions, must take many positions into account, and then reach compromise decisions. The need for these tradeoffs are not always understood by nongovernment people. The reports, being statements of demands for government policies in the interests of the participants, inevitably put the government in a position where it generally had to say "no" to the requests. However, about sixty changes were passed up to the cabinet for implementation, affecting seven or eight separate departments of government. These were signed by the then minister of industry, trade and commerce, Jack Horner, and some were in fact implemented. However, seen from the outside, the general impression was left that the mountain had brought forth a mouse.

On the positive side, business and labour leaders were brought together for a common consideration of the most outstanding problems facing them, and some positive results were forthcoming from this. For example, the Major Projects Task Force, a cooperative study respecting megaprojects for the Canadian economy, was set up cooperatively by the labour and business leaders meeting in this forum.

Both business and labour were suspicious of government in its pre-election situation. They feared being coopted and exploited for political reasons. Therefore, they insisted that the Tier I and Tier II meetings take place in secret. The fact that there were no clear objectives stated for the meetings also caused some suspicion. However, both sides agreed that the exchange of views and cooperation between the two sides constituted a first step towards positive action. This, however, did not extend to the actual agreement on priorities. Canada was still in 1978 too rich a country for that!

Perhaps the major criticism of the operation was that by simply saying to the private sector, "Tell us what you want," the government was encouraging it to avoid the hard choices and articulate its demands without having to confront the price both to itself and the community. In that sense, the operation must be considered as a kind of first step in an ongoing process. If, in fact, it had been followed up by a well-planned series of subsequent encounters, the experiment may well have produced positive results. The unfortunate fact is that political events were to foreclose that possibility for a considerable period of time. The federal elections of 1979 and 1980 so disrupted the governmental pattern that the initiative was lost.

The year 1978, therefore, was a year of promises dashed. Both the federal-provincial conferences on the economy and the Tier I and Tier II task forces constituted a bringing together of the major players in the Canadian economic game. The former was a kind of horizontal federal-provincial governmental consideration, and the latter a vertical labour-industry-government approach. Both involved getting major leaders in the nation's political and economic life to focus their attention on the major problems of the Canadian economy. This was the only time in the entire history of the country that this kind of concerted attention by both government and business leaders was directed towards the structural problems of the economy. It represented, therefore, a rare opportunity lost, at a time when the country was moving even deeper into economically troubled waters. The failure to come to any significant understanding either at the federal-provincial level or at the government–private sector interface would leave the country unable to mobilize its resources to meet the coming economic problems.

Since 1978, federal-provincial relations and relations between the government and the private sector have been buffeted by destabilizing forces. The double-election disruption meant that the foundations laid in 1978 for both of these two areas of collaboration were neglected. The essential following-up of the initiatives simply did not take place. The Clark government, during its short term in office, did take economic questions seriously. It placed its leading economic expert, Senator Robert de Cotret, in charge of the economic development portfolio; he decided to hold a large conference to follow up on the Tier I and Tier II initiatives. However, the government was defeated before this event could take place.

When the Liberals returned to office in 1980, there were new ministers in the various economic portfolios and the Clark interregnum had broken the connection between earlier initiatives and the government's preoccupations in 1980. The prime minister was determined to achieve his objectives of constitutional change, and to do this he launched a vigorous offensive to enlist provincial support. This unilateral federal action was at first opposed by eight of the provinces, and the general rancour and bitterness involved in the ongoing struggle undermined any continuity there was in the field of federal-provincial economic relations. While the prime minister succeeded finally in reaching a compromise over the Constitution with all of the English-speaking provinces, the estrangement of Quebec was complete and bitter. The atmosphere was not conducive to reaching compromise on the complex and difficult questions involved in dealing with the national economy. Moreover, the economy itself had been declining and was moving into a situation of recession, if not of crisis. It was obvious that something had to be done, even though the atmosphere prevailing between the federal government and the provinces was one of tension and suspicion.

The newly re-elected Liberal government did not appear to have a strategy worked out to deal with these worsening economic conditions. Its most recent economic strategy dated from 1972, when conditions were vastly different. Its rather vague enthusiasm for megaprojects, especially in the energy sector, appeared increasingly threatened as the recession deepened. Very high interest rates, low consumer demand and general economic malaise discouraged investment in the private sector, and had its effect also on the government. Falling demand for goods led to declining demand for energy and a weakening of the price for petroleum on the international market. Clearly this was no time to mortgage the future to expand energy production in Canada. The megaprojects would have to wait. But what was to be done?

In November of 1981 the government issued *Economic Development for Canada in the 1980s* with its budget papers — a plan for the Canadian economy. While this document touched all the bases, it was clear that the government was planning to rely most heavily upon the resource sector as the major engine for economic growth in the period ahead.

The federal government realized early in 1982 the urgent need to focus on Canada's competitiveness in the international economy. The reorganization of its departmental structures favoured the development of an overall economic strategy to end the government's habit of conducting contradictory economic policies at one and the same time. DREE's program, for example, burdened the competitiveness of the Canadian economy in international markets, and retarded the economic adaptation of Canada by discouraging people from moving from unproductive or inefficient sectors into those sectors that could pay higher wages and salaries because of greater economic efficiency or market appeal. Similar effects could be ascribed to the generous unemployment benefits that did much to ease the pain of joblessness for workers, but diminished their eagerness to seek employment in other parts of Canada. UIC benefits also encouraged workers to remain in their present industrial sectors awaiting re-employment, rather than seeking retraining in order to enter sectors where jobs were to be found.

Obviously, the government was bound to move cautiously in such a politically sensitive area as this. It prepared its way by ending the separate existence of the Department of Regional Economic Expansion, and scattering its various parts between MSED and IT&C, creating MSERD (see chapter 9). The new ministry brought together regional questions and the industrial reorganization of the country as a whole. This pan-Canadian economic preoccupation was also reflected in the transferring of the trade commissioner service to the Department of External Affairs.

In the course of several cabinet shuffles in 1981 and 1982, the prime minister moved away from his economic nationalist posture assumed during the election of 1980 when he had undertaken to strengthen the Foreign Investment Review Agency and give it responsibility for reviewing cases of foreign-owned firms already in Canada that were considering entering new fields of economic endeavour. He also had considered extending the principles of the National Energy Policy to other fields of economic activity dominated by foreign investment.

184

However, after the violent and somewhat threatening statements of the Reagan administration, which talked about "retaliation" against Canada, the government backed off these initiatives. Trudeau transferred Herb Gray, his nationalist minister of trade and commerce, to the politically less sensitive presidency of the Treasury Board. Ministers with a more business-oriented or right-wing orientation, such as Ed Lumley and Don Johnston, were moved to key economic portfolios. The government appeared to be on the defensive.

Part 4

The Canadian Dilemma: Possible Ways Out

Looking to Coordination 14

It is fairly obvious that some measures should be undertaken to coordinate the efforts of the two levels of government and to end a situation where the efforts of one government are, wittingly or unwittingly, nullified by the other. This, however, is difficult to achieve for a number of reasons. Governments, like other organizations, seek as much freedom of action as possible. This simplifies their problems of decision-making and flatters their corporate egos by giving them a sense of autonomy and of power. In addition, there is the reality of simple inertia. It is much easier to continue doing what one has been doing than to think out and follow new initiatives. Busy officials and politicians are not inclined to look for additional work. Nor are they inclined to inform themselves about the activities of other levels of government unless there is a clear advantage in doing so. To seek out the other level of government for a comprehensive integration of policies is to invite the questioning of one's own motives and policies, and raises the possibility of friction with the other level. Therefore, under normal conditions it is clearly easier to go one's own way than to undertake the time-consuming and cumbersome effort of policy coordination with other agencies.

Moreover, governments work within a structure of incentives. They are primarily concerned about retaining electoral support to ensure re-election. This involves showing vigilance in defending the interests of the province and its people against outsiders, among whom must be counted the other provinces and their people. Thus, the structure of federalism in itself is an incentive to view political issues in zero-sum terms. Each provincial government is a team directed at defending provincial interests — with the opposition constituting an alternative team to be sent in if the incumbent one is seen to be performing less than satisfactorily.

To strengthen their efforts, provincial governments have constructed substantial expert bureaucracies; a large and efficient machine exists in each provincial capital to defend provincial interests against those of the federal government and the other provinces. Large vested interests have, therefore, been created to sustain a status quo situation of watchful defence of individual provincial interests.

Despite this situation there has been, since the Second World War, a great proliferation of consultative committees set up between the federal government and the provinces at various levels. At the top there is the federal-provincial conference at which the first ministers meet roughly once a year. This is a widely publicized event. The major speeches of the first ministers are televised and reported in the press, with the usual posturing for political advantage. This format has not encouraged the kind of informal cooperation that would be most fruitful. On the contrary, it has emphasized postures of heroic defence of the rights of one's own area or level of government, and the laying of blame on others for whatever appears to be going wrong. All agree that the most fruitful sessions are those that are held in private and that deal with the most concrete issues upon which actual compromises can be reached.

To serve these federal-provincial meetings, there are meetings of officials, at the deputy minister and more subordinate levels, dealing with more specific questions. The more junior the level at which the meeting takes place, the more likely cooperative understandings can be reached. This is because at these lower levels the party political factors are less important, and the desire for concrete results is greater. As one moves up to the deputy minister level, one gets closer to the party political concerns, and compromise is therefore more difficult. Since most understandings reached between subordinate officials of both levels of government have to be ratified at the deputy ministerial or ministerial level, the substance of agreement reached is often not very great. Deputy ministers tend to reflect the attitudes and postures of their principals.

Now let us consider the options among which we must choose: more of the same, leadership by the federal government, the acceptance of provincial autonomy, and the creation of a new federal-provincial institution to build collaboration.

More of the Same
It must be emphasized that the cooperative efforts that have been undertaken to date are positive achievements that point the way to an

improvement of our federal-provincial relations. If these steps can be enhanced and extended, then progress will be made. However, it must be recognized that this is essentially an *ad hoc* approach with no particular plan or purpose. It amounts to "doing what comes naturally." If one hopes to see improvement made in a fairly short time, a more concerted approach would be required.

It is probably correct to say that Prime Minister Trudeau's confrontational style and jesuitical form of argumentation have tended to exacerbate relations between the federal government and the provinces. This contrasts with the extreme solicitousness of Lester Pearson, whose concern for "cooperative federalism" led him to make many generous concessions to the provinces. The result was relatively good relations between the two levels of government at that time. No doubt the federal government could not have continued to be as generous in subsequent years, and Mr. Trudeau's arrival may well have corresponded to a hardening of the federal position that would have developed in any case.

As well, the subjects of discussion were different in the two periods. In the Sixties the first ministers and their staffs dealt with the sharing of income tax and succession duties, the tax rental and later tax collection agreements, the principle of equalization, and the various shared-cost programs, such as hospital insurance and the Trans-Canada Highway. Then came the protracted negotiations over the Canada Pension Plan. In the Seventies constitutional change became an important question, as did medicare and tax reform. These were subjects much less amenable to harmonious resolution than the earlier ones. By the mid-Seventies the contentious natural resources question, inflation and the block funding arrangements for federal-provincial transfers were dominant. By the late Seventies the question of restraint in expenditures, the Constitution, general economic questions, such as aid to industry and development of the economy, and matters of trade were dealt with. The most contentious issue was over the sharing of natural resource rents. Revenue sharing did not have the importance it had formerly had, having given way to matters of economic policy. These, of course, are much more regionally sensitive and therefore more likely to be areas of disagreement.[1]

The Sixties and Seventies saw Canadian governments, both provincial and federal, extend their activities and build up complex programs, which led one government to impinge on the concerns of another. Some people think that governments overextended themselves and took on responsibilities beyond their capacities. The result has been a growing cynicism among the public towards government. To avoid these frustrations and entanglements, many provinces are seeking to solve their own problems in isolation from the federal government. They have been able to contemplate this because they now have their own highly sophisticated public services that are able to function in complex situations. This has been taking place at a time of growing regional consciousness. The Atlantic provinces are increasingly aware of their relatively deprived situation; Quebec has become more nationalistic; and the western provinces have developed a new feeling of efficacy based on their new-found, resource-based wealth. These developments threaten the old dominance of the imperial provinces of Ontario and, naturally, have their consequences in intergovernmental relations.

The growing claims to responsibility of government and their increasing involvement in the concerns of everyday life have led all levels of government to encounter each other where their jurisdictions overlap. Therefore, it has been necessary to increase the mechanisms for intergovernmental liaison. There were only 5 of these federal-provincial committees involving ministers in 1957, but by 1977 there were 31. At the administrative level the increase is no less impressive: 59 federal-provincial committees of civil servants in 1957 as against 127 in 1977.

These bodies are mostly concentrated in three sectors: natural resources and primary industry, transportation and communications, and general government services.[2] This proliferation has produced a new class of experts in intergovernmental relations whose main task is to defend the interests of their particular jurisdiction in the numerous meetings with the others. No doubt this growth was inevitable as governments became increasingly interdependent, especially after the Great Depression, when the positive state developed. Cooperation was needed to mobilize the nation's wealth and to set up the modern social service structure. The result is growing interdependence between the federal government and the provinces. The policy of one affects the other, and therefore the autonomy of each is diminished. There is need for continuous concertation, which requires this new breed of public servant. This has produced a bureaucratization of intergovernmental relations, as a complex structure of coordination has to be constantly attended to. The number of meetings increases, and as policies become more complex, confusion is likely to occur where one level of government's activity crosses another. Since the situation is inherently adversarial, there is always a temptation for the specialist in intergovernmental relations to create tensions to justify himself, and to steal a march for his own jurisdiction against the others.

This new intermingling of jurisdictions means constant attention to ever-changing arrangements. Relations become increasingly important and fragile. "The more governments speak to each other, the less they understand one another."[3]

These intergovernmental relationships resemble diplomatic ones. Each party sends a competent representative to defend its interests and to secure the greatest advantage for its own jurisdiction. The encounters are frequent, but they are discrete and separate from one another. The agents sally forth from their headquarters to encounter each other, and return to assess the results of their meetings. Intergovernmental relationships do not have an ongoing corporate existence, but rather they are an arena for competitive if not conflictual encounters. There is a bias in the institutional structure which favours confrontation, competition and ultimately conflict. The meetings, whether they be of first ministers or of officials, tend to lack fixed dates, established agendas and, most important, a corporate existence. They are conducted in isolation from the other mechanisms of democratic government, such as the legislatures. Given their episodic nature, there is inevitably a frustrating degree of delay in reaching decisions. Each level of government, in order to carry out its intergovernmental responsibilities, is inclined to overbuild its central agencies and intergovernmental departments; therefore, a complicating extra level of bureaucracy is added to an already substantial machine. In the meetings themselves, the representatives, often with fairly rigid instructions or perceptions of their position, tend to stick to their guns; so compromise is extremely difficult to achieve.

The media merely compound these problems. The regional press tends to emphasize the need to avoid compromising the interests of the province, and to focus upon the gladiatorial role of the participants.[4]

The factor of secrecy adds its element of complication. When negotiations take place behind closed doors, suspicion builds up about the possibility of undesirable compromises or even "sellouts." The lack of public accountability of such secret sessions adds to the suspicion, and is itself an unhealthy aspect of otherwise democratic government. Yet when agreements are undertaken to hold some sessions in public with the media present, the atmosphere changes to a kind of combat in which each side plays to the gallery of its own jurisdiction, and thereby decreases the likelihood of public commitments being undertaken that later cannot be abandoned in negotiation.

We seem to have contrived to have the maximum disadvantage of both secrecy and open diplomacy. These meetings are "occasions." There is nothing ongoing and routine about them that would permit participants to behave in a normal and relaxed manner.

At federal-provincial meetings the application of federal programs is often discussed. Thus, the provinces increasingly assume that they have a rightful say concerning programs in the federal area of jurisdiction. Federal initiatives are checked and discussed, while provincial ones generally only come up in the small bilateral meetings between the federal government and the province concerned. Consequently, the provinces frequently unite in common fronts to challenge the federal government in order to secure a better result for themselves. This has produced a resentment and reluctance on the part of the federal government, heightening tension on both sides.[5]

This development arises more from the provinces following the expedient course of uniting for greater strength in encountering the federal government, than from differing views of the channels of accountability in a federal state. However, there are these two different views: the prevailing Canadian one, that governmental jurisdiction is divided between the two levels, each of which is accountable to its electorate through its parliamentary institution; and another, that the federal government is the creature of the provinces and is therefore, in a sense, accountable to them. This latter view, often called the compact theory of confederation, would justify provincial scrutiny of federal proposals, while no comparable questioning of provincial initiatives would be authorized. The latter view has no standing in law, but it has found provincial defenders through the years, and at the present time.

This situation has produced differing attitudes in the various governments of Canada. In Quebec, perceptions are most critical. Louis Bernard commented that the federal government is tending to act increasingly unilaterally in abandoning mutual programs, or is imposing financial limits on its commitments of funds to them: for example, its unilateral change in the equalization formula. The result, he says, is that federal-provincial conferences are becoming forums for recrimination in which the game is not worth the candle. The difficulty of conducting intergovernmental relations adds to the problems of long-term planning, when the country needs a strategy for economic development but encounters federal unilateralism. "La perte de confiance réciproque est si profonde qu'elle devient elle-même une problème qui s'ajoute à tous les autres. Elle devient une entrave qui pousse les gouvernements à s'enfoncer plus avant dans l'unilatéralisme. Et c'est le circle vicieux.''[6]

Professor Donald Smiley points out that what he calls executive federalism is inclined to favour the interests of governments and territorial interests over other interests, such as those of citizens, classes and so on. It tends, therefore, to perpetuate inequalities and produce conflict where there is little cause for it.[7]

What might be done to relieve this regrettable condition? The fault clearly stems from the fact that each participant seeks to maximize the advantage of his own jurisdiction. The structures in no way encourage priority going to the development and maintenance of harmonious relationships, or to the creation of a corporate identity for the ongoing process of Canadian federalism. It is easy enough to say that the solution lies in a changed spirit or attitude. How can this be achieved? Surely the answer lies in finding some sort of ongoing corporate existence for intergovernmental relations. If they took place in a forum which itself was an institutionalized part of Canadian government, then the provinces would become part of the decision-making process for the whole in a continuous way.

Perhaps if we could construct an institution of a corporate sort to contain the intergovernmental relations, such as the proposed House of the Provinces modelled on the German Bundesrat, we might succeed in developing a greater sense of trust and purpose, a greater political will and sense of direction for the country. Goals might then be more easily agreed upon and conflicts thereby reduced. Such a change might create new conditions so that the game would cease to be an end in itself.

Provinces now express concern with fields clearly within federal jurisdiction; this probably reflects a decline in the importance of the generally perceived role of Parliament. With the tightening of party discipline, members appear to be merely counters for their parties in the registration process that parliamentary divisions have become. Furthermore, the parties have seen their legitimacy decline as responsible exponents of public opinion. The broadly representative party system has given way to parties that each speak for only part of the country. Gone are the days when regional tradeoffs could be worked out in the caucus of the government party. Now there are no Liberal members elected west of Winnipeg, the Conservatives are dead in Quebec, and there are no New Democratic MPs elected east of Oshawa. The provinces, in a sense, have been drawn in as the only legitimate spokesmen for regional concerns, as Parliament has lost this capacity. This strengthens the argument that the country is a "community of communities,"[8] in which the provinces have a right to be heard even on issues clearly and solely within the jurisdiction of the federal Parliament. It should surprise no one if the federal government shows reluctance to make such issues the subject of federal-provincial conferences, or, if these do creep onto the agenda, that the prime minister declines to march to the provincial drummer.

Federal Leadership

A second option goes back to 1867, when the British North American colonies came together. Then it was assumed that the federal government would exercise the leading role. Since governments at that time did very little by present standards, and since the major economic activities of the day were under federal jurisdiction, the provinces were left with "matters of a local or private nature." This arrangement reflected the desire of the major business interests in Montreal and Toronto to build a "commercial empire" based on the St. Lawrence drainage basin and extending east to the Maritimes and west across the Prairies. To do this they required the federal government to exercise the major economic powers. On the other hand, the concerns of the French Canadian elite of the time, and of the Catholic church in Quebec, were for the provincial government to control education and matters relating to religion, morals and culture. Therefore, "property and civil rights in the province" were assigned to the provinces. The federation was thus an agreement between the English-speaking economic elite and the French Canadian elite centred in the liberal professions and in the church.

To exercise its mandate, the federal government undertook the building of the Inter-Colonial Railway from Montreal to Halifax and the Canadian Pacific west to Vancouver. These undertakings were the physical foundations on which the National Policy was based. This involved a protective tariff to encourage the establishment of manufacturing enterprises in Canada and to supply a revenue source for the federal government, enabling it to support the building of the railways and other development schemes.

This policy of economic development was built upon dominant federal powers: an extensive constitutional jurisdiction and an unlimited power to tax. While the policy was slow in showing its effectiveness because of generally depressed economic conditions in the 1870s and 1880s, it was a resounding success in the two decades or so that preceded the outbreak of the First World War.

Federal dominance in the economic field gradually came to be challenged on several fronts. The Judicial Committee of the Privy Council favoured the provincial authority when matters of jurisdiction came before it. It enunciated an "aspects doctrine," under which it discovered areas of federal jurisdiction in which some aspects of a given question should be reserved to the control of the provincial legislatures. Moreover, as governments came to show an interest in matters of public health and welfare, the courts tended to find these areas generally within provincial jurisdiction.

During the Depression, the federal government found itself, because of judicial decisions, barred from acting in certain ways. For example, it was unable to implement Canada's commitments to the International Labour Organization.

The tendency to divide jurisdiction over a single subject between the federal government and the provinces often meant that effective action by either the federal government or the provinces was difficult. For example, in attempting to regulate the grain trade, both the federal and some of the provincial governments found that they were unable to develop legislative instruments that did not encroach on the jurisdiction of the other level of government. The result was that effective legislation became virtually impossible to frame.

With the crisis of the Depression and the trend towards urbanization and industrialization, Canada, like other Western countries, sought to implement the various social security measures and other interventionist policies that we identify as the positive state, where government serves as well as polices its citizens. Most of these new areas of activity came to be considered by the courts as falling within provincial jurisdiction. The cumulative effect of this trend was to enhance provincial government powers and diminish those of the federal government. In order to act, the federal government was compelled to seek the cooperation and active collaboration of the provincial governments. Under these conditions it became easy for one level of government to frustrate the other, and the federal government found it increasingly difficult to exercise leadership.

Despite these growing problems the federal government did succeed, with provincial cooperation, in erecting a comprehensive social security system for Canada. By the end of the 1960s, Canada had systems of comprehensive hospitalization and medical care, family allowances, and a broad program of support for the handicapped, the elderly, and the needy generally. In addition, a system of unemployment insurance was put in place.

These costly programs, along with other governmental initiatives, greatly expanded the need for public revenues. To cope with this the federal government followed the pattern established during the Second World War when it rented the provincial powers to levy income taxes, corporation taxes and succession duties. This set the pattern for the subsequent tax-sharing arrangements between the two levels of government. Since there is so much at stake and the interests of the various provinces and the federal government often diverge, this question has led to periodic friction between the two levels of government beginning in the 1960s.

The "Quiet Revolution" in Quebec saw the provincial government assume an activist role in making its citizens "masters in our own house." This involved nationalizing the hydroelectric power industry, establishing a provincial department of education, and developing a comprehensive system of technical, scientific and administrative educational programs to equip French Canadians for the new sophisticated technological society. This created a greater demand by the provincial government for revenues, thus producing friction with the federal government. This in turn led to disputes over jurisdiction, since the province sought to enlarge its role at the expense of the federal government.

Quebec's example was followed by other provinces, and serious disputes developed over powers to tax the rents from natural resources, particularly hydrocarbons. The federal government was challenged by provinces reflecting either regional economic interests or concentrated cultural and language groups. It continued to exercise supremacy in external affairs, national defence, criminal law, interprovincial trade and foreign trade. However, in some cases, even these areas attracted provincial interest and sometimes encroachment. For example, Quebec sought its own external representation, opening offices abroad and undertaking policies of cooperation, most notably with France.

The federal government found that the constitutional powers which had made it clearly superior at first (such as its power to reserve or disallow provincial legislation and its general grant of power to make laws for the peace, order and good government of Canada) no longer assured federal predominance. Much of the jurisdiction for social security questions was clearly provincial, and with the development of natural resources, provincial powers over public lands became increasingly important. The major social and economic activities of the twentieth century largely fell under provincial jurisdiction. Cultural and linguistic particularism grew into strong regional interests challenging the federal government; so the provincial authorities were given further motivation to defend their turf.

As noted earlier, the policy of the Pearson government (1963–68) was one of cooperative federalism, involving a willingness to make concessions to the provinces (at that time especially Quebec) in the interests of preserving good relations. This policy failed to satisfy provincial demands, and may well have whetted the appetites not only of Quebec but of other provincial governments, who found the Quebec example a profitable one to follow.

Pearson's successor, Pierre Trudeau, lost little time in dissociating himself from the policy of his predecessor. He has sought to satisfy the aspirations of French Canada by a policy of equal rights and privileges for both language groups across Canada. This involved a substantial program of "bilingualizing" the public service and opening new career opportunities for French-speaking Canadians in government employment and elsewhere.

Trudeau wished to reassert the power of the federal government. He began by enlarging the functions of the Prime Minister's Office and the Privy Council Office so as to be in a position to exert leadership over the vast expanse of the federal bureaucracy. He and his colleagues greatly improved the position of French Canadians within the federal public service and sought to work out a policy of fiscal harmonization, in which the federal government and the provinces would cooperate in delivering services to Canadians. The tax-sharing arrangements and the equalization programs begun at an earlier time were continued, but the federal government, anxious to protect its powers, further exerted itself against growing provincial pressures. The friction has been aggravated by the election of the Parti Québécois in 1976 and by the growing economic crisis, in which the Canadian economy has faced serious inflation and unemployment.

In this crisis, Canadians have looked to the federal government for leadership even though its power to take initiatives in the field of economic policy has been attenuated by the reality of provincial power and jurisdiction. Also, many Canadians, especially in Quebec and western Canada, are no longer content to see the federal government exercise the predominant role, and this naturally inhibits the federal authorities.

As a result, the federal government has been more active in the less developed parts of Canada, where the provincial governments have been anxious to secure federal support through its program of regional economic expansion and other special assistance arrangements. A growing number of joint programs have been worked out on an *ad hoc* basis, with substantial federal financial support. As we have seen, the actual provision of the service has usually been performed by the province, and this means that the federal government receives less than its share of political credit — hence its growing tendency to deliver its own programs unilaterally in the provinces.[9]

This constitutes an attempt by the federal government to exercise more direct control over economic development in Canada, relying less upon provincial cooperation. The government will be free to develop its own strategies independent of the provinces, and to favour development in one region over another. If it follows the strategy laid down in the budget of November 1981 in the paper *Economic Development for Canada in the 1980s,*[10] the government will stress the development of the resource industries. There it proposed allocating $42 billion to economic development expenditures and another $18.2 billion to energy development expenditures in the period 1981/82 to 1985/86.

Linked to this, the government proposed to follow the line laid down by the Major Projects Task Force, which identified $440 billion worth of potential projects in the energy and resource sectors. To supply machinery, equipment and materials for these developments, the Canadian manufacturing industry would have to greatly enlarge its production level. The strategy would see over half of the funds invested in major projects in western Canada, which in turn would greatly increase the demand for labour there. The government proposed to assist workers to move to where the jobs will be created. This would necessitate the free flow of capital and labour across provincial boundaries, and therefore might encounter resistance from provinces which have been erecting barriers to movement in recent years. Provincial cooperation for such a policy is essential if it is to succeed. Similarly, collaboration with large business organizations is called for. The program also includes plans to develop export services to sell Canadian products abroad, the upgrading of technical training to provide skilled labour for the proposed projects, and aid to industries generally to assist them in becoming more internationally competitive.

In his January 1982 policy statement, the prime minister focused on regional economic development and the vigorous pursuit of international markets. All this stresses unilateral federal activity. Indeed the prime minister proposed the creation of a Regional Fund based on money "freed up as the existing GDA's [General Development

Agreements] expire . . . to support special regional economic development efforts. The fund should reach 200 million dollars by 1984–1985."[11] As outlined in chapter 9, the main agency for implementing and supervising regional development, the Ministry of State for Economic and Regional Development, has a regional office in every province headed by a federal economic development coordinator of senior rank. His task is "to transmit government policy back to the regions."[12]

The new Department of Regional Industrial Expansion is concerned to see that Canada derives industrial benefits from major projects. Its Office of Industrial and Regional Benefits is charged with the responsibility of ensuring that the megaprojects make maximum possible use of Canadian planning skills, project development ability, and machinery and material supply capability. The government will also help some firms to modernize or to diversify through an Office of Industrial Adjustment. This will help declining industries such as textiles, clothing and footwear.[13]

It is clear from this that the Trudeau government is determined to reassert the federal role in matters of economic development. This is seen as a return to classical federalism, in which the federal government looked after such infrastructure as transportation and services. By reducing the need to work with the provinces, the government hopes that confrontation, unpopular with the voters, can be reduced. A new visibility of the federal government as it renders direct services to the citizens is expected to add to its visibility and therefore its popularity.

With the departmental reorganization announced in January 1982 (see chapter 9), the federal government will be in a stronger position to undertake its own initiatives. These moves prepare the way for dealing singly with the provinces, thereby preventing the provinces from "ganging up" on it. The new approach should open the door to collaboration with cooperative provinces, such as Ontario, Manitoba and Nova Scotia. On the other hand, if Quebec wishes to go its own way, the federal government can demonstrate that this is its own choice. Since the Quebec economy is in serious trouble, this may serve to show up the Parti Québécois government as a poor manager. The policy, therefore, has a flexibility to it and reveals a readiness on the part of the federal government to work cooperatively with those provinces disposed to do so. The provinces can be expected to encourage development spending within their borders, even if this bolsters the image of the federal government.

However, the federal government must be careful to avoid appearing to be trying to dominate the provinces. By beginning with economic development, which is primarily a federal matter, it begins on fairly solid ground. Provided it can field a team of impartial and competent experts, it can expect some success. If the federal government clearly claims the initiative, Quebec may be, to some extent, forced to play the federal government's game. Alberta, on the other hand, with its Heritage Fund and its wealth of oil royalties, does not have to accept federal leadership and, therefore, may choose to confront the federal policy or seek to bend it to its own purposes.

What does this mean for the struggle between Alberta and Ontario over the location of the petrochemicals industry? The federal government will face a difficult dilemma if it must choose between these two forces. This illustrates the extreme delicacy of the federal policy. The provinces now are aroused and committed. Quebec under the Parti Québécois will not be tamed, and Alberta and Newfoundland appear to have nailed their colours to the mast. There is too much provincial feeling and too deep a sense of proprietorship in natural resources to expect the provincial owners to supinely accept federal policies if they do not suit provincial preferences.

On the other hand, of course, there are clear advantages to the federal position. It will provide one clear authority for initiatives in planning. There is a greater possibility of efficiency under this policy than where compromise has to be sought at every level. The move may well involve a return to the kind of economic rationality that was suggested by the Royal Commission on Canada's Economic Prospects back in the late 1950s. This would likely favour the regions best located in terms in economic development opportunities (and this probably means Ontario and the resource-rich western provinces), and mean a return to maximizing per capita income through efficiency, and therefore the downgrading of the development of the poorer regions. This, in turn, suggests encouraging internal population migration. With more concentration of decision-making power in the hands of the federal government, small-scale and local interests would have less power, although the large ones would continue to deal effectively with Ottawa. The overall result would enable Canada to better confront foreign unitary governments in the economic marketplace because of a greater emphasis upon economic efficiency.

All this suggests that the federal government is finally coming to view favourably the idea of a national industrial strategy, and is prepared to act alone to implement it. Since the federal government has most of the relevant constitutional jurisdiction and taxing power, the way appears to be open if it has the will. The recent constitutional changes support this posture, but a major problem appears in the timing of the initiative. It comes when provincial disaffection, especially in Quebec, Alberta and Newfoundland, is at an all-time high, and when other provinces too are coming to feel uneasy about their positions in the Canadian federation. Could such an initiative really succeed if pursued unilaterally in the face of this growing disaffection? It is significant that when it came to constitutional change, the federal government felt compelled to enlist widespread provincial support. It enlarged its agreement from two provinces to nine to make this possible. One wonders why economic development should be different. Certainly the question is an open one. Unilateralism may be dangerous.

There are two possible federal perceptions of this situation. The first sees the decline in federal power and influence to be mainly a consequence of weak-willed compliance by past federal governments in the face of truculent provincial politicians and bureaucrats who were anxious to enlarge their powers but who lacked substantial support from their populations. The remedy, therefore, is for the federal government to summon up the nerve shown by the Macdonald and Laurier governments, and exercise the leadership that the country longs for and, if offered, would readily accept ("The fault, dear Brutus, is not in our stars but in ourselves that we are underlings").[14]

The other interpretation sees the federal powers really reduced by secular changes in the country. Improved communications make the provinces able to take issue with federal initiatives. Uneven development permits wealthy provinces to strike out on their own, using their own resources. The unforeseen importance of natural resources, which are under provincial jurisdiction, has given great power to provincial governments, especially richly endowed ones. The great social transformation of French Canada has made Quebec no longer willing to accept federal predominance. The growth of north-south economic links since 1918, and particularly since 1945, has attenuated the east-west integrative economic linkage, which emphasized federal power. Cultural Americanization has diminished the emotional commitment to the nation and weakened federal authority. Therefore, the federal government has no real choice but to acquiesce in this reduced condition, act as a facilitator and middleman for the provinces, and carry out a reduced national role, complemented by its newer function as equalizer of revenues between persons and regions.

There is truth in both of these caricatures, but the whole truth in neither. The most important fundamental challenge to our governments is to get the federal-provincial relationship functioning properly for today, and forget nostalgic recollections of faded federal grandeur.

Acceptance of Provincial Autonomy

An obvious and somewhat simplistic solution to the Canadian problem of federal-provincial conflict and rivalry would be for the federal government to cut back its functions in the field of economic development in order to make way for the initiatives of the provincial governments. This would appear to accommodate the burgeoning demands of Quebec for greater autonomy, and would probably be viewed on the whole favourably by Alberta and perhaps British Columbia. To follow such a course of action, the federal government would have to continue its equalization arrangements if a general impoverishment of the have-not provinces is to be avoided. The problems of restructuring and dismantling much of the cooperative machinery that has been put in place would itself pose significant problems. However, if it were decided that this is the best way in which to purchase internal peace and to avoid endless friction and rivalry, it could conceivably be contemplated.

The advantages of such a course of action are roughly four.

First, it appears to offer a reduction of the conflict of overlapping federal and provincial powers, and would reduce the inevitable rivalries and conflicting policy preferences. This course might be welcomed by provinces rich enough to be net contributors towards current federal programs, but those on the receiving end would be put in a more vulnerable position. They would have to press for the continuation and extension of federal government equalization programs. However, since they would not be participating in a joint effort, their position as an advantaged collaborator would give way to that of an external supplicant. The federal government would find it increasingly difficult to keep up, much less expand, payments to the have-not provinces, since by accepting the principle of provincial autonomy, the federal government would really be conceding the right of the richer provinces to live of their own.

Second, such a policy would have the advantage of giving the provincial governments full opportunity to develop their own

204

initiatives and to improve their own institutions and programs according to their own preferences. This could well open the door to fruitful experimentation with new policy forms. In addition, it would be an answer to the growing claims of the provinces, especially Quebec and Alberta but also Saskatchewan, British Columbia and Ontario, for elbow room to undertake their own policies. Obviously such an advantage for the richer provinces would be translated into disadvantages for the have-not provinces. They would be under political pressure to provide services roughly equivalent to those in the more prosperous parts of the country; yet they would not have the means to do this adequately. The federal government would find it extremely difficult to help them beyond the very limited agreed-upon level of equalization. Thus, the liberation of the creative forces of the provinces would be an advantage for the richer provinces, but would merely be an embarrassment and a problem for the rest.

Third, this course of action would cut back on the federal government's use of its spending power, which is perceived by some provincial spokesmen as a device for invading the provincial area of jurisdiction. With this change, the spending power would be exercised mainly through the federal government's equalization program, and through various manifestations of the old protective function of operating the national defence establishment, the policing arrangements, and the other items falling under the enumerated heads of section 91 of the Constitution. While the federal role would probably still include the regulation of interprovincial trade, it could be held down to more of a referee function than one of underlying policy initiatives and instituting programs.

Fourth, such a course would release the creative and competitive powers of the provincial governments, and develop a competitive spirit of enterprise in their policy-making circles. A corollary would be to give greater power to the business community, which would have only one significant level of government to deal with — the provincial one, which is much more narrowly based than the federal. At least in the case of the smaller provinces, the provincial government would fall even more under the domination of the larger business organizations than is currently the case. Even the larger provinces could very well find the power of their major business interests so great that they would be obliged to accept considerable policy input from them. This arrangement, therefore, is one that would find the advocates of free enterprise and of the government policy of *laisser-faire* as its major defenders. The large business interests would have only the provincial governments to confront, which lack the strength and broad national base of the federal government. Consequently, the public interest would be less vigorously defended than at present. Since these larger business enterprises are often multinationals headquartered in the United States and other countries, the effect of such a policy would be to augment the powers of these externally controlled interests and to diminish those of the local authorities, who ostensibly are being favoured by such a policy. In reality, there is reason to think that the provincial governments would be less autonomous under such arrangements than they are under the current ones.

However attractive in the abstract such proposals may be to the romantics of a bygone age and to the ideological champions of old-fashioned capitalism, these ideas are clearly out of the question in these last decades of the twentieth century. Nowhere are governments relaxing their hold upon the national economy. We live in an age of vigorous competition between countries for markets. Governments are being mobilized to assist their business communities in this enterprise — so *laisser-faire* is no longer possible. Indeed, in those countries such as the United States and Britain under their current governments, we find the business community mobilizing the governments to act vigorously in their own defence by protecting the home market, and by undertaking policies that will strengthen business against labour and will reduce its tax burden and the impediments of regulation. The ultimate purpose of the newer monetarist policies is to increase the relative efficiency of the national firms against foreign competitors by containing inflation. Therefore, to suggest that the federal government deliberately withdraw into the minimum police and equalization functions is to counsel a return to a past that is out of phase with what is being done in the international market, and therefore a policy that no national government can contemplate. This suggests a passive stand where aggressiveness is needed to counter a general mobilization of strength in other countries in an increasingly competitive scramble for economic advantage.

To talk about the federal government withdrawing is just an academic game. Clearly it is one that the federal government shows absolutely no intention of playing. Indeed, given the current weaknesses of the Canadian economy, all pressures appear to be working in the opposite direction, in favour of greater federal government action to strengthen and protect the national economy.

While the richer provinces and Quebec might well advocate such a course either as a serious option or as a form of argumentation to justify their claim to specific federal powers, the poorer provinces and Ontario could be counted upon to resist such a change. The Atlantic provinces would have the most to lose and could be expected to act in their own self-interest. They will resist being turned into simple pensioners of the federal government, living on equalization payments that would have to come from the richer provinces, which would be withdrawing from the cooperative enterprise of Confederation in order to develop their own economies. The richer provinces' willingness to continue a given level of equalization can be expected to weaken as they come to concentrate more on their own affairs, thereby putting the poorer provinces at some risk.

Ontario has other reasons for refusing this option. Despite its relative decline from an earlier position of wealth and hegemony, the province remains at about the national average in per capita income. While technically it is entitled to receive equalization payments at present, these are too small to induce the provincial government to accept the embarrassment of classifying itself among the have-not provinces. The whole position of the Ontario government has been to emphasize the prosperity and dynamism of the provincial economy. The 1981 federal budget, in any case, made Ontario the standard by which other provinces will be judged in the matter of equalization.

Ontario's economy is the most "national" of all the provincial economies. It is the workshop of Canada in the sense that it does over half of the secondary manufacturing for the whole country. Since it depends upon a national market, it favours the integration of Ontario with the rest of the country. It can be counted upon to resist any policies that would encourage other provinces to engage in protectionism. It is surely no accident that Ontario has undertaken to be the ally of the federal government on the Constitution as well as on other questions. With its substantial block of seats in the House of Commons, greater than any other province, with its economic clout as the producer of about 40 per cent of the gross national product, and with its role as the economic heartland of Canada, it can be counted upon to resist any loosening of the economic ties with the other provinces, which would mean a reduction of its role as the economic centre for Canada.

Moreover, on the world stage Ontario is still too small to be effective in the international competition for markets. Since it is already host to many of the multinational corporations, especially in manufacturing and mining, it would be in a vulnerable position, open to manipulation by these powerful international actors.

There are other reasons too why Ontario could be counted upon to resist such a change. Its role in history as the major initiator of the Confederation idea, its unwavering support for Confederation (it has never had a separatist or autonomist movement), the undisputed advantages that have flowed to Ontario as the industrial centre throughout Canada's history, would lead it to seek its continued integration with the four provinces to the west and five to the east. Ontario's position without the other provinces would simply be one of vulnerable dependency on the United States.

A province whose attitude seems somewhat difficult to predict if such a policy of shifting economic powers to the provinces is to gain momentum, is Manitoba. It is a western province in the perception of its population, and also as viewed by the rest of Canada. It would therefore be difficult to imagine Manitoba departing drastically from the attitudes and positions of the other western provinces. However, looked at realistically, Manitoba is the westernmost extension of central Canada. Its economy is much the weakest of the four western provinces, and the most similar to that of Ontario, given the importance of the city of Winnipeg with its manufacturing and distribution functions. It is the longest settled of the Prairie provinces, with political attitudes that are more similar to those of Ontario, with its traditional pragmatism, than to the populism of Alberta and British Columbia or to the agrarian collectivism of Saskatchewan. As a generally have-not province, Manitoba's interests appear to lie with the status quo rather than with the devolution of economic powers to the provincial governments.

British Columbia's attitude is also relatively hard to predict. One would expect it to side with its western neighbours with whom it shares vast natural resource wealth and a high per capita income. It might welcome the possibility of developing its own economic policies and its own trading relationship with Japan and the other countries of the Pacific rim.

The province with the greatest economic incentive to go along with such a program is Alberta. With its enormous wealth in natural resources, developed at the moment (1983) to what is probably their most profitable stage, the province would be encouraged to use these revenues for its own development and resist sharing them with its poorer neighbours. Its current emphasis on province-building would be greatly encouraged and sustained by such a policy.

Saskatchewan is less predictable but would be economically advantaged by such a policy because of its natural resource wealth. On the other hand, its tradition of pan-Canadianism suggests less enthusiasm for a policy that diminishes the importance of the national economy. Of all the provinces, it is the most social democratic in its policy preferences, and therefore might well be encouraged by the possibility of undertaking its own initiatives without the need to seek compromises with its more conservative neighbours and the federal government.

It is likely that Quebec would favour the federal government cutting back its role in order to leave more room for the province to undertake its own economic development initiatives. It has already shown an inclination to opt out of cooperative programs and to seek financial compensation. Such a course of action is bound to be perceived both by the government and the people of Quebec as a *de facto* separation in matters of economic affairs, which might well be followed in due course by a *de jure* separation. Therefore, the policy would become unacceptable to Canadians who wish to preserve the nation — a fair indication that as a policy, devolution of economic functions to the provinces is a nonstarter.

The adoption of such devolution is bound to lead to the further drifting apart of the provinces, with a reduced saliency of the Canadian nation in the consciousness of all citizens. The richer provinces would develop attitudes towards the poorer ones rather similar to those already shared by Canadians towards underdeveloped countries. In this sphere our record is one of parsimonious indifference. Probably in the beginning at least, the richer provinces might be disposed to be somewhat more generous, but aid to less developed provinces is bound in the long run to be viewed with disfavour. The poor provinces would undoubtedly be unhappy with the relationship, so obviously one of the rich brother aiding the poor one in perpetuity. There is an indignity attached to such a relationship, especially when the importance of the overall national family is diminished or downgraded. Without federal leadership there would appear to be little likelihood of the poor provinces developing their economies; the kind of lumpy capital input that brings about development would be difficult to provide under equalization payments, which are geared essentially to sustaining income and public services. The less developed provinces would therefore be trapped in a dependency relationship with little likelihood of escaping through development by substantial capital investment.

It is clear that this option of diminishing the federal responsibility appears to be somewhat of a chimera. It is rendered unlikely because it is a step out of harmony with the movement of modern governments at the present time. It would constitute an act of self-mutilation by the Canadian nation. Governments do not willingly give up their powers. Indeed the federal government would be strengthened in its resolve to retain and expand power by the influence of the poorer provinces, by the influence of Ontario, and by the strength of pan-Canadian sentiment, which, however weakened it may be, still remains the predominant loyalty of the overwhelming majority of Canadian citizens. Surely it is reasonable, therefore, to put aside this "option" and concentrate on the others, which are politically feasible.

A New Federal-Provincial Institution

Now we have examined the advantages and disadvantages of the status quo, of a policy of federal leadership and predominance, and of a policy of growing provincial autonomy in economic affairs. We have concluded that the last option is clearly out of the question, and in the case of the status quo, there would continue friction, frustration and recrimination as one level of government impedes the other in carrying out its chosen programs. The posture of dealing at a distance one with another adds to the problems. The option of federal leadership, while superficially and in a simplistic sense attractive, would certainly be resisted by Quebec and probably by two or more of the western provinces. Even Ontario might be disposed to object to some aspects of such a policy. We appear then to be confronted by three unpromising options. There is, however, a fourth possibility that we should explore.

Canada is, and must remain, a profoundly federal country. However, the current adversarial stance of the two levels of government towards one another must be changed. We could develop institutions to help in the integration of one level of government with the other. This is the argument of those who have favoured the substitution of a House of the Provinces for the Senate. The idea would be to involve the provinces with the federal government in a common venture of making policy for the country in areas where this seems appropriate. Under this arrangement the House of the Provinces would be a means whereby provincial representatives — that is, representatives of the provincial governments — would participate in the making of federal government policy; it was hoped that by making their views known and their weight felt they would come to support the policies once elaborated. This would tend to reduce the rivalries between two separate levels of government and introduce an ongoing common participation in an enterprise of policy-making for the whole country.

210

This proposal has been unattractive to the Canadian government because it appears to be a one-way street. The provinces would participate in federal policy-making, but the federal government would have little or no input in the making of provincial government policy. Certainly in cases such as resource management and vocational training, where provincial policies have a direct effect on the welfare of Canada as a whole, there is a strong case for the federal government's voice being heard. However, in matters predominantly the concern of the residents of a given province, there is less reason to demand a federal voice. We should get away from seeing the two levels of government as separate participants entitled to equal rights, and come to see them as complementary mechanisms for governing the people of Canada. The same people are citizens of the several provinces and citizens of Canada. When we engage in federal-provincial strife, we are fighting with ourselves — and we are the losers.

While integration through Senate reform appears unattractive for several reasons, policy integration itself is clearly an idea looking for an effective institutional manifestation. The logical place is in policy areas that are important, mutual in interest between the federal government and the provinces, and amenable to some kind of institutional incarnation. Surely the field of economic development policy-making is an obvious place where such an approach should be canvassed.

We must first ask the question why Canadian governments do not plan — at least the prevailing view is that they do not. On closer examination we find that this is a generally shared folk attitude that has long been bypassed by events. We have hung on to our view that Canada is a free enterprise country, with business taking the initiatives as the "engine of economic growth." However, as outlined in earlier chapters, the years since 1945 have seen a remarkable proliferation of activity at all three levels of government. Relationships between business and government have grown complex and interdependent. Both federal and provincial governments are embarked on a course of increasingly intense policy-making for economic development. These programs require coordination so that they do not impede or frustrate one another. Currently we rely on a congeries of federal-provincial committees and other cooperative arrangements, vaguely coordinated under the periodic meetings of the first ministers. These arrangements operate through occasional meetings of representatives of the two levels of government, coming together to coordinate their activities and work out their differences. There is a certain bias in such a relationship: it encourages an attitude of watchful suspicion of one level of government towards the other. Each level is anxious to maximize its own advantage.

There is a great difference between this pattern of complex modern government and one of indicative planning. The present arrangements are extensive and involve many competent policy-making mechanisms at various levels in the government structure. However, at the apex of the structure, both at the federal and provincial levels, integration is not systematically brought about. As we have seen, new and expanded central agencies have been put in place, but no single one has been given the responsibility for working out the overall government policy for economic development. Hence no longer-term strategies have been implemented, and no effective means of integrating federal and provincial policies has developed.

Why is this? No doubt there are many reasons, but surely the main one is inertia. Canada has experienced a prolonged period of prosperity and growth since 1945. The structures in place seemed to be working, and they took on a life of their own that made them resistant to change. Each part of the complex mechanism defended its own position — and there was no effective agent from outside to force change, although, as we have seen, Trudeau and his team did try before they were assimilated by the system.

Another factor is the dominance of party politics. The ruling party has had to face election every four years or so. Longer-term thinking was effectively blocked, as ministers were anxious to keep their discretionary powers to meet these trials. And finally, the country continued the federal-provincial zero-sum game with a new tenacity as government activities expanded and the stakes grew greater.

However, the major reason why these habits and mechanisms remained in place is that they were not challenged. The country was satisfied with its progress and well-being. It was a successful participant in the international trading system.

Now things are different. The country is clearly falling behind rapidly in secondary manufacturing and in research and development. The old ways are no longer adequate, and there is a growing willingness to abandon the old mechanisms and attitudes for new ones. But what will they be?

What we need most of all is an arrangement in which the incentive system works towards cooperation and integration rather than in the direction of competition and confrontation. This can only be brought about if we create a new institution, with a life of its own, whose mission is the harmonious integration of the two levels of government in a given policy area. Only in such an institution with its own staff of experts and support personnel, and in which success is to be measured in terms of the achievement made in policy integration, can the inherent negative bias of the status quo be turned around. What is required is an economic development policy secretariat, staffed by competent professional people, expert in the relevant aspects of economics, with some also having an expertise in such areas as sociology, political science and law. Such a body, charged with the mandate of working out the national development policies that are reconcilable with the interests of both levels of government, offers some hope that Canada might be able to match the vigorous policy integration and execution of such successful modern economies as France, Germany and Japan.

The agency would have to be *federal-provincial*; that is, it would have to answer to *both* levels of government. The secretariat would have to be led by a person enjoying the confidence and trust of *both* levels of government, who would offer leadership and diplomatic skills. There would have to be a directing council for the body, nominated in *equal* numbers by both levels of government and answering to their principals. The professional staff would be employed on the basis of their expertise, with an adequate support staff to assure their capacity to do their jobs effectively.

The point is that the new body would not be under either level of government but would be a cooperative institution answering to both levels, charged with the mission of building bridges of cooperation and integrated policy to maximize the effectiveness of Canada in the international economic contest.

The staff, therefore, would have to develop scenarios for cooperation, which would be discussed and accepted in principle by the board. Then, under these general blueprints, detailed policy would be elaborated for implementation by the Parliament of Canada and, where necessary, by the legislatures of the provinces affected.

It is obvious that in the process of negotiating tradeoffs between the interests of various regions and provinces of Canada there would be difficulties. From time to time there would be deadlock. When that occurs, and one hopes that this would be much less frequent under this arrangement than under the status quo, either that particular line of policy would have to be dropped for a time or the possibility held out of working out bilateral relations among the willing participants. In addition to the obvious advantages of implementing policies to further the economic effectiveness of Canada would be the carrot of federal money to back proposals, alongside money from the cooperating provinces. In addition, of course, there are federal powers that may at times be resorted to as a kind of stick to prod recalcitrants on. These factors are no great change from the current situation, but they may be more effective within the framework of an institution committed to developing a cooperative policy package.

In fact the creation of such a new institution implies much greater integration than at present. We should call things by their names: we are talking of a system of indicative planning. This lays on the new authority the task of using its professional expertise to elaborate a plan for the economic development of Canada that confronts the numerous questions and works out strategies and solutions acceptable, after tradeoffs have occurred, to the regional interests within Canada. While there is no reason to be dogmatic about the details of an institution yet to be created, we should enumerate what is likely to be meant by planning in the Canadian context.

Obviously the operation would have to be democratic and consensual to fit into the Canadian tradition. Its role would be to study the problems of the Canadian economy in depth, prior to developing strategies to prod the agents of the Canadian economy, public and private, to develop viable, competitive industry. This would mean identifying the areas in which Canada is equipped to compete, and also preparing plans for getting out of areas in which we cannot compete effectively with a minimum of dislocation and loss. Since the plans would have to be approved, once adopted and fully discussed, by the provinces and the major private sector actors, the process would have to be consensual.

However, if agreement is to be reached, the planner would have to be in a position to offer incentives so that the changes proposed would take place. There would be an important role reserved for the federal government, and in some cases the provinces, to come through with the funding of essential research and investment and/or rules and directives to bring about the desired results. Governments would be called upon to wield more carrots and sticks in a more coherent and cooperative way than in the past, informed by an expert staff operating under the new incentive structure with pan-Canadian objectives uniting provincial and federal governments.

While one would hope that this would lead to greater harmony and enlightenment in decision-making, there would probably be times of stress and disagreement. The planning agency, with support from some governments, might encounter resistance from other provincial governments or private interests. When this occurs, the life of the planning authority is endangered and the leadership and capacity of its leading personnel would be put to the test. It might fail — but surely the very existence of such a body, with its strong capacities, would be a force in the balance tilting the result towards successful agreement. By mapping out proposals for the direction of development, it would clarify the field for private decision-makers, who would find it easier to develop their own separate strategies.

To be successful, planning of this sort must avoid dogmatism and confrontation, and there must be room for flexibility of response. How quickly the megaproject strategy became too costly and unsuitable with the advent of the economic crisis! But this is not to say that such a strategy cannot contain a reserve plan that could be implemented should a return of effective demand for energy resources at higher than current prices occur. Successful indicative planning must avoid a mandatory posture. Instead it must rely on careful studies of the country's economic sectors to discover what the various possibilities are, the elaboration of possible development strategies, followed by the discussion of these with the affected parties. While the major instruments are likely to be the channelling of investment credits and other incentives, and the elaboration of possible legislation in support of specific strategies, there could well be other means of operation, such as proposals for the retraining of labour or for the conversion of plants and equipment to more promising lines of production. There is no limit to what might be undertaken, and no point in enumerating what the many initiatives might be.

Given the Canadian tradition, the approach would be pragmatic. The important factor is the will to put research and good faith to work in the interest of the harmonious integration of the Canadian economy through the cooperation of both levels of government in support of the private sector. The French example, probably the best known, need not be a prototype for Canada, where the factor of federal-provincial integration is a key element. France, after all, is a unitary state.

Also there are stages in indicative planning. France was deeply involved in government–private sector collaboration when it was building up its infrastructure and modern productive capacity. The planning commission had a less active role to play once this was done. Now some consider planning as a less important factor than in the past, and that is because there is less need for fundamental transformation of the economic structure. This could well be the Canadian experience. Concertation is more important in the process of economic transformation and fundamental building than in the process of day-to-day management.

Also, we must be careful not to overestimate the payoff from such rational planning. It may well improve the competitiveness of our economy — but it cannot make it crisis- or recession-proof. All countries are experiencing serious problems in the recession of the early Eighties. Those that plan and manage their economies will fare better; yet all are affected, and so it would be for Canada.

One problem will have to be confronted from the beginning: the demand by some provinces for the privilege of opting out of policies thus elaborated. Some will even press for financial compensation for losses incurred by not participating. Surely the principle of opting out is so well established in Canadian federal-provincial relations that it would be unrealistic to contemplate ending it. One would simply hope that it would be used less frequently than at present. However, there will be the question of financial compensation to those who do not participate. Here we encounter a problem where attitudes appear to be changing. The recent constitutional agreement involved the refusal by those signing the accord to concede the right of any opting-out province to automatic financial compensation. This position is the one taken by the federal government and the nine English-speaking provinces. Quebec, of course, does not accept this and claims the right to compensation. Presumably, these attitudes would apply to just such a new arrangement as we are considering. Certainly withholding the automatic right to financial compensation would give greater power and effectiveness to the new planning secretariat. It is to be hoped that all the provinces will perceive the advantages in such an arrangement, but that is something that will have to be worked out in future.

In any event, the need or the desirability of opting out might well decline, since programs elaborated by a federal-provincial secretariat with a staff whose loyalties are to the new federal-provincial body and who are concerned to secure mutually satisfactory arrangements would be more likely to produce agreement than does the status quo situation, associated as it is with federal government unilateralism and the unwillingness of some provinces, for their own reasons, to participate. Perhaps a suitable arrangement that would attract the support of the nine agreeing provinces plus Quebec would be one in which ordinary compensation for opting-out provinces would apply only in cases where the subject matter is one in which cultural or educational matters

216

(and perhaps other matters under clearly provincial jurisdiction) were concerned. In other matters, such as the general area of economic development, which is clearly within federal jurisdiction, there should under normal conditions not be an automatic right of compensation to opting-out provinces.

In cases where the initiative directly affects only the federal government and some of the provinces, or in cases where some provinces specifically wish to be excluded from a program that others are anxious to pursue, it seems appropriate that the possibility be left open for bilateral arrangements between the willing participants. Obviously there would be a problem of reconciling these bilateral arrangements with the overall agreed-upon objectives and policy frameworks accepted by all participants. Care would have to be taken to make certain that such bilateral arrangements not seriously counteract the overall objectives and not involve an unfair transfer of financial resources to some of the participants at the expense of others. There would, of course, be the present problems of reconciling the objectives of maximum national productivity, and therefore economic competitiveness, with the internal problems of redistribution of wealth, which were the responsibility of the Department of Regional Economic Expansion. The new commission would offer an opportunity for these problems of reconciliation to be tackled by teams of competent specialists owing responsibility to both levels of government and to all regions of the country. The possibilities of equitable tradeoffs under these conditions would be considerably better than under the fragmented and complex arrangements currently existing.

Obviously the task of the chairman and council of the new body would be extremely onerous and would require a considerable effort of will to make the new institution function. The very fact that the participants would have agreed to its formation would in itself be testimony of their will to make a success of the cooperative economic endeavour. There is no doubt that great skills of diplomacy, absolute integrity and a high level of competence would be necessary. It is also clear that if the country could see fit to create such an institution, it would greatly increase the likelihood of success for Canada in the area of international competition among developed, sophisticated, modern states. In this contest the race clearly goes to those countries with the best mechanisms for the integration of their economic efforts in the most rational and coherent fashion. This is the major success of Japan, France and Germany — countries that have succeeded in reconciling their democratic institutions with the need for rational, coherent

217

integration, guided by the rigours of technical competence and shrewd judgement. There is no room for institutional incoherence that encourages fractious efforts that impede the high level of cooperation needed for success in a highly competitive world.

There may well be objections to the commission idea from those who cherish the role of Parliament as the highest representative of Canadian public opinion. Surely, they would say, the commission would involve a usurpation to some extent of Parliament's role. The response here is twofold. First, the commission would not be a representative body; rather it would be one of expertise, reporting to both levels of government. It would have no power that the respective legislatures had not given it and could not rescind. It would be their servant seeking to find a common ground of agreement in the common interest. Second, Parliament, regrettably, no longer represents and integrates Canadian public opinion, moulding it into a common policy pattern. The regions of the country have diverged, and the perceived common views have diminished. Parliament reflects this by returning regional concentrations of MPs: Liberals from Quebec, Conservatives and New Democrats from the West. Only in Ontario and the Atlantic provinces are the two old parties balanced, but there the NDP component is tiny in the one and nonexistent in the other. Such a Parliament has no chance of reaching interregional compromises in such complex areas as economic policy. Moreover, whatever it does produce will have very little legitimacy in the parts of the country returning opposition members in concentration. Parliament and the new-found regional spokesmen, the premiers, speaking for their legislatures, need expert help in finding common policy positions. It is this service that the commission would render.

Building the Structure 15

Our previous survey showed the general tendency in the developed economies for increasing concentration since the Second World War. The predominance of the federal government in the United States has been further enhanced, and the development of the EEC has substituted a common European authority for the individual smaller states of Western Europe. The Treaty of Rome assures freedom of movement for labour, capital and goods, creating a common market greater than that constituted by the United States itself. This tendency towards very large trading areas makes Canada's market and scale of operations appear to be very small indeed by comparison.

Add to this the fact that, particularly in Western Europe and in Japan but also in the United States in its own way, business and government are beginning to work closely together. Labour too, at least in some jurisdictions, is coming to be involved in this concerted effort. In short, there has been a growing corporatist intermediation developing among great centres of power in Western societies: government, business and labour. Powerful economic concentrations have been built up, which offer strong competition.

We have also seen how the tendency in Canada has in many ways been in the opposite direction. The new assertiveness of the provinces and the growing regional tensions have pushed the country in the direction of economic balkanization. The early 1980s economic recession, which is hitting Canada much harder than its developed trading partners, shows up the need for urgent changes in the economic organization of Canada. The problem is: How can these changes be brought about?

The Federal Initiative
In order to establish the kind of concertation that we have discussed in the previous chapter, we must develop a strategy for putting such a

219

mechanism in place. Current federal-provincial relations hardly concede pride of place to the federal government over the provinces. However, since it alone is responsible to the nation as a whole, and since it has responsibility for fiscal and economic management of the national economy, it is still the government that should take the responsibility for initiating discussions — without federal government support, such a proposal would be stillborn. How should it do this to enhance the likelihood of success?

There are really two basic approaches. The federal government could work out a complete proposal, elaborating all the structures and indicating the relationship of the planning body to the provincial and federal governments. While it would probably do this in any case, the question is whether it would further the chances of acceptance by presenting a detailed package at the beginning. This would depend very much on the complex interpersonal relations between federal and provincial personnel at any particular time. Given the current state of rivalry and tension, to do so probably would present a target for one or more of the provincial leaders to launch a demagogic charge that the federal government was seeking to extend its powers.

It would probably be preferable for the federal government to approach the provinces on their own ground, going back to proposals that have been made by the provincial premiers and other officials at recent federal-provincial meetings. As we saw in chapter 12, the premier of British Columbia brought forward at the federal-provincial conference on the economy in 1978 a proposal for a federal-provincial planning authority. This is the sort of thing that could be built upon and elaborated by the federal government in order to present to the provincial leaders a proposal that has been endorsed by one or more of their number.

There are other provincial initiatives that could be referred to. For example, we have already discussed the publication by Larry Grossman, then minister of industry and tourism in Ontario, *Interprovincial Economic Co-operation: Towards the Development of a Canadian Common Market* (1981). This proposal for concerted interprovincial action is an indication of the Province of Ontario's willingness to collaborate in economic matters with other provinces.

It has already been noted that in interprovincial and federal-provincial negotiations the highest degree of cooperation is to be found between line officials at the intermediate rather than the highest levels. No doubt this is because these people are more concerned with the substantive matters with which they are entrusted than with the

220

political rivalry that is the stuff of the premiers and their immediate associates. Therefore, it would probably be best if discussions of a federal-provincial planning arrangement could be undertaken at several levels at the same time. Obviously it makes no sense to bypass the highest level because its general assent for discussions is necessary. On the other hand, it makes a great deal of sense to involve the substantive policy makers in the various relevant aspects of government at both intermediate and senior levels. Persons concerned with economic policy making, with policy in areas of joint jurisdiction, and persons concerned with governmental organization and structure should all be involved in ongoing discussions of how collaborative arrangements might be worked out in the common interest.

After a period of such informal discussion back and forth between the federal government and the provinces, and also among the provinces, it would become relatively clear in what areas of collaboration lay the best hopes for success. Also, one would be able to identify where support lay, where there was indifference, and where to expect opposition.

At this point, and after the way had been prepared, there would have to be a formal meeting between the federal government and the provinces, probably a federal-provincial conference, to discuss the proposals. If the national economy continues in a pattern of recession and crisis, the likelihood of a positive response would be greater. Politicians would be less willing to run the risk of appearing to sabotage an initiative that holds some hope of improving the economic condition of the country.

The Provincial Response

One could anticipate, to some degree, the probable response of different provinces to such an initiative. We can predict with some confidence that Quebec, if still governed by the Parti Québécois, would have very serious reservations about such a proposal. Clearly it does not fit into the strategy of that political party to go along with further integration of Quebec into the Canadian national economy. On the other hand, that party must face re-election and wishes to maximize its chances. Therefore, it would be careful to avoid being seen as a spoiler of an initiative that promises to improve the province's economic condition at a time of serious economic difficulty. Since the isolation of Quebec in the constitutional revision of 1981, Premier Lévesque, while wishing to minimize his contacts with the federal government and the other provinces, has maintained contact in economic matters. This contact is obviously not to be interpreted as a full-fledged willingness to cooperate with other governments; nonetheless the door remains ajar for continued discussion. If federalism can be shown to be profitable (*"rentable"*), it may, in some of its aspects, even be acceptable to the Parti Québécois. Previously the Liberal party under Bourassa saw this as a major justification for Quebec's continuation in the Canadian federal union.

In short, there is some hope that the government of Quebec would not simply sabotage the initiative by refusing all cooperation, but more probably it would adopt a wait-and-see attitude, combined with a somewhat critical posture towards federal initiatives. Quebec is the province most likely to object to the proposal on fundamental grounds of party policy and because of its perception of Quebec as a nation. On the other hand, there is the factor that Quebec is in a more serious economic situation than all of the provinces west of the Ottawa River. It could not afford, in its own interest, to refuse all cooperation.

Another province that may be hesitant to cooperate in such a scheme is Alberta. Despite the recession this province remains the richest province per capita in Canada, and the one with the greatest endowment of petroleum and natural gas in the country. It could well consider proposals for economic collaboration as likely to lead to subsidization by Alberta of activities in other provinces. Since Alberta has made clear its desire to develop its own industry, based on its own natural resources, and wishes to support this by government initiatives, it may be hesitant to become involved in national planning, which would assign the role of industrial development in certain areas to the other provinces as well. To attract the support of Alberta, it would have to be shown that the province would be better off overall by collaborating in such an arrangement than it would be by isolating itself from it, or attempting to abort it entirely. This realistic assessment would of course bias, to some extent, the nature of the planning arrangements.

Since one is starting with relatively autonomous units, one would have to get their consent in order to begin to plan. This was not a problem for the French in setting up their planning arrangements after the Second World War. The country was already a highly centralized one. However, in a federal democracy, it is necessary to secure the consent of the various participants, and this is particularly true of a fundamental organizational arrangement such as this.

What is true for Alberta would apply in a somewhat diminished way to British Columbia. Both are resource-rich provinces that would be apprehensive of close collaboration with poorer eastern provinces. Furthermore, the political philosophy predominating in these two westernmost provinces is more conservative, more oriented towards suspicion of government initiatives, more stridently capitalist or favourable to free enterprise, than is the case with the other provinces. This ideological factor could be important, especially if the discussions become general and theoretical rather than practical and related to concrete proposals.

It is more difficult to comment with assurance about Saskatchewan, polarized as it is between the NDP favouring government initiatives in the productive sectors on the one hand, and a populist Conservative party with attitudes not unlike those of the Alberta and B.C. governments on the other. Probably its rich natural resource base would lead it to share many of the attitudes of its western neighbours.

The position of Canada's largest and most industrialized province, Ontario, is more predictable. The interprovincial economic rivalries of the early 1980s are largely traceable to an attempt by other provinces to favour their own industry over that of Ontario. Any arrangement that would substitute for this a rational, cooperative effort at economic integration is bound to be beneficial to Ontario. This is particularly evident when one considers the very substantial political and economic clout that this province possesses. Also, Ontario is already on record as favouring cooperative efforts, as it is well aware of the negative consequences of the current state of affairs. Therefore, vis-à-vis the other provinces, one can confidently expect that Ontario would be cooperative and accommodating. In relation to the federal government, however, Ontario's posture is less predictable. In some ways it has benefited from federal policy and been extremely cooperative, especially with the Department of Industry, Trade and Commerce. As "Ontario's DREE," this department has long defended Canadian manufacturing, which is largely situated within the province. On the other hand, the province has had reservations about federal initiatives that have run counter to Ontario interests. For example, when the Department of Regional Economic Expansion undertook to develop the salt reserves of the Magdalene Islands in Quebec, Ontario reacted negatively because this would adversely affect the continuing development of the Ontario deposits in Goderich and were less economically viable. The reconciliation of the Ontario interests with those of the rest of Canada and of the federal government will therefore depend largely upon the strategy undertaken by the planning agency. This might shove the cart before the horse in the sense that in order for

223

the planning arrangements to be acceptable, it may be necessary to bias them in advance in favour of certain types of economic development over others. This obviously would add to the difficulty of seeking compromises between the various interests, but on the other hand, once the compromises were secured, there would be the promise of a greater success in the future for the operation.

From a purely economically rational perspective, there is little doubt that the Atlantic provinces and Manitoba should not object to a federal-provincial planning initiative that would be compelled to take their interests into account, and thereby improve their lot in the Canadian federation. Since their political power is probably greater than their economic power, such an arrangement would likely improve their position because this political power (five provincial governments out of ten) would be bound to accomplish more than their relatively weak economic power could by itself.

Politics, however, is not only a matter of the calculation of rational economic advantage. Some provinces have adopted a long-term strategy of cooperation, whereas others have undertaken confrontational positions in order to improve their lot. One thinks of the Peckford government of Newfoundland, which has chosen to confront the federal government on the question of the offshore oil reserves. While this may delay development of exploration and production, no doubt it is calculated to pressure the federal government to be more generous towards the province in the sharing of resource rents. The background of such a maximalist strategy does not bode well for the future of a cooperative planning arrangement. There is, however, some possibility that the province might be brought around to the view that an arrangement in which the provinces were equal partners with the federal government was one offering them the maximum opportunity for their own economic advantage. Since the recession has reduced the economic activity in the offshore, a more accommodating atmosphere has developed between the federal government and the government of Newfoundland.

The position of the Maritime provinces has traditionally been one of cooperation. They have long recognized their reliance upon federal revenues in order to maintain the level of government services to their citizens. Only recently have they felt sufficiently confident that this was assured no matter what happened, to diverge seriously from federal government initiatives. Perhaps the Newfoundland precedent has served as a teaching example. However, the basic posture of the Maritime provinces remains one of accommodation. In 1983 Nova

224

Scotia signed an agreement of cooperation with the federal government to develop its own offshore oil resources, and this in turn has been used as a lever to induce Newfoundland to follow suit. Both Nova Scotia and New Brunswick have been host to substantial DREE projects, which have followed the earlier ARDA and FRED initiatives back in the Sixties. One would expect that this habit of cooperation would extend to a willingness to entertain a federal proposal for economic planning and development.

The province of Prince Edward Island has gone furthest in welcoming federal government economic initiatives. It has signed an agreement giving substantial initiative to federal authorities to develop the island's resources and plan its future (see chapter 11). This commitment is likely to bias the province in favour of cooperation.

A Federal-Provincial Cooperative Initiative

So far we have been assuming that the federal government would take the initiative in proposing a joint planning agency. Another approach would be for the federal government and the provinces to negotiate quietly in an *ad hoc* fashion to elaborate such an arrangement, and then call a federal-provincial conference, or a meeting of a similar kind, to discuss the matter in a public forum to inform and educate public opinion. Such an approach assumes a considerable degree of common acceptance of the basic principles of the scheme. If this were found to exist, it would obviously be preferable to an initiative taken by only one level of government. The advantage would be that no participant would be free to seize the opportunity to "grandstand" against the proposal and bring it down in acrimonious controversy. If there were enough agreement to permit both levels of government to sponsor such an initiative, the chances of success would obviously be greatly enhanced.

Staffing a Planning Agency

The problem of staffing has to be approached on two levels: the practical aspect of recruiting the best possible personnel to serve the agency; and the public relations aspect of developing elite and public support. Obviously the major interest groups, public servants, federal and provincial, and politically active persons must give their assent to such an initiative. We shall first consider the practical staffing problem.

It is bound to be difficult to assemble on short notice the best-qualified and best-motivated persons to serve on such an agency.

In addition, there will be problems in integrating such an agency into the governmental structure of the country alongside the many policy-making bodies and other think tanks that already exist. Some such agencies have been carrying out a function similar to a modern planning agency. One thinks of the Economic Council of Canada and the Science Council of Canada. These bodies have on their staffs the kind of expert personnel required. Furthermore, they have the structures and administrative arrangements for conducting studies and preparing policy documents. Such ongoing institutions would be invaluable to a planning body, and care should be taken to relate the proposed planning agency to their present activity. This study is not the place to discuss the future role of these agencies in the Canadian governmental structure. Suffice it to say that their cooperation should be enlisted, and the opportunity presented to their personnel to seek employment in the new agency. The same could be said for the many provincial economic councils and private think tanks across the country.

Recruitment, however, should not be confined to existing governmental and quasi-governmental bodies, but should be extended to the wider area of Canadian academic, bureaucratic and business life. This would involve an extensive canvas of available personnel, as well as a campaign to attract the applications of qualified persons.

The setting up of such an agency is a relatively complex operation, which itself requires careful planning. Charts and blueprints must be prepared outlining the characteristics of the new body with establishments for the different categories of personnel. These plans would have to involve arrangements to include the appropriate proportion of English-speaking and French-speaking persons, and of people from the various regions of Canada. While the importance of economists is obvious in such an agency, care must be taken to supplement their expertise with that of sociologists, demographers, political scientists, engineers, urban and regional planners, and so on.

One must guard against hiring too many personnel. Agencies that are assembled on a crash basis, without careful forethought as to the functions to be performed, often find that they have employed people with nothing to do. Morale is quickly undermined, and such agencies soon decay from within. It would be preferable to have a strong but small agency drawn from high-calibre individuals to carry out an essentially planning and allocation function. Much of the detailed work and studies could, at least at the beginning, be farmed out to other agencies or be handled on a contract basis.

The single most important task in setting up the agency is the appointment of its director. The choice of the right person is crucial both from the point of view of the efficient operation of the agency, and also in order to enlist general support for it. A person of obvious first-class competence is required, one who is also well known and highly regarded as someone who gets things done, has vision and is trusted as a reliable and public-spirited citizen. There have been, over the years, people who have come to enjoy immense public respect and prestige and who have been called upon to accomplish that sort of public task which involves enlisting widespread support. One thinks of the late John J. Deutsch, the late Donald Gordon, and Senator Carl Goldenberg. This task would require a person who has great executive ability, respect for rational economic planning, and a degree of sophistication in that area sufficient to win the respect and confidence of the professionals.

The director would have to be the sort of person who would be accepted in the leadership role for a crucial function. He would have to avoid being simply a conciliator between contesting interests; he would have to be capable of conceptualizing along with his experts the strategy to be undertaken, and of negotiating in concert with leaders from political and business life the path to be followed.

The point of such an agency is to bring expertise and careful study to the fore in the making of economic policy so that it will be informed by such knowledge, and will not simply be the output of a process of elite accommodation in which various interest groups press for their own advantage and claim their pound of flesh. This point is a very delicate one. Obviously a policy defying the major interests in the country has no chance of success. On the other hand, the policy that simply clips together the interests of the various components of our national economy is no change from the present and is not likely to lead us anywhere. It is important to inject careful, dispassionate analysis of the various multifaceted issues of Canadian economic life.

The job of winning over the elites is most important and delicate. What is proposed is a profound change in the way we make our basic economic policy decisions. It will be hard to persuade the people who presently occupy key decision-making roles to accept new processes in which their own positions are less assured. Yet only if they can be so convinced will our proposal succeed. The fact that similar arrangements are in place in many of our successful economic-rival states is some evidence of the advantage of such change; so is the rapid decline in Canadian economic performance in competition with them. The challenge to Canada, is therefore, to put our house in order or to face the consequences. With the situation seen in these terms, Canadian elites have a clear choice before them.

Winning over public opinion could also be difficult. The Canadian media are not accustomed to serious consideration of complex questions. Rather they are prone to see issues in terms of stereotypes such as free enterprise, limited government and so forth. It would not be easy to get a serious and informed discussion launched so as to prevent a few enthusiastic scribes from leading the pack in summary rejection of the proposal before it has been fully elaborated. Care must be taken to show the public that the new economic environment in which Canada must compete is one in which states mobilize their economic strength behind complex development strategies involving business, labour and government in concerted cooperation. If Canada cannot do as much, our economic future is bleak.

A Fallback Strategy

Our discussion so far suggests an uncharacteristically high level of consensus among Canadian decision-makers. Past experience suggests that there are likely to be some elements in the country that would be unwilling to go along with such a proposal, despite the economic condition of the country. For reasons we all understand, Quebec may be unwilling to cooperate. Some rich provinces may think that to go along with such a proposal is merely to expose themselves to exploitation by their less wealthy neighbours. While there are many things that could go wrong in such a bold venture, there are three obvious contingencies that we must consider: the refusal of one or more provincial governments to participate, the possible apprehension of the business community, and finally the possibility of deadlock within the large federal government structure.

If One Province Refuses Cooperation

Assuming that the federal government and most of the provinces are prepared to go along with such an arrangement, what should be done if one or more of the provinces refuses to participate? Clearly there is a point beyond which it is impossible to persevere. If the cooperation of Ontario and most of the English-speaking provinces is not forthcoming, surely it would be unwise to take any positive steps beyond attempting to convince those who remain opposed. However, if there is a substantial body of agreement among the federal government and most of the provinces, then the refusal of a minority should not be sufficient to prevent initial steps being taken to set up the agency. Only if the agency does appear to take on some real substance will it become at all clear both to the participants and to the recalcitrants, what the true nature of the agency is and what the advantages of association really are.

Past Canadian experience should be useful at this point. When the tax rental agreements were first proposed by the federal government as a means of carrying the wartime arrangements on into the postwar period, Quebec and Ontario, each for their own reasons, at first refused to participate. The federal government was therefore in the position where it had to devise options which, if offered to the provinces, would turn out to be to the economic advantage of each to participate. While Ontario entered shortly after it became evident that its economic advantage would be served by participation, Quebec for a time did remain outside. It did so even though its economic advantage would have been served by participation. Finally, however, it did succomb when the arrangements were made sufficiently attractive and when no actual signature of agreement was required.

This experience is useful in this context. Refusal to participate should be interpreted as a signal to the federal government and the sponsoring provinces that it is necessary to redraft the terms of agreement so that the recalcitrants will be tempted to participate.

It is obvious that this poses a very considerable challenge to those responsible for the agency and the sponsoring governments. In the purely rational context of economic advantage, Quebec does not pose a great difficulty. It is obvious that the province must be offered economic advantages by entering, but it is also obvious, given the state of that province's economy, that it would be offered these in any case. The challenge of Quebec is the challenge of convincing its leaders and its people that it would to be their advantage to participate in such a common planning agency, despite their interest in maintaining the authentic Quebec culture and society. No doubt the example of the participating countries in the European Economic Community would be relevant here. They have all lived through the history of separate national status, and yet they perceive it as to their advantage to participate in the EEC. Surely as much could be said for Quebec in participating in a pan-Canadian economic community.

It may be somewhat more difficult to convince the resource-rich and outward-looking western provinces of the virtues of collaboration. Again the EEC example is relevant in that the richer inner six (Germany, France, Italy and the low countries) have accepted the

United Kingdom and Ireland despite their poorer economic circumstances, and they are now in the process of including Greece, Spain and Portugal. This suggests that rich countries have more to gain than to lose from participating in a common market with poorer ones. The richer provinces must be made to see the advantages of the overall Canadian market for their goods, and perhaps more important, of the clout in international economic relations that comes from being part of a large and prosperous country able to take significant initiatives abroad.

No doubt it would be a dramatic moment in the life of such a planning authority if one or more provinces should announce publicly their opposition to participation. This would be a test of the determination of the agreeing provinces and governments. If they were to persevere and give substance to their project, they may very well win over the unconvinced as they demonstrate the value of their initiative. If they allow such refusal to prevent the birth of the agency, clearly nothing can be done. One would hope that any province that chose not to participate would at least refrain from launching a full-scale attack upon the whole idea of cooperation towards economic integration. If the project escapes into the realm of heated rhetoric and demagogic declarations, little is to be expected. Let us hope that we have reached that stage of political maturity where such opportunistic posturing will not be rewarded with political success.

If the Business Community Seeks to Remain Aloof

We have become accustomed to hearing business leaders criticize government initiatives as interference with the free market. Despite the the obvious and deep interrelationship between business and government, one still hears the familiar incantation. It must be made clear that in proposing such a planning agency for Canada, one is proposing what the leaders of major corporations have long been doing: rational planning of economic enterprise on the basis of expert knowledge and informed opinion. All business leaders practise this at the level of their own corporations, so why not also at the level of the national economy?

What we are suggesting is not a socialistic experiment, but rather the rational development of a free market. We are suggesting measures to strike down the counterproductive restrictions on markets that operate to the economic disadvantage of Canadians. If they have sufficient confidence in government-related bodies and are willing to work with other interests in the country, businessmen should be willing to collaborate with such an initiative in the rational planning and allocation of resources. The problem, therefore, is to convince the business leaders of the essential nature of the enterprise, and to avoid the kind of misunderstanding that would lead them to withhold support.

The analogy could be made with the economy of France that was successfully revived by the process of indicative planning under the talented leadership of Jean Monnet in the difficult years of postwar reconstruction. This was a process in which the planning secretariat set up by the government secured the endorsement and cooperation of the business community, local authorities and voluntary groups — and to some extent the trade unions — throughout the country. This was a highly successful experiment, and it is interesting to note that as the country became less committed to these arrangements, it fell victim to the economic difficulties we have all experienced in recent years. In the successful period, Monnet and his associates succeeded in convincing business of the need for concerted national planning to develop those industries that offered the best future for the country. With this cooperation, investment was secured with public backing, initiatives were taken, and France became a leading exporter in areas in which before the war it had been only a minor participant. Chemicals, cement, the aerospace industry, household appliances, et cetera, all received their initial stimulus from this program of planned investment.

At first business was sceptical. This approach had not been tried before in their experience, and it appeared to fly in the face of all the traditional beliefs of business. Despite this, the program succeeded as the businessmen were shown what could be accomplished by cooperative and concerted effort, with government collaborating with business and other sectors, guided by careful, realistic analysis and planning.

Surely Canadian business would be no less capable of perceiving the advantages to itself of such a course of action. The major problem for Canadian business is the fact that such a large component of it is foreign controlled. Those businesses that are part of multinational economic organizations are already participating in substantial planning on an international basis. They may very well perceive a Canadian indicative planning agency as a challenge to their home international organization. On the other hand, those that allow some degree of autonomy to their Canadian subsidiaries, even going so far as to admit global product mandating, may see the advantages of

231

participation in such a scheme. Certainly apprehensions about the attitude of foreign-controlled business should not prevent the initiative from going forward. One may well be suprised to find a large segment of foreign-controlled business willing to participate. After all, they are already accustomed to a substantial planning operation and will perceive the advantages to be gained by participation (making their opinion felt) over aloofness and consequent ineffectiveness.

In short, one should not be discouraged by the habitual rhetoric coming out of the business community. In a military metaphor, it is much like covering fire from artillary and machine guns, calculated to keep the enemies' heads down. Such rhetoric is part of the ongoing defensive strategy that business has been mounting, and it should not be perceived as an indication of a refusal to think through serious economic problems. If businessmen are given concrete proposals to consider, they will study them. Their philosophy is to act rationally and in the interests of their shareholders. As long as the planning arrangements are consistent with this, there is no substantial reason to prevent them from cooperating. Care should be taken to make clear that what one is proposing is not a wild experiment drawn from some kind of doctrinaire economic theory, but rather the simple application of rational economic and social analysis to practical problems from which business, among others, can benefit.

The task, however, of convincing business leaders is not one that is going to be accomplished overnight. They will respond better to demonstrations of practical advantage through action, than to prolonged argumentation. The advantages of participation will become apparent when there is something tangible in which to participate.

The Possibility of Deadlock within the Federal Government
Since the Second World War, the Canadian government has proliferated as never before. The number of civil servants has vastly increased, but, more important, the number of agencies has multiplied. Each of these has a life of its own and is concerned to protect its own interest. While in theory the cabinet, responsible to Parliament, directs the activities of the various departments of government, in fact there is a high degree of autonomy simply because of the immensity of the governmental apparatus — and therefore the impossibility of effective scrutiny by two or three dozen ministers. Moreover, the proliferation of government has involved the setting up of many independent and quasi-independent bodies, each charged with a separate area of responsibility. With the passage of time, these bodies develop their

own policies, indeed their own cultures, with ongoing relationships with each other and with the departments of government, relationships which become highly institutionalized and rigid. The natural reaction of all organizations when threatened with change or disruption of any kind, is to resist the implementation of the proposed change in order to protect a quiet life. Unless the directing personnel of these many government agencies can be made to perceive the advantages to Canada, and ultimately to themselves, of the implementation of our proposed federal-provincial planning authority, we must expect an initial stonewalling reaction.

In Canada the central agencies (the Privy Council Office, the Treasury Board and the Department of Finance) have been created to integrate the overall government structure; with their support our planning initiative would be greatly facilitated. On the other hand, if they were to oppose, they could offer powerful resistance. Clearly, they would have to be "on side."

This suggests that from the beginning the leaders of the many public agencies must be involved in discussions about the proposed planning authority on the understanding that their points of view will be taken into account and their interests protected. If they perceive advantages to the country, and generally to their own agencies, they will probably cooperate. If, on the other hand, they are confronted with a threatening monster that is likely to be imposed from above, their natural reaction will be to resist it or otherwise subvert it.

This suggests that much more than a conventional public relations campaign is necessary. There must be a legitimate, honest consultation of higher public servants both within the departments and in the semi-independent agencies. These people have much to contribute and are bound to be affected by such an agency. If their cooperation can be enlisted, the agency may proceed with strength and on a firm foundation of realistic analysis and advice. Without it, immeasurable difficulties will be encountered.

Problems to Overcome

When one contemplates such a far-reaching change to our ways of conceptualizing our economic goals, we must anticipate some serious attitudinal obstacles ahead. Let us consider four specific problems: the basic attitudes or philosophy of our business community; the federal-provincial rivalry that has developed and become a kind of institutional pattern in Canada; the system of political parties that we have developed, with each cast in the role of debunking whatever the

233

other proposes; and, finally, Canada's relationship with its large and powerful neighbour, the United States.

Attitudes of the Business Community

Traditionally in Canada business leaders have enjoyed a high level of prestige and considerable autonomy in conducting their own affairs. If Canada has an elite group, surely it is its business leaders. These are the people who make the major investment decisions, who have more influence than any other group over governments, and who therefore possess a high degree of autonomous power. It will surprise no one that business leaders are anxious to protect this privileged position and, if possible, to improve it. Their means of accomplishing these objectives involve maintaining a close working relationship with leaders of government, both within the public service and in political life. This relationship of elite accommodation has been amply demonstrated by Robert Presthus[1] and other writers on interest groups in Canada. Consistent with business in other countries, Canadian business supports an ideological position that sanctifies the free market and abhores government intervention, viewing it as socialism, bureaucracy or statism. They identify such intervention with lumbering inefficiency, incompetence and uncontrolled expenditure. It must be admitted that these relatively simplistic attitudes seem to correspond with some real problems in the late years of the twentieth century. With mounting deficits and enormous public expenditures, which seem to many to be out of control, there appears to be substance in this horrific picture of government activity.

If our governments have lost the confidence of business and, to some extent, of the community because of the problems of inflation and economic dislocation, it is obviously difficult to convince businessmen that the answer is to be found in additional activity involving government.

Here the approach must be based not upon doctrine or prejudice but rather upon sound, objective analysis. Businessmen must be shown that for a planning agency to be successful, it must involve more than economic experts and governmental participation. It involves also the collaboration and cooperation of business leaders; they must be convinced of the objectives and proposals involved in planning arrangements before they are put into effect. What is proposed, therefore, is not a radical change from current practice, but rather a systematic structure lending coherence to a relationship of collaboration that already exists. Governments already consult businessmen on a

234

somewhat *ad hoc* basis, and produce policies consistent with their interests, while other governments do the same with other businessmen. The overall effect is somewhat incoherent and contradictory, but the ongoing relationship between business and government remains. What we are asking for is that this relationship be institutionalized on a national, federal-provincial basis and in a coherent fashion, informed by the well-targeted studies of the best experts in the field in question. When stated in such terms, one is merely pleading for the kind of behaviour that businessmen themselves are prone to praise.

If this can be perceived, then there is some chance of enlisting the support of key elements in the business community. They must become aware that this does not mean a diminution of their power and influence, but merely a mobilization of it in a more rational and coherent fashion, and informed by sound analysis of specific problems.

There is one peculiarly Canadian problem that is bound to create difficulty. This is the key position of the foreign-controlled subsidiary, particularly in the resource sector and in secondary manufacturing. In some cases, the Canadian chief executive officers of these corporations are merely subordinate agents acting on orders from headquarters located outside of Canada. Such men do not have the authority to lend support to the proposed agency, and can be expected to resort to a more negative attitude in order to preserve the status quo to which they are accustomed. However, other foreign firms have granted considerable autonomy to their Canadian operations, and they could be expected to approach the problem in a more analytical way.

In any case, events are developing in Canada such that the day is now past when foreign-controlled enterprises can have their own way in the Canadian political context. In recent years the Canadian government has undertaken controversial policies to protect the autonomy of Canadian business and to prevent the rents from Canadian natural resources from being exported or capitalized by non-Canadian interests. Businessmen are very flexible. They respond to the realities of the situation. Already they are making their peace with these new governmental initiatives and are operating within them. One can expect that they will similarly adapt themselves to such a planning agency, cooperate with it in order to have their voices heard, and exercise what influence they can. While it may be more difficult to set up an indicative planning agency in Canada because of this substantial foreign presence, it should not be impossible. Indeed, if it proves to be impossible, this gives us very bad news about the degree of real autonomy Canadians possess in their own country.

We are testing the "good corporate citizenship" of these foreign businesses in Canada; we are trying to convince them of the need for cooperation with the overall national economic plan for their own economic enterprises to survive and prosper. If Canada does not come to grips with the inherent structural weaknesses of its own economic arrangement and deal with them, then these firms, along with all the others, can only suffer.

If the business leaders can be convinced of the competence, impartiality and open-mindedness of the planning agency, they can be expected to cooperate. On the other hand, if they view it with suspicion as an agency of the government that does not have their interests at heart, they will resist it. They must come to see, as we all must, that Canadians must hang together or hang separately. This involves the collaboration of government and business and all other segments of the community in a coherent and cooperative effort of rational, long-term economic development.

Canada's economy difficulties of the early Eighties are tragic for Canadians. These difficulties, however, will probably bring Canadians to see that they must work together if they are to overcome them. Their economy must be made more competitive and more productive. This can only be done if efficient structures replace inefficient ones, and cooperation replaces confrontation.

The establishment of a planning agency may also open the door to a new collaboration between labour and business, which have hitherto had a relationship frought with confrontation and bitterness. Canada has the highest rate of industrial stoppages in the Western world, exceeded only from time to time by Italy. The existence of some kind of economic planning arrangement, perceived to be both impartial and competent, could do much to win the confidence of both business and labour, leading them to the kind of collaboration other countries, such as Sweden and Germany, have achieved.

Federal-Provincial Rivalry
Recent years have seen a serious exacerbation of the rivalry between the federal government and the provinces. This has passed through ongoing disagreements over the sharing of revenues, through the quarrels over the federal share in the rents from natural resources, particularly oil, gas and potash, and came to a head in the 1981–82 negotiations over constitutional change. This posture of federal-

provincial confrontation is in danger of becoming institutionalized as a permanent feature of Canadian life. This is a serious and decidedly unpleasant prospect. It has already created the serious balkanization of what used to be a Canadian common market, as the development of nontariff barriers has opened the way for provincial governments to interfere with trade between their own jurisdictions and others. Provincial politicians have perceived the advantages in making the federal government a kind of opponent in order to secure re-election; we have seen as recently as 1982 the federal government leader attacking the provincial leaders for their desire to trade off "rights for fish," for creating "a confederation of shopping centres," and so on. These outbursts are symptomatic of a developing mind-set in which political leaders preserve themselves and their interests at the expense of the nation as a whole. We are in serious danger of settling into the kind of economic fragmentation that undermined the economic viability of medieval Europe, or was characteristic of the German states before unification. In today's world with huge markets in the United States, the Soviet Union and the EEC, Canada will go the road of economic balkanization at its peril. Surely a way out of this destructive provincialism is to be found in elaborating new structures of cooperation among the federal government and the provinces. No one can seriously question the rights of both levels of government to exist and to preserve their powers and jurisdictions. There is no reason why they cannot, however, while retaining possession of these, use them cooperatively in a common national interest. In this sense the planning agency will go beyond merely economic concerns, and will prepare the way for a new spirit of cooperation based on rational, professional analysis.

The Political Parties
The Canadian political party system involves very little ideological cleavage. The Liberals and the Conservatives are essentially brokerage parties seeking to offer programs that will attract the maximum public support at election time and that are pleasing to business and other leaders with which they carry on the process of elite accommodation. This has meant that the parties have grown increasingly estranged from the traditional stances that identified them in the early years of this century. Neither has had a particularly consistent policy record, especially since the Second World War. Since they tend to take their policies from the representations made to them by interest groups, or else from public opinion surveys showing majority support for a given

237

initiative, they have neglected the most important task of a political party, namely, the development of a philosophy and program to be offered to the public at election time. Consequently, policy in Canada has developed on an incremental basis, with one party remaining in office for long periods. This incrementalism has tended to make Canadian policy particularly short term and oriented to the electoral cycle. Longer-term policies have been neglected, and clear choices have not been presented to the electorate. Instead of Canada being equipped to plan its economic development strategy in the international struggle for markets and economic advantage, we have relied on a relatively blind incrementalism, without much weighing of longer-term economic advantages.

This situation may well have been acceptable at a time when other countries followed similar practices and government played a relatively minor role in economic life. Neither of these conditions obtains today. Canada confronts large trading blocs that are informed by careful planning and analysis of economic advantages, and that develop careful strategies for enhancing their economic position and performance. The striking success of Japan in the international market both for complex goods of mass consumption, such as automobiles, and for high-technology items is a warning to Canada as well as other countries.

A possible way out of this impasse can surely be found in equipping the Canadian governmental structure, both provincial and federal, with a rational economic planning capability that can lay out and secure support for a coherent policy of economic development. If this were to occur, and such plans were generally accepted by the community, the political parties would be bound to follow. This has been the French experience since the Second World War, where the planning arrangements have not been a subject for party disagreement in the electoral process.

Since the Canadian approach to politics is largely empirical and material, and since ideological distinctions play a relatively small role in Canadian party politics, there is some reason to think that Canadian political leaders would be disposed to accept the objectives defined by the planning authority. The problem lies in convincing party leaders of the soundness of setting up a planning mechanism. Once the structures are in place and the policies elaborated, they would probably be supported by party leaders, who would then recognize the political saliency of collaboration. Party rivalries of course, must remain. The substance of their discourse, however, would be enriched by national objectives that have been widely discussed and generally supported by Canadian elites.

The existence of such a planning agency may well have as a by-product the rooting of Canadian political discourse in a common bed of sound and generally accepted analysis, providing a basis for coherent political discussion. At least we would be injecting an element of professional analysis into the free-wheeling gambit of political party rhetoric. We may even escape from some of the incrementalism of the past through the substitution of planned policy development.

Possible U.S. Apprehension

There are really two sides to this question: the possibility of actual American reaction to the Canadian initiative and, secondly, Canadian fears and uncertainties as to what to expect from the United States. Let us consider first of all the substantive question of possible U.S. reaction.

As we look over the past experience of Canada-U.S. economic relations we find a remarkable story of amicable and close relations between the two parties who engage in the largest international exchange of goods and services taking place in the world.

Generally speaking, the United States has avoided bullying its smaller neighbour, and Canada on the other hand as been careful to keep American interests high on its list of considerations in making economic policy. When the United States has undertaken important changes in economic policy that affect foreign countries, the usual Canadian reaction has been to send a delegation to Washington to ask that Canada be made an exception to the regulation. The United States has usually acceded to this request because of the particularly intimate relationship existing between the two countries. The cumulative effect of this "exemptionalism" has been to create a considerable measure of Canadian dependence on the United States, thus making Canada extremely vulnerable should it fall out of favour with the United States. Add to this the consequences of the enormous American investment in Canada, its influence in Canada through the sale of its mass-produced products, the extension of its television and radio broadcasting area into Canadian airspace, and the immense cultural influence of the United States as the great generator of modern English-language mass culture.

Canadians therefore must be concerned about the reaction of the United States. What might it be? To begin with, the United States would respect Canada's sovereign right to organize its affairs as it sees fit, but of course the U.S. would reserve to itself the right to take countermeasures if it thought that Canadian initiatives were harmful to American interests. In the case of the federal-provincial planning agency, there is no reason to think that the United States would disapprove, since the proposal is no threat to legitimate American interests and is in no way ideologically deviant. The fact that Canada decides to make its economic decisions rationally on the basis of objective analysis should not trouble American policy-makers. It is not a radical scheme; so it should not excite American ideological susceptibilities, provided its nature was understood.

The real problem would arise if some American corporation were to perceive that its interests might be adversely affected; for example, a pan-Canadian planning agency might wish to terminate some excessively generous give-aways that have already been conceded by vulnerable provincial governments. We have already seen this kind of reaction when U.S. resource industries found their freedom to move within the Canadian economy limited by such programs as the National Energy Program (NEP) or other legislation, both federal and provincial. The point to be made here is that the United States has no *legitimate* cause for objection to a federal-provincial planning agency. It may, however, be goaded into concern lest certain of its corporations see their special advantages threatened. Surely this is not the sort of situation that should cow Canadians into inaction when faced with their own economic interest in a legitimate and honourable sense.

Some Americans may well be advantaged when the Canadian economy is balkanized, and therefore vulnerable and weak. The fact that Canadian provincial governments are sometimes led to develop excessive dependence upon major investors can be counted as a situation favourable to American interests. By the same token, it is clearly a situation unfavourable to Canadian interests, and is one that should be brought to an end. The general pattern of incremental improvisation that has characterized Canadian policy-making may also be perceived as serving American interests. Certainly it does not serve Canadian ones.

However, one must hope that the United States would take a long-term view of such problems. Surely it is more in the interest of the United States to have a neighbour that runs its affairs soundly and is therefore a stable and prosperous associate, rather than to have a highly vulnerable Canada with a declining economy sliding into worsening economic conditions and, perhaps, political instability.

240

One would hope that Canada's efforts to solve its own economic problems would serve more as an example to be followed rather than as a threat to be countered. The United States has not taken exception to another Western country when it so ordered its economic house. While the United States has been economically threatened by the highly effective economic organization and consequent productivity of such countries as Japan, France and Germany, it has never counted them as its opponents or threatened them with measures other than the conventional instruments used by all countries engaged in international trade. In short, in an objective sense, there does not appear to be any sound reason to expect the United States to do other than accept the Canadian initiative for what it is: a legitimate right by a hard-pressed neighbour to puts its own economic house in order.

A more serious problem concerns Canadian fears of American reaction. Canada has long followed a policy of cautious accommodation to American wishes. We have even put up with American extraterritoriality affecting our business operations, and we have all too often assumed a cap-in-hand posture in dealing with the United States. We have tried to attract its capital and, until recent years, have done little to deal with the control over our economy that this has involved. Our business community especially is prone to be extremely sensitive to American preferences and perhaps to anticipate objections where none could be found, or at least where nothing substantial exists.

There is therefore considerable likelihood that Canadian governments and Canadian elites may feel apprehensive about undertaking a program of cooperative federal-provincial economic planning because they wish to avoid any possibility of cross-border recriminations. In addition, such discussions might jeopardize the parties in power by exposing them to attack from their political oppositions. However, in substantive terms there would appear to be little to fear from American reaction. We have always tended to be overly cautious about American attitudes. It would behoove us now to give thought to our *own* advantage through a course of action that is honourable, rational and expeditious. We must remember that Canada's relations with the United States have long been peaceful, involving mutual understandings. Those Canadians are surely wrong who think that the United States claims any right to determine Canadian internal policy. It has not done so in the past and there is no reason to expect it to do so in the future. It is no tribute to the United States to behave as if we thought they would not permit us the freedom of action that all sovereign countries rightly claim.

241

Conclusion

16

We have now canvassed the experience of France, Germany, the U.S.A. and Britain in the matter of making economic policy; we have looked at the relations between government and business, and have reviewed the Canadian experience. A few simple conclusions stand out. First, success in terms of developing a productive, growing economy has gone to those countries that have put their economic house in order. That is to say, the countries that have been the winners have developed relationships of trust between government and the private sector, permitting them to erect structures for planning rationally and with wide participation. Canada has not been among these for several reasons. At the heart of our difficulties is the fact that we have developed a relationship of deadlock in federal-provincial relations that has set the pace for other relations, especially between business and government. This has prevented us from agreeing on our economic goals. Instead our attention has been drawn to the struggle between our governments. We have become fascinated by the manoeuvres, the victories of one side, the defeats of another. We have allowed this sterile process to prevent us from making rational allocations of our resources, to plan for the maximization of productivity in order to succeed in the scramble that the international market has become.

This failure to order our affairs rationally according to plan at the highest level has had most serious consequences: our economy has become balkanized and our politics confrontational, leading us to dissipate our top decision-making resources on struggles of allocation between regions, provinces, industries and so on, instead of building a consensus around an agreed-upon program of development. And as a by-product of our preoccupation with dividing our economic pie, we have produced allocations that featherbed many inefficient sectors.

Each of these arrangements pleases the beneficiaries but adds to the accumulation of inefficiency and uncompetitiveness of our economy. At the same time our rivals in the international market have been concentrating on improving their product and their prices through research and development, efficient management and sound investment. Our current difficulties are a warning. We must organize our structures so that we too can make the best use of our efforts and our resources.

The years since the Second World War have seen Canada move deeper into the situation Samuel Beer calls "pluralist stagnation"[1] — a state in which interest groups have become vested interests that have gained certain rights and privileges from government (subsidies for one industry, quotas to protect another, monopoly privileges for trade unions, prerogatives for provincial governments, special "rights" for given classes, sexes, ethnic and cultural groups, regions, etc.). These become *situations acquises* (acquired positions) that are not to be challenged. Each can be defended individually, especially in the face of the existence of all the others. But the cumulative effect is a lumbering, inefficient system that produces far below its capacity. This is a waste of resources at any time, but when other nations are arranging their incentive systems and decision-making structures to maximize efficiency and productivity, it is a formula for disaster.

The key, the way out of the trap, as we have long known, is in the rational planning of our actions. The Trudeau government in the early Seventies recognized this, and set up not one but three systems of planning — the Privy Council Office, the Treasury Board and the Department of Finance. In addition, every department created its own planning staffs, adding enormous numbers of highly trained and well-paid systems analysts, planners and the like to the public payroll. But instead of coherence and efficiency we got confrontation, bureaucratic infighting and a draining of morale. Why?

The reason is simple. There must be an overall, master plan within which the lower levels of economic planning fit as part of a whole. First one must decide what the unit is: Canada, a province, a region, an industry, or what? Then the plan must be elaborated, and it must be sold to those elites both within and outside government who are expected to carry it out, and whose lives will be deeply affected by it. The process is one of developing coherence.

Instead of doing this, we merely put the newly acquired planning skills to work in the service of the old confrontational politics. Each level of government got better at defending its turf, more effective in planning its programs to steal a march on the others. The wars between levels of government, between departments in government and between branches of a single department were carried on at much greater expense than before — but the level of confrontation did not decline. It may even have increased.

Now we must go back and get the basic structure right. We require not *several* but only *one* planning agency at the apex of our national governmental structure. It must answer to both federal and provincial levels of government, since each is strong enough to frustrate the other. They must be brought together around one basic plan that is fair, competently elaborated and able to serve as a basis for discussions leading to implementation on a basis of consent.

To do this we must constitute a board of directors for the planning agency drawn *equally* from the two levels of government. A first thought suggests one from each province and one from each of the ten federal departments most involved in economic development. No doubt this is too simplistic. Ontario would have to have more weight than Prince Edward Island, Quebec than New Brunswick, and so on. So we could allot the provincial seats on a regional basis: two for Quebec, two for Ontario, two for British Columbia, two from the Atlantic provinces, and two from the Prairies to be chosen as they decide. The point is that there must be parity between the federal and provincial levels, and reasonable equity among the provinces. How these levels are determined must depend on the parties themselves.

Once the board is in place and the chairman appointed, the staff must be assembled and the plan prepared. Then it must go for discussion and approval to the agency's board. Approval by Parliament and the provincial legislatures would help establish the legitimacy of the instrument, and would commit the governments to working together to bring about the results proposed. Then business, local governments, labour organizations and others affected would discuss the aspects affecting them in order to develop an overall national consensus, thus producing concerted action.

Here one must face the accusation: Is this not naive, too simplistic, too idealistic? I think not, for several reasons. The problem Canada faces now is a lack of leadership, and this is because the confrontational state into which we have fallen prevents agreement and therefore leadership. The only escape from this is to transcend it by defiantly setting up consensual instruments, in the hope that they will be welcomed by elites sickened by the years of futile and self-defeating confrontation. This initiative would play the role of the grain of sand in the oyster: the nucleus around which the pearl of consensus and purposive action can form.

Secondly, the country must now face the reality that it can no longer afford to deliberately mutilate its productive capacity by shoring up, and indeed creating, nonviable economic operations. A means must be found to break out from the pattern of supporting unproductive operations out of general revenues. Since our competitors are not doing this, we cannot do it either if we are to survive in competition. The only fair way to reorient our initiatives is through rational planning around a national consensus. Otherwise we shall simply be compelled to go on crippling ourselves in the name of equity, making ourselves poorer because we cannot escape from the trap we have made for ourselves.

Cynics will say that those who have reaped the benefits from the public treasury will not give up what they have won. If that is true, we are indeed trapped. The situation will deteriorate until those bearing the burden will opt out. Our country will either break apart or simply grow increasingly uncompetitive.

Careful planning can lead us to a better solution. But we must be prepared to contemplate workers changing jobs, people moving to regions where opportunities exist, industries that cannot pay their way closing to make way for others that can. If we plan the transition and support the people who must move, or retrain, we can regain our competitiveness. Unless we plan the transition, however, those affected have no choice but to dig in and defend their positions, even if by so doing they are holding back the country's adaptation.

If we have a competent planning mechanism in place, then we have the capacity to work out the strategies of development that we need, and we also have the means of getting general support for these strategies. For Canada to find a role for itself in the new competitive and complex world of post-industrialism is indeed not easy. It is too difficult for the present structures that we have. The answer is not that all of us in our competing and confrontational postures should try to develop such a strategy. Rather we should move in steps. We should begin by creating a competent structure that is assigned the problem as a pan-Canadian one and that is responsible to us all — federal and provincial governments, managers and trade unionists, in all parts of the country.

But even before this comes the leap of faith — the decision and collective will to set up the machinery around which a consensus can be built on a basis of rational planning for agreed-upon objectives. If we cannot agree to do that, then we cannot do anything.

245

Notes

Chapter 2

[1] W. T. Easterbrook and H. G. J. Aitken, *Canadian Economic History* (Toronto: Macmillan, 1956), p. 406.

[2] Ibid., p. 521.

[3] Fifteen of the largest forty industrial enterprises in Canada are more than 50 per cent foreign owned. Of the two hundred largest industrials, sixty-nine were 100 per cent owned by foreigners and another forty-one were more than 50 per cent foreign owned in 1978. *Financial Post* 300, summer 1978, cited in Christopher Greene, *Canadian Industrial Organization and Policy* (Toronto: McGraw-Hill Ryerson, 1980), p. 18.

[4] Ibid., p. 25.

[5] See Stephen Clarkson, *Canada and the Reagan Challenge* (Toronto: Lorimer/Canadian Institute for Economic Policy, 1982).

Chapter 3

[1] See Robert Gilpin, "Economic Interdependence and National Security in Historial Perspective," in K. Knorr and S. N. Trager, *Economic Issues and National Security* (Lawrence, Kansas: National Security Education Program, 1977), pp. 19–66.

[2] A good comprehensive review of the approaches of the major European countries can be found in Peter Katzenstein, ed., *Between Power and Plenty: Foreign Economic Policies of Advanced Industrial States* (Madison: University of Wisconsin Press, 1978).

[3] See André Blais and Philippe Faucher, "La Politique industrielle dans les économies capitalistes avancées," *Canadian Journal of Political Science*, vol. 14, no. 1 (March 1981), pp. 3–35.

Chapter 4

[1] See John Hackett and A. M. Hackett, *Economic Planning in France* (London: George Allen and Unwin, 1963), p. 26.

[2] See Diana Green, "The Budget and the Plan," in P. G. Cerny and M. A. Schain, *French Politics and Public Policy* (London and New York: Methuen, 1981), pp. 115–20.

[3] See William Keegan and R. Pennant-Rea, *Who Runs the Economy?* (London: Maurice Temple Smith, 1979).

[4] See Samuel Beer, *Britain Against Itself* (New York: W. W. Norton & Co., 1982), pp. 23–47, 67–76.

Chapter 5

[1] See Stephen D. Krasner, "United States Commercial and Monetary Policy: Unraveling the Paradox of External Strength and Internal Weakness," in P. J. Katzenstein, ed., *Between Power and Plenty* (Madison: University of Wisconsin Press, 1978), p. 85.

[2] See Andrew Shonfield, *Modern Capitalism* (New York: Oxford University Press, 1965), p. 297.

[3] See Michael Kreile, "West Germany: The Dynamics of Expansion," in Katzenstein, *Between Power and Plenty*, pp. 191–224.

[4] Ibid., p. 210.

[5] Ibid., p. 221.

Chapter 6

[1] For more details see: Thomas A. Hockin, *Apex of Power*, 2nd ed. (Toronto: Prentice Hall, 1977); Colin Campbell and George J. Szablowski, *The Super Bureaucrats* (Toronto: Macmillan, Toronto, 1979); and Richard D. French, *How Ottawa Decides* (Toronto: Lorimer/Canadian Institute for Economic Policy, 1980).

[2] See Mitchell Sharp, "Decision-Making in the Federal Cabinet," in French, *How Ottawa Decides*, p. 66.

[3] For a good discussion of the cabinet committee system see French, *How Ottawa Decides*, pp. 1–8.

[4] Ibid., p. 7.

[5] Ibid., p. 42.

[6] Ibid., p. 44.

[7] Ibid., p. 45.

[8] Ibid., p. 51.

[9] Ibid., p. 52.

[10] Ibid., p. 83.

[11] Ibid., pp. 32–41, 53–58.

[12] Ibid., p. 35.

[13] Quoted in ibid., pp. 36–37.

[14] Ibid., p. 40.

[15] Richard W. Phidd and G. Bruce Doern, *The Politics and Management of Canadian Economic Policy* (Toronto: Macmillan, 1978), p. 197.

[16] See Canada, Standing Committee on National Finance, Senate of Canada, "Growth, Employment and Price Stability" (Ottawa, 1971); and A. Breton, "Modelling the Behaviour of Exchequers," in L. J. Officer and L. B. Smith, eds., *Issues in Canadian Economics* (Toronto: McGraw-Hill Ryerson, 1974), pp. 107–14.

[17] Phidd and Doern, *Politics and Management*, p. 218.

[18] French, *How Ottawa Decides*, p. 32.

[19] Quoted in ibid., p. 73.

Chapter 7

[1] Richard W. Phidd and G. Bruce Doern, *The Politics and Management of Canadian Economic Policy* (Toronto: Macmillan, 1978), p. 292.

[2] Ibid., p. 320.

[3] Ibid., p. 322.

[4] *Globe and Mail*, 13 August 1981.

[5] Ibid.

Chapter 8

1 Economic Council of Canada Act, 1973, cited in Richard W. Phidd and G. Bruce Doern, *The Politics and Management of Canadian Economic Policy* (Toronto: Macmillan, 1978), p. 183.
2 From an interview with the chairman of the Economic Council of Canada.
3 G. Bruce Doern, "The Role of Central Advisory Councils: The Science Council of Canada," in G. Bruce Doern and Peter Aucoin, *The Structures of Policy-Making in Canada* (Toronto: Macmillan, 1971), p. 247.
4 For details see ibid., p. 256.
5 John N. H. Britton and James M. Gilmour, *The Weakest Link: A Technological Perspective on Canadian Industrial Underdevelopment* (Ottawa: Science Council of Canada, 1978), p. 197.
6 *Canadian Public Policy*, vol. 5, no. 3 (Summer 1979), pp. 304–35.
7 Ibid., p. 304.
8 Ibid., p. 332.
9 Kristian Palda, *The Science Council's Weakest Link* (Vancouver: Fraser Institute, 1979).
10 Ibid., p. 44.
11 Ibid., p. 3.
12 Ibid., pp. 8, 9.
13 *Science Council of Canada Annual Review 1980* (Ottawa, 1980), p. 19.
14 Ibid., pp. 23–26.
15 Ibid., pp. 32–36.

Chapter 9

1 In January 1982 the government announced a major reorganization of government departments. For details see last section of this chapter.
2 Canada, Ministry of State for Economic Development, *ABC: Assistance to Business in Canada* (Ottawa, 1979).
3 Agenda for Economic Development in the 1980s, Notes for Remarks by Senator H. A. Olson, P.C. M.P. Ottawa, Ontario, 20 October 1980 (a press release issued by the department).

Chapter 10

1 W. T. Easterbrook and Hugh G. Aitken, *Canadian Economic History* (Toronto: Macmillan, 1956), p. 406.
2 Marsha A. Chandler and William M. Chandler, *Public Policy and Provincial Politics* (Toronto: Methuen, 1979), p. 257.
3 Ibid., p. 259.
4 See A. E. Safarian, "Impediments to the International Mobility of Labour in Canada," *L'Economiste*, 1979.
5 See Judith Maxwell and Caroline Pestieau, *Economic Realities of Contemporary Federation* (Montreal: C. D. Howe Research Institute, 1980), pp. 85–87, for a listing of provincial restrictive practices. Also, R. E. Haack, D. R. Hughes and R. G. Shapiro, *The Splintered Market* (Toronto: Lorimer/Canadian Institute of Economic Policy, 1981), presents a detailed picture of provincial policies in relation to agriculture.
6 Gerry T. Gartner, "A Review of Cooperation among the Western Provinces," *Canadian Public Administration*, vol. 20, no. 1 (1977), pp. 174–87.

[7] *Alberta Heritage Savings Trust Fund, Annual Report, 1979* (Edmonton: Department of the Treasury).

[8] L. Pratt and J. Richards, *Prairie Capitalism — Power and Influence in the New West* (Toronto: McClelland and Stewart, 1979).

[9] See British Columbia Ministry of Finance, *Financial and Economic Review* (Victoria, 1979), pp. 792–97; and Canada, Department of Industry, Trade and Commerce, *Canada's Trade Performance, 1960-1977* (Ottawa, 1978), pp. 79–86.

[10] British Columbia, *Financial and Economic Review*, p. 81.

[11] See British Columbia, Ministry of Consumer and Corporate Affairs, "Revision of Securities Regulation in British Columbia: A Discussion Paper" (Victoria, October 1979).

[12] See Pratt and Richards, *Prairie Capitalism*, pp. 142–43.

[13] Ibid., pp. 262–72.

[14] Ibid., p. 272.

[15] See W. MacDonald, "Central Planning in Saskatchewan: 1944 to the Present" (Unpublished paper, Saskatchewan Planning Bureau, 1980), p. 1.

[16] Saskatchewan, Department of Industry and Commerce, *Saskatchewan: Industrial Development Site Selection Handbook, 1979*.

[17] Ibid.

[18] Richard Cleroux, *Globe and Mail*, 26 April 1983.

[19] Professor J. C. Weldon, interview, 19 August 1980.

[20] *1981 Manitoba Budget Address*.

[21] *Editeur Officiel du Quebec, 1979*, p. 523.

[22] See the Quebec government publication DM 77-19, 26 January 1977, for the seven rules on government purchasing.

[23] Government of Quebec, *Le Virage Technologique* (Quebec, 1982), p. 23.

[24] Ibid., p. 204.

[25] Government of Quebec, *Challenges for Quebec* (English summary of *Bâtir le Québec*), p. 38.

[26] Ibid., p. 38.

[27] Ibid., p. 37.

[28] Ibid., p. 47.

[29] Ibid., p. 50.

[30] Bernard Descoteaux, "Les Super-ministres," *le Devoir*, 16 and 18 August 1980.

Chapter 11

[1] See A. A. Lomas, "The Council of Maritime Premiers: A Report and Evaluation After Five Years," *Canadian Public Administration*, vol. 20, no. 1 (Spring 1977), pp. 188–99.

[2] Ibid.

[3] Interview with the executive vice-president, APEC.

[4] Hans K. Larsen and William Y. Smith, "The Case for Indicative Planning," *Policy Options*, vol. 3, no. 6 (1982), pp. 19–21.

[5] See Donald Savoie, *Federal-Provincial Economic Collaboration: The Canada-New Brunswick General Development Agreement* (Montreal: McGill-Queen's University Press, 1981).

[6] New Brunswick, Department of Commerce and Development, *Manufacturing in New Brunswick: An Industrial Development Strategy* (Fredericton, March 1982).

[7] Canada, Department of Regional Economic Expansion, *Development Plan for Prince Edward Island* (Ottawa, 1975).

[8] D. C. MacDonald, *Government and Politics in Ontario* (Toronto: Macmillan, 1975), pp. 114–19.

[9] Energy, Resources Development, Natural Resources, Northern Affairs, Education and Labour.

[10] Innovation Development for Employment Advancement.

[11] Ontario, Ministry of Industry and Tourism, *Annual Review* (Toronto, 1981), p. 3.

[12] Ibid., p. 16.

[13] Ibid., p. 17.

[14] Ibid., p. 25.

[15] Published in Toronto in 1981.

[16] Ibid., p. 21.

Chapter 12

[1] Government of Alberta, *Inventory of Federal-Provincial Programs in Alberta* (Edmonton, 1981).

[2] M. S. Whittington, "CCREM: An Experiment in Interjurisdictional Coordination" (Unpublished report for the Science Council of Canada, 1978).

[3] *The Council of Ministers of Education of Canada, Annual Report 1980–81* (Ottawa, 1981).

[4] See Richard D. French, *How Ottawa Decides* (Toronto: Lorimer/Canadian Institute for Economic Policy, 1980), pp. 79–80.

[5] See Douglas Brown and Julia Eastman, *The Limits of Consultation* (Institute of Intergovernmental Relations, Queen's University, and the Science Council of Canada, May 1981).

[6] "An Economic Development Policy for Canada," presented by Hon. W. G. Davis, Premier of Ontario, to the Federal-Provincial Conference of First Ministers, Ottawa, 13-15 February 1978, p. 26.

[7] Brown and Eastman, *Limits*.

[8] Ibid., pp. 66–72.

[9] Ibid., pp. 101–5.

Chapter 13

[1] The detail relating to the Tier I and Tier II consultation is drawn from Dougas Brown and Julia Eastman, *The Limits of Consultation* (Institute of Intergovernmental Relations, Queen's University, and the Science Council of Canada, May 1981), plus some interview material.

[2] *A Report by the Second Tier Committee on Policies to Improve Canadian Competitiveness* (Ottawa, October 1978), p. 15.

Chapter 14

[1] G. Veilleux, "Intergovernmental Canada: Government by Conference? A Fiscal and Economic Perspective," in *Canadian Public Administration*, vol. 23(1) (Spring 1980), pp. 33–36.

[2] See G. Veilleux, "Evolution des méchanismes de liaison intergouvernementale," in R. Simeon, ed., *Confrontation and Collaboration — Intergovernmental Relations in Canada Today* (Ottawa: Institute of Public Administration of Canada, 1979), pp. 37–46.

[3] Ibid., p. 46.

[4] See Don Stevenson, "The Role of Intergovernmental Conferences and Decision-Making," in Simeon, *Confrontation,* pp. 89–94.

[5] Gordon Robertson, "The Role of Interministerial Conferences in the Decision-Making Process," in Simeon, *Confrontation*, pp. 78–80.

[6] Louis Bernard, "La conjoncture actuelle des relations intergouvernementales," in Simeon, *Confrontation*. ("The reciprocal loss of confidence is so deep that it becomes itself a problem which is added to all the others. It becomes a trap which pushes the governments to go even more deeply along the unilateralist path. It is a vicious circle.")

[7] See D. V. Smiley, "An Outsider's Observation of Federal-Provincial Relations Among Consenting Adults," in Simeon, *Confrontation*, pp. 105–10.

[8] The term is Joe Clark's, the past Conservative leader.

[9] *Globe and Mail*, 13 August 1981.

[10] Canada, Department of Finance, *Economic Development for Canada in the 1980s* (Ottawa, 1981).

[11] Press Release, Prime Minister's Office, 12 January 1982, *Reorganization for Economic Development*, p. 4.

[12] Ibid.

[13] Ibid., pp. 5, 6.

[14] Shakespeare, *Julius Caesar*.

Chapter 15

[1] R. Presthus, *Elite Accommodation in Canadian Politics* (Toronto: Macmillan, 1973).

Chapter 16

[1] Samuel Beer, *Britain Against Itself* (New York: W. W. Norton & Co., 1982), pp. 23–106.

The Canadian Institute for Economic Policy Series

252

Canada's Population Outlook: Demographic Futures and Economic Challenges
David K. Foot

Financing the Future: Canada's Capital Markets in the Eighties
Arthur W. Donner

Controlling Inflation: Learning from Experience in Canada, Europe, and Japan
Clarence J. Barber and John C.P. McCallum

Canada and the Reagan Challenge: Crisis in the Canadian-American Relationship
Stephen Clarkson

The Future of Canada's Auto Industry: The Big Three and the Japanese Challenge
Ross Perry

Canadian Manufacturing: A Study of Productivity and Technological Change
Volume I: Sector Performance and Industrial Strategy
Volume II: Industry Studies 1946-1977
Uri Zohar

Canada's Cultural Industries: Broadcasting, Publishing, Records and Film
Paul Audley

Canada's Video Revolution: Home Video, Pay-TV and Beyond
Peter Lyman

Marketing Canada's Energy: A Strategy for Security in Oil and Gas
I.A. McDougall

Offshore Oil: Opportunities for Industrial Development and Job Creation
Roger Voyer

The above titles are available from:

James Lorimer & Company, Publishers
Egerton Ryerson Memorial Building
35 Britain Street
Toronto, Ontario M5A 1R7